Immigration Madness

A SAPIENT Being's Guide to the Biden Border Crisis, Illegal Immigrant Costs, Laws, Reform & More

By

Corey Lee Wilson

Immigration Madness

Fratire Publishing books can be purchased in bulk with exclusive discounts for educational purposes, association gifts, sales promotions, and special editions can be created to specifications. All inquiries for such can be made below.

FRATIRE PUBLISHING LLC
4533 Temescal Canyon Rd. # 308
Corona, CA 92883 USA
www.FratirePublishing.com
FratirePublishing@att.net
1+ (951) 638-5502

FratirePublishing
Relevant Books for **SAPIENT** Beings

Fratire Publishing is all about common sense and relevant books for sapient beings. If this sounds like you and you can never have enough common sense, wisdom, and relevancy, then visit us and learn more about the 40 *MADNESS* series of book titles at www.fratirepublishing.com/madnessbooks.

Printed paperback and eBook ePUB by Ingram Spark in La Vergne, Tennessee, USA
Copyright © 2024: First Edition February 2024
ISBN 978-0-9994603-6-8 (Paperback)
ISBN 978-1-953319-40-1 (eBook)
Immigration Madness-01-PDF (pdf)
LCCN 2024901682

Special thanks for the cover design by Jenny Barroso, J20Graphics, j20graphics@gmail.com and ebook conversion by Jahurul Md. Islam at Upwork.

Contents

Acknowledgements

We owe a debt of gratitude to the following for "heavily" borrowing at times pieces of their and/or outright sections. We do this unashamedly to use the sapient phrase, "if it ain't broke—don't try to fix it." Most of the borrowed works and research cannot be improved upon—so why try? It's better to assemble these meaningful parts, profound messages, and eloquent arguments into a cohesive whole, told with high school and college students in mind, and that's what we've done and where our talent lies.

Below in alphabetical order are the major contributors to *Immigration Madness* that we borrowed verbatim, quoted, and conceptualized much of their content from a little to a lot. Wherever this happened, we did our best to acknowledge the source. If we didn't at times within the 15 chapters, we did so intentionally because doing so would have distracted from their message. Nonetheless, they are more than acknowledged in the References and Index sections of this textbook.

Bernstein, Brittany: Is a news writer for *National Review*, with a focus on national politics and elections and has written for various publications including Yahoo Finance, Yahoo News, RealClear Education, and Live Action.

Camarota, Steven A.: Serves as the Director of Research for the Center for Immigration Studies (CIS), a Washington, D.C.-based research institute that examines the consequences of legal and illegal immigration on the United States.

Center for Immigration Studies (CIS): Is an independent, non-partisan, non-profit, research organization that has pursued a single mission–providing immigration policymakers, the academic community, news media, and concerned citizens with reliable information about the social, economic, environmental, security, and fiscal consequences of legal and illegal immigration into the United States. Our staff has testified before Congress over 140 times.

Downey, Caroline: Is a news writer for *National Review*, with a focus on national issues in the United States and her work has also been featured in publications such as the *New York Post*, Yahoo News, *Washington Examiner*, and *Newsweek*.

Dwinell, Erin: Was a Senior Research Associate in the Border Security and Immigration Center at the Heritage Foundation.

Federation for American Immigration Reform (FAIR): FAIR seeks to reduce overall immigration to a more normal level. Reducing legal immigration levels from well over one million at present to a very generous 300,000 a year over a sustained period will allow America to manage growth, address environmental concerns, and maintain a high quality of life.

Hankinson, Simon: A former State Department official, Simon Hankinson is a senior research fellow in the Heritage Foundation's Davis Institute for National Security and Foreign Affairs.

Hans von Spakovsky: Is Senior Legal Fellow and Manager of the Election Law Reform Initiative in the Edwin Meese III Center for Legal and Judicial Studies at the Heritage Foundation. Charles Stimson is Senior Legal Fellow and Manager in the National Security Law Program at the Heritage Foundation.

Heritage Foundation, The: Is an American conservative think tank that is primarily geared toward public policy and the foundation took a leading role in the conservative movement during the presidency of Ronald Reagan, whose policies were taken from Heritage's policy study Mandate for Leadership. The Heritage Foundation has had a major influence in U.S. public policy making and is among the most influential conservative public policy organizations in America.

Migration Policy Institute (MPI): The non-partisan institute seeks to improve immigration and integration policies through authoritative research and analysis, opportunities for learning and dialogue, the development of new ideas to address complex policy questions.

Morgan, Mark: Is an American law enforcement official who served as the Chief Operating Officer and acting Commissioner of U.S. Customs and Border Protection from July 5, 2019, to January 20, 2021.

*National Review***:** Is an American semi-monthly editorial magazine, focusing on news and commentary pieces on political, social, and cultural affairs and its authors contributed a considerable number of articles to this textbook. The magazine was founded by the author William F. Buckley Jr. in 1955 and has played a significant role in the development of conservatism in the United States, and is a leading voice on the American right.

Rappaport, Nolan: Was detailed to the House Judiciary Committee as an Executive Branch Immigration Law Expert for three years and subsequently served as an immigration counsel for the Subcommittee on Immigration, Border Security and Claims for four years and has wrote decisions for the Board of Immigration Appeals for 20 years.

Ries, Lora: Is Director of the Border Security and Immigration Center at the Heritage Foundation with over 26 years' experience in the immigration and homeland security arena. Ries twice worked at the Department of Homeland Security on management and immigration policy and operations issues, most recently as the Acting Deputy Chief of Staff.

Zimmermann, David: Is a news writer for *National Review*, with a focus on national news and his articles cover a range of topics including politics, current events, and policy issues.

A SAPIENT Being's Preface

Presently, immigration is more relevant than it has ever been. As the United States continues to grow and flourish, continually proving itself to be the greatest and most exceptional nation in the world, more and more immigrants arrive to pursue their own idea of the American Dream.

In a country made up of people from every race and nationality on earth, it is pertinent we preserve the significance of legal immigration, assimilation, and the process of becoming a naturalized American citizen.

Since the very formation of the United States, millions of people have entered this great nation as pilgrims, refugees, entrepreneurs, opportunists, nomads, missionaries, and pioneers as eloquently noted in this section by sapient author Cole P. Zail in his *AMAC Magazine* Summer 2018 article "Immigration: Solidarity, Identity, and the American Dream."

These millions of immigrants made their way to the United States in pursuit of the American Dream, seeking a land in which life was richer, fuller, and more free. Depending on their country of origin, they had varying conceptions of the American Dream, whether it meant freedom from government oppression, social mobility, a safe future for their children, economic prosperity, or simply the promise of an overall better life than that from which they came.

This mass migration and legal immigration is part of the foundation America was built upon. The contributions of hard-working, naturalized American citizens have helped make our country strong, our culture robust, and our national spirit unparalleled. At its core, the United States of America is a country that unites people, however vast their differences may be, in the pride and exceptionalism of being able to call oneself an American.

The 13-letter phrase *e pluribus unum* aptly used to encapsulate this unity is a Latin phrase that means "Out of many, one," and originated from the union of the thirteen American colonies, referencing how they emerged from the Revolutionary War as a single united nation.

While we should celebrate our unique differences, we should, perhaps more importantly, celebrate the fact that we have joined together and blended ourselves into one nation, in spite of these vast differences. America's Founding Fathers were wise; they knew that our national strength could be preserved through unity. However, individuals who are not citizens do not have a right to American citizenship without the consent of the American people as expressed through the laws of the United States.

As such, *e pluribus unum* exemplifies this unity and distills the essence of the United States, highlighting how we are a nation of individuals united by shared ideas and values, rather than by race or origin. Our populace is not bonded together by blood or birthplace, rather, we are united by our adherence to mutual values and our commitment to the Constitution. Becoming an American citizen has nothing to do with ancestry or ethnic identity; being American is a state of mind and a devotion to beliefs.

This spirit of unity, this celebration of American citizenship, this shared faith in a national ideal—this is the true majesty of our great nation. Unfortunately for America and its legalized citizens—illegal immigration does not abide by these ideals—and its inherent costs to America's taxpayers, its assault on the core principles of the American Dream, and its disregard of American immigrations laws—all present clear and present dangers as this textbook will clearly, concisely and factually demonstrate.

Like all MADNESS textbooks, *Immigration Madness* offers an opportunity to be part of the solution to these many problems. For some of you this MADNESS book will be a revelation, an epiphany, a sapient being moment. For others, it will be a triggering event, denial of truth, and a painful intervention.

Are you interested in learning about the depth and breadth of Biden's borders crisis, the shocking costs of illegal immigration, its intentional lack of enforcement, how to fix America's broken immigration system, and working together to address these issues? If yes, please read on and if you also believe in the message of this book and willing to fight for it—please considering joining or participating in one of the three SAPIENT Being programs below.

Sapient Conservative Textbooks (SCT) Program is a relevant and current events textbooks program (published by Fratire Publishing LLC) to help return conservative values, viewpoint diversity, and sapience to high school and college campuses—and enlighten them on the many blessings to humankind that are the direct result of Western European culture, American exceptionalism, and Judeo-Christian values.

Free Speech Alumni Ambassador (FSAA) Program helps create faculty and administrative positions, throughout America's predominantly liberally staffed college campuses, that can serve as much needed conservative club advisors—because conservative students are facing many obstacles when they attempt to start and charter a right-leaning student organization on campus due to faculty members fearful of losing their jobs or tenure for becoming these organization's advisors.

Make Free Speech Again On Campus (MFSAOC) Program is an interactive opportunity and nexus for high school and college students to start SAPIENT Being campus clubs, chapters, and alliances where independent, liberal, and conservative minded students can meet, discuss, and debate important issues by utilizing the sapient principles of viewpoint diversity, freedom of speech, and intellectual humility—and develop sapience in the process.

Are You a Sapient Being or Want to Be One?

Sapience, also known as wisdom, is the ability to think and act using knowledge, experience, understanding, common sense and insight. Sapience is associated with attributes such as intelligence, enlightenment, unbiased judgment, compassion, experiential self-knowledge, self-actualization, and virtues such as ethics and benevolence.

Being a sapient being is not about identity politics, it's about doing what is right and borrows many of the essential qualities of Centrism that supports strength, tradition, open mindedness, and policy based on evidence not ideology.

Sapient beings are independent minded thinkers that achieve common sense solutions that appropriately address America's and the world's most pressing issues. They gauge situations based on context and reason, consideration, and probability. They are open minded and exercise conviction and willing to fight for it on the intellectual battlefield. Sapient beings don't blindly and recklessly follow their feelings or emotions.

Their unifying ideology is based on the truth, reason, logic, scientific method, and pragmatism—and not necessarily defined by compromise, moderation, or any particular faith—but is considerate of them.

Most importantly, per a letter written by Princeton professor Robert George in 2017 and endorsed by 28 professors from three Ivy League universities for incoming freshmen, "Think for yourself!"

George's letter continues:

Thinking for yourself means questioning dominant ideas even when others insist on their being treated as unquestionable. It means deciding what one believes not by conforming to fashionable opinions, but by taking the trouble to learn and honestly consider the strongest arguments to be advanced on both or all sides of questions—including arguments for positions that others revile and want to stigmatize and against positions others seek to immunize from critical scrutiny.

The love of truth and the desire to attain it should motivate you to think for yourself. The crucial point of a college education is to seek truth and to learn the skills and acquire the virtues necessary to be a lifelong truth-seeker. Open-mindedness, critical thinking, and debate are essential to discovering the truth. Moreover, they are our best antidotes to bigotry.

Merriam-Webster's first definition of the word "bigot" is a person "who is obstinately or intolerantly devoted to his or her own opinions and prejudices." The only people who need fear open-minded inquiry and robust debate are the actual bigots, including those on campuses or in the broader society who seek to protect the hegemony of their opinions by claiming that to question those opinions is itself bigotry.

So, don't be tyrannized by public opinion. Don't get trapped in an echo chamber. Whether you in the end reject or embrace a view, make sure you decide where you stand by critically assessing the arguments for the competing positions. Think for yourself. Good luck to you in college!

Now, that might sound easy. But you will find—as you may have discovered already in high school—that thinking for yourself can be a challenge. It always demands self-discipline, and these days can require courage.

In today's climate, it's all-too-easy to allow your views and outlook to be shaped by dominant opinion on your campus or in the broader academic culture. The danger any student—or faculty member—faces today is falling into the vice of conformism, yielding to groupthink, the orthodoxy.

At many colleges and universities what John Stuart Mill called "the tyranny of public opinion" does more than merely discourage students from dissenting from prevailing views on moral, political, and other types of questions. It leads them to suppose that dominant views are so obviously correct that only a bigot or a crank could question them.

Since no one wants to be, or be thought of as, a bigot or a crank, the easy, lazy way to proceed is simply by falling into line with campus orthodoxies. Don't do it!

To be sure, our overly-politicized culture has a tough time viewing any "verbal cacophony" as a sign of strength and vibrancy. And perhaps nowhere is this truer than on many college campuses where political correctness is rampant, groupthink is common, and social media "mobs" arise in a flash to intimidate anyone who openly strays from the prevailing orthodoxy.

At the SAPIENT Being we're not intimidated—and our primary purpose is to seek the truth by enhancing viewpoint diversity, promoting intellectual humility, protecting freedom of speech and expression while developing sapience in the process—no matter what the cost on the intellectual battlefield, campus classroom, and marketplace of ideas. This is our ethos! Is it yours?

Best regards and sapiently yours,

Corey Lee Wilson

Corey Lee Wilson

S.A.P.I.E.N.T. Being

1 – America: The World's Top Destination for Legal & Illegal Immigrants

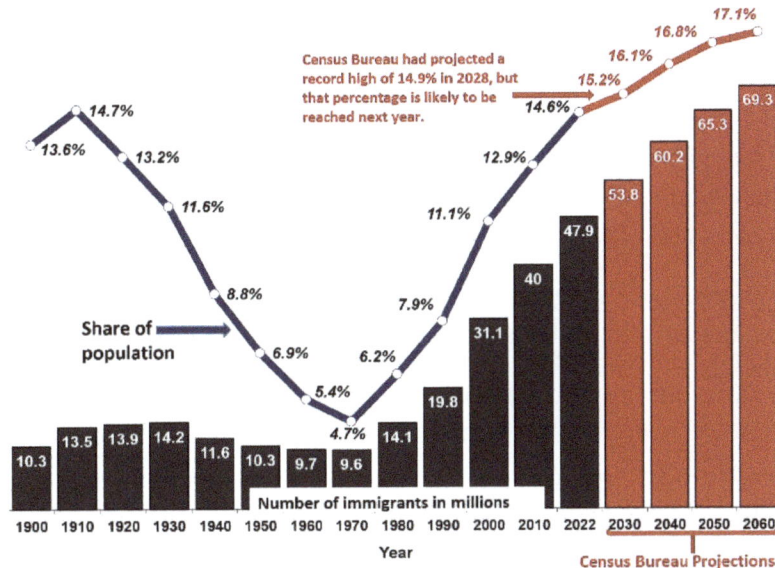

Credit: CIS tabulation of data from U.S. Census Bureau.

From the David Zimmermann "Biden Administration Failed to Remove 99 Percent of Illegal Immigrants Released Into U.S., GOP Report Shows" *National Review* October 2023 article:

Since January 2021, the Biden administration has failed to remove more than 99 percent of the illegal immigrants who have been released into the U.S., according to a 61-page report led by House Republicans titled THE BIDEN BORDER CRISIS: NEW DATA AND TESTIMONY SHOW HOW THE BIDEN ADMINISTRATION OPENED THE SOUTHWEST BORDER AND ABANDONED INTERIOR ENFORCEMENT. A link for the full report can be found in the Appendix.

House Judiciary Committee chairman Jim Jordan (R., Ohio) and Immigration Subcommittee chairman Tom McClintock (R., Calif.) published new data that showed how the Biden administration and Department of Homeland Security secretary Alejandro Mayorkas have been downplaying the border crisis despite the extraordinary numbers.

At least 2,148,738 illegal aliens were released into the country, from President Joe Biden's inauguration to March 31, 2023, according to their findings, and only 108,102 have been removed from the country by immigration authorities. Of those removals, DHS deported only 5,993 illegals through official immigration-court proceedings, accounting for less than 0.3 percent of the total number of aliens released.

Furthermore, of the more than 5.6 million illegal aliens encountered at the southern border during that 26-month period, at least 2,464,424 had no confirmed departure from the U.S. as of March 2023.

"These data contradict Secretary Mayorkas's statements that the southwest border is closed and that illegal aliens are 'quickly' removed," the 61-page report reads. "Instead, with more than 99 percent of illegal aliens staying inside the United States after being released by the Biden administration, there is virtually no enforcement of our immigration laws."

Notably, only 6 percent of illegal immigrants were found to have a legitimate fear of persecution in the past two years, debunking Mayorkas's claim they are just asylum-seekers looking for a new home.

"The vast majority of those individuals have not sought to evade law enforcement but have actually surrendered themselves to law enforcement and made a claim for relief under our laws," Mayorkas told CNN host Chris Wallace in February 2023, the report notes.

It also mentions that, owing to the record number of illegals crossing into the U.S. and Biden's lax policies, border officials often can't fulfill their immigration duties.

"Because of the unprecedented border crisis, some Immigration and Customs Enforcement (ICE) officers have been forced to abandon arrests and removals of aliens, including criminal aliens, to process the illegal aliens who have arrived at the southwest border," the report adds. "Meanwhile, the Biden administration's own policies and so-called enforcement 'priorities' have contributed to reduced arrests and lower removals of aliens."

Senate Republicans' Report Condemns "Biden's Border Crisis"

Per the Simon Hankinson "Senate Republicans' Report Condemns 'Biden's Border Crisis'" Heritage Foundation June 2022 article: Illegal crossings at the U.S. border are at "astronomical and record-breaking levels," as detailed in a June 2022 report from the Republican minority on the Senate Foreign Relations Committee puts it.

The 47-page Senate report led by Idaho Senator James E. Risch, "Biden's Border Crisis: Examining Policies That Encourage Illegal Migration," describes the ongoing disgrace on our southern border and the utter failure of the Obama and Biden administrations to address it, concluding with some recommendations for immediate action to secure our country from uncontrolled illegal immigration. A link to the full report can be found in the Appendix.

First, the numbers: The report says that 234,088 foreigners were encountered by U.S. Customs and Border Protection at the border attempting to illegally enter the country in April 2022. That's the highest-ever monthly total (back then and many times surpassed since then through 2023).

That staggering record was already broken, even as the report was being written. In May 2022, "there were 239,416 encounters along the southwest land border," according to government figures.

That doesn't count the unknown (and unknowable) number that evaded detection entirely. One estimate puts that number—the "got-aways"—at about a third (32%) of those caught, which would mean more than 600,000 last year.

According to the report, most illegal crossers still come from Mexico and the Northern Triangle countries of Central America (El Salvador, Guatemala, and Honduras), but the number from elsewhere increased nearly nine times between President Joe Biden's inauguration in January 2021 and March of this year to more than 88,000.

It seems not just Ecuadorians, Haitians, and Cubans, but also Cameroonians, Bangladeshis, and Chinese have received the message from the Biden administration that the border is wide open to illegal crossing without credible repercussions.

To summarize the report's conclusion, we have spent billions of dollars in foreign assistance in failed efforts to tackle the "root causes" of immigration. No doubt some of it reached the target countries, but much will have gone in administration and overhead fees to the "Beltway bandits" run by non-governmental organizations (NGO) with government connections.

The Obama administration's Strategy for Engagement in Central America failed and was built on the fantasy that any amount of U.S. money (in that case, $3.6 billion) could fix what ails the countries to our south. The idea that we can spend enough on noble but vague goals such as security cooperation, promoting economic prosperity, encouraging good government, and fighting corruption in El Salvador, Honduras, or Guatemala in time to deter their youth from leaving right now is ludicrous.

In the words of the State Department's senior Latin American official in 2019, "This approach failed." There is no realistic correlation between U.S. aid dollars spent in Mexico and the Northern Triangle, and any reduction in illegal crossings of our border by the targeted nations, much less from places such as Eritrea and India, which the "root causes" aid faucet does not even touch.

With an official policy of "prosecutorial discretion" not to deport them, work authorization, schooling for their children, health care in emergency rooms, and even driver's licenses and "free" in-state college tuition in many states, illegal residents of the U.S are highly incentivized to stay.

The Biden administration came to power with an open-borders mentality, determined to undo everything former President Donald Trump had done to control the border. Biden ended the successful Migrant Protection Protocols, which, by sending would-be illegal immigrants back into Mexico while their cases were decided, deterred fraudulent and frivolous asylum claims by economic migrants.

Biden also ended the promising Asylum Cooperative Agreements with Northern Triangle countries, and through regulatory overreach and prosecutorial discretion—which in practice means telling prosecutors not to do their jobs—undid efforts to streamline the asylum-processing system. U.S. immigration courts already have 1.7 million pending cases, and that impossible backlog is rapidly increasing.

The Biden regime was also determined to end Title 42, the health-related provision enacted by Trump because of COVID-19 that allows Customs and Border Protection (CBP) to expel illegal immigrants before they can be admitted and claim asylum.

The disdain with which this administration treats career border officials and agents who attempt to enforce the law is disgraceful, from Biden's silence when Texas National Guardsman Bishop Evans died saving illegal immigrants from drowning to the White House's refusal to apologize to mounted Border Patrol agents after falsely accusing them of using their reins to whip Haitians crossing into the U.S. illegally.

The consequences of Biden's abject refusal to enforce our immigration laws are obvious, if slow to unfurl. At current rates, the Biden border is allowing in enough illegal immigrants to fill a city the size of Houston or Chicago in a year. Among them, CBP will likely arrest more than 10,000 criminals per year.

Immigration: Solidarity, Identity, and the American Dream

As per the inspirational Cole P. Zail "Immigration: Solidarity, Identity, And The American Dream" *AMAC Magazine* Summer 2018 article: "Give me your tired, your poor, Your huddled masses yearning to breathe free, The wretched refuse of your teeming shore. Send these, the homeless, tempest-tost to me, I lift my lamp beside the golden door!"

The pedestal of New York Harbor's Statue of Liberty is adorned with an inscription from the classic American poem, "The New Colossus" by Emma Lazarus. Written in 1883, the excerpt of the poem featured on the statue's base has become a celebrated piece of American history and culture, widely credited with shaping the idea of New York's Statue of Liberty as a welcoming beacon to incoming immigrants.

Since the very formation of the United States, millions of people have entered this great nation as pilgrims, refugees, entrepreneurs, opportunists, nomads, missionaries, and pioneers. These immigrants made their way to the United States in pursuit of the American Dream, seeking a land in which life was richer, fuller, and more free.

Depending on their country of origin, these immigrants had varying conceptions of the American Dream, whether it meant freedom from government oppression, social mobility, a safe future for their children, economic prosperity, or simply the promise of an overall better life than that from which they came. Whatever their motivation, these people came from the farthest corners of the world to live in the greatest nation on earth, the United States of America.

This mass migration-legal immigration-is part of the foundation our great nation was built upon. The contributions of hard-working, naturalized American citizens have helped make our country strong, our culture robust, and our national spirit unparalleled. At its core, the United States of America is a country that unites people, however vast their differences may be, in the pride and exceptionalism of being able to call oneself an American.

"...Yearning to Breathe Free"

The United States has experienced several major waves of immigration since its inception.

While the Pilgrims of the 1600s came to this country in search of religious freedom, later waves of immigrants arrived seeking greater economic opportunity and relief from government oppression. Most immigrants during the mid-1800s came from countries in Northern and Western Europe, as well as Latin America and Canada.

With the 1848 discovery of gold in California and the subsequent construction of the transcontinental railroad beginning in 1862, a wave of Asian immigrants soon arrived on the West Coast, hailing mainly from China and Japan.

By the turn of the century, the largest mass migration in the history of the world was underway. In 1907, approximately 1.25 million immigrants were processed at New York Harbor's Ellis Island immigration station alone—the bulk of which came from Southern and Eastern Europe.

Today, immigrants continue to make up a sizable percentage of the United States population. While the majority of immigrants throughout the past century were of European descent, today's immigrant population comes mainly from Mexico, Latin America, China, India, southeast Asia, Middle East, and Africa.

As these immigrants continue coming into the country, the words of Lazarus' poem ring true- the United States is the "golden door" where those from the farthest corners of the world can come to build new lives for themselves as American citizens.

Census Bureau: No End in Sight to Record-Breaking Immigration

Noting the Jason Richwine "Census Bureau: No End in Sight to Record-Breaking Immigration" *National Review* November 2023 article:

In 1910, in the midst of a high immigration period known as the Great Wave, the Census Bureau found that 14.7 percent of the U.S. population was foreign-born, close to the record of 14.8 percent set in 1890. The onset of World War I would soon lessen the flow, however, and restrictive legislation passed in the 1920s kept immigration low for the next four decades. The years 1890 and 1910 stood as the high-water marks of immigration in the U.S.—until now.

According to the Center for Immigration Studies (CIS), the foreign-born share hit roughly 15 percent in August 2023. Although there is some sampling error involved in that estimate, the U.S. is clearly at or near a new record.

Optimists may cite the Great Wave as proof that the U.S. can absorb the high levels of immigration that we are experiencing today. The problem with that analogy is that the Great Wave was followed by a long period of low immigration, giving newcomers time to integrate. By contrast, new population projections out today from the Census Bureau show no expected slowdown in immigration. The bureau projects that the foreign-born share will keep increasing throughout the century, setting new records year after year.

In the bureau's main analysis, the foreign-born share will approach 20 percent by the end of the century, and in the alternative "high immigration" scenario it would rise to nearly 25 percent. As my colleague Steven Camarota notes, the acceleration of immigration under President Biden probably makes the "high" scenario the more likely one.

Absent a change in policy, our country's absorptive capacity will soon be tested as it never has been before.

The Immigrant Population is Growing Rapidly

The total foreign-born population reached a record 47 million in April 2022, according to a new information provided by Steven Camarota and Karen Ziegler that is covered in the Mark Krikorian "The Immigrant Population Is Growing Rapidly" report in the *National Review in* June 2022:

While that's the largest number ever recorded, and the total number of immigrants is important in itself, the simple fact of a record number is maybe the least interesting finding of the report; after all, a growing population of any kind sets a new record every year.

But the pace of that growth is remarkable. The report, based on the Census Bureau's monthly Current Population Survey, noted that the 47 million number is half-again more than in 2000. Going back further, the total size of the foreign-born population has doubled since 1990, tripled since 1980, and quintupled since 1970. (The total U.S. population has grown only by about half since 1970.)

In addition to the size of the foreign-born population, the percentage also matters. The foreign-born now account for one in seven U.S. residents (14.3 percent)—the highest percentage since 1910. As recently as 1990 they were about one in 13 (7.9 percent) U.S. residents. The numbers are growing so fast that if present trends continue, the foreign-born share of the population will reach about 15 percent by the end of 2023, higher than at any time in the nation's 246-year history.

Considering this rapid growth in numbers, and the approaching record percentage, you'd think lawmakers would want to consider the impacts on schools, health-care systems, welfare programs, physical infrastructure, the job market, quality of life, etc.

Maybe even more important, where is the national leader who even asks how many people we can successfully assimilate? The last great wave of immigration, from the 1870s to the 1920s, was brought to an end when immigration was greatly curtailed by legislation, contributing hugely to the successful assimilation of those already here. This, even more than the disaster at the border, is the most pressing issue in immigration policy.

Immigration Backlashes Spread Around the World

From the Tom Fairless "Immigration Backlashes Spread Around the World" *Wall Street Journal* July 2023 article: Record immigration to affluent countries is sparking bigger backlashes across the world, boosting populist parties and putting pressure on governments to tighten policies to stem the migration wave.

But the jump in arrivals, along with increases in illegal immigration to the U.S. and Europe, is making more voters uneasy. The influx since the end of the pandemic is altering societies, with many people blaming immigrants for increases in crime and higher housing costs.

The Dutch government collapsed in July 2023 after parties failed to agree on new measures to restrict immigration that has soared to record levels, triggering new elections in the fall. Anti-immigrant parties recently took power in Italy and Finland, and have started backing a minority government in Sweden. Austria's far-right Freedom Party is leading national polls.

Around five million more people moved to affluent countries last year than left them, as Covid-era travel restrictions eased, rich-world labor shortages intensified, and economic problems in the developing world worsened. That was up 80% from pre-pandemic levels, according to a *Wall Street Journal* data analysis.

Polls across affluent countries show a jump in opposition to immigration, including in places that have been most welcoming to newcomers.

Roughly half of Canadians think the government's new target of about a half-million immigrants a year is too many in a country of 40 million, while three-quarters worry the plan will result in excessive demand for housing and health and social services, according to a poll by Léger, a Montreal-based research company.

In the U.K., which has eased rules to attract more college graduates from abroad to fill skills shortages, nearly half of people think legal migration is too high, according to a March 2023 poll by Public First, a research consultancy.

In the U.S., where a large percentage of the population has long opposed immigration, attitudes have hardened over the past year.

Americans' satisfaction with the level of immigration into the U.S. declined to 28% in February 2023, the lowest reading in a decade, from 34% a year earlier, according to Gallup polls.

And in France, which has been convulsed by violent protests after police shot and killed a teenager of North African origin, recent polls suggest that French far-right National Front leader Marine Le Pen, who favors tighter rules on immigration, could win the country's next presidential election.

Voters' concerns typically center on illegal immigration, which tends to weigh on wages and social-welfare systems. Illegal entries across the Mediterranean into Europe and from Mexico to the U.S. have surged to record levels in recent years.

Europe is expanding efforts, launched before the pandemic, to build hundreds of miles of new barriers on land and sea to stem an increase in illegal migration. Finland is building a 125-mile high-tech fence along its border with Russia, while Greek Prime Minister Kyriakos Mitsotakis said in March the country would complete a 90-mile steel fence along its border with Turkey to prevent illegal crossings.

In Europe especially, "you definitely have a strong mismatch between the kind of people our labor markets need and the kind of people actually coming in," said Roland Freudenstein, Brussels-based vice president of the independent think tank Globsec.

Many immigrants to Europe are motivated by generous social-welfare systems in places such as Sweden and Germany, Freudenstein said. That differs from the U.S., where immigrants are more motivated by work, in part because social benefits are less generous, he said.

In 2015-16, surging immigration into the U.S. and Europe helped fuel the discontent that drove Britain's exit from the European Union and Donald Trump's ascent to the presidency. "We are seeing a similar push now that might go even further," Freudenstein said.

What Happened When Immigration Fell?

Per the Steven A. Camarota "What Happened When Immigration Fell?" *National Review* May 2023 article: We are often told that America must have very high levels of immigration—otherwise, businesses will be deprived of the labor needed to expand. CEOs from retail to technology have recently made this case, as have allied politicians from both sides of the aisle.

But is it really true?

The period between 2016 and 2019 represents a good test of this argument because both legal and illegal immigration fell substantially. If immigration enthusiasts were right, the economy should have sputtered, but that's not what happened. In fact, GDP grew, inflation remained low, and—perhaps most significantly—wages for less educated American workers not only grew but grew at a faster rate than for high-skill workers.

After peaking at 1.75 million in 2016, the total number of new immigrants (legal and illegal) fell to 1.45 million in 2017, followed by 1.34 million and 1.36 million in 2018 and 2019, respectively. Of course, there is always some undercount in Census Bureau survey data, but the rate of undercount tends not to change from year to year, so there is little question that new arrivals declined significantly.

Moreover, the Census Bureau estimated that net migration—the difference between the number of people arriving in the country versus the number leaving—also fell significantly. Fewer immigrants came, and more of the people already here left.

A stronger economy traditionally encourages more immigrants to come, especially illegal immigrants, but that was not true in the first three years of the Trump administration. Immigration slowed almost certainly because of the administration's restrictive policies—including a reduction in refugee admissions, efforts to curtail welfare eligibility for new immigrants, the Remain in Mexico policy for asylum seekers, more worksite enforcement against employers who hire illegal immigrants, increased fencing at the border, efforts to end temporary protected status and Deferred Action for Childhood Arrivals, as well as some smaller administrative changes that cumulatively made a difference.

So what, if any, impact did the decline in immigration have?

First, total GDP growth in these three years was actually higher than in the preceding three years—7.5 versus 6.7 percent. The inflation rate, which is now such a concern, was about the same in the first three years of the Trump presidency as it had been in the years before.

Importantly, real (inflation-adjusted) weekly earnings for full-time U.S.-born workers without a bachelor's degree grew 3.2 percent between the fourth quarters of 2016 and 2019, whereas it had actually declined slightly from 2012 to 2016. In addition to an increase in earnings, the labor-force-participation rate—the share of working-age adults either employed or actively looking for work—also increased for the less educated U.S.-born. In contrast, there was little improvement in labor-force participation in the years before 2016, after the rate bottomed out in 2013 as a result of the Great Recession.

These workers earn much less on average than those with a college education, and their earnings had increased little in recent decades. Those without a college degree make up the overwhelming majority of the working poor, particularly those with children. Moreover, they are the primary beneficiaries of the earned-income tax credit and refundable child tax credits aimed at low-income workers. If they earn more in the labor market, the cost of the welfare state will lessen.

So, what's happened since 2019? Covid-19 hit at the beginning of 2020, and the accompanying shutdowns had a very negative impact on the economy. Real earnings for virtually all workers, immigrant and U.S.-born, declined from 2020 to 2022, in part because of the high inflation. However, the decline in earnings also coincides with a dramatic rebound in immigration.

While we cannot say with certainty because all the data have not been released, the available information indicates that more than 4 million immigrants (legal and illegal) settled in the United States in 2021 and 2022. The decline in earnings for virtually all workers, particularly lower paid and less educated Americans, should give pause to those advocates now calling for more immigration to reduce inflation by lowering wages even more.

The immigration slowdown in the years just before the pandemic illustrates what can happen when government policy reduces immigration during an economic expansion. The available evidence from 2016 to 2019 indicates that less educated American-born workers did better, although of course we cannot establish a causal relationship with certainty.

What we can say with certainty is that immigration fell, the economy expanded, and lower paid American workers did well—all without sparking inflation. This runs directly counter to the oft-heard argument that very high levels of immigration are necessary for the American economy to prosper.

Well-known economist Paul Samuelson observed six decades ago: "After World War I, laws were passed severely limiting immigration. Only a trickle of immigrants has been admitted since then. . . . By keeping labor supply down, immigration policy tends to keep wages high." The short-lived immigration slowdown a few years ago seems to confirm this truth. It turns out that the basic laws of supply and demand apply to immigration, after all.

Biden 2.0: The US Could Double its Undocumented Immigrant Population

Per the Nolan Rappaport "Biden 2.0: The US Could Double Its Undocumented Immigrant Population" published in *The Hill* in November 2023:

President Joe Biden initially sought to reform our "broken" immigration system through legislative means. On his first day in office, he sent his U.S. Citizenship Act of 2021 to Congress. It would establish numerous immigration benefits, including the largest legalization program in U.S. history, increased opportunities for lawful immigration and humane treatment of migrants at the border.

When this didn't work, he shifted his focus to administrative actions. This included bypassing the visa system by bringing migrants here through new legal pathways, catch and release at the border and restricting interior enforcement. Apparently, by "broken," he means that existing law doesn't permit enough immigrants to come here and subjects the ones here unlawfully to the threat of deportation.

This has caused serious, presumably unanticipated consequences, such as a record-breaking increase in illegal border crossings and an immigration court backlog crisis that can't be fixed.

Border security expert Todd Bensman claims that whether migrants are willing to pay big fees to be smuggled into the country depends on how likely it is that they will be able to get in and stay—and the likelihood of being able to do this has been extraordinarily high during the Biden presidency.

This is not likely to change if Biden is re-elected.

Catch and release and "lawful pathways" let them in without visas.

Border Patrol has encountered more than 5.6 million illegal border crossers on the Southwest border during the first three years of the Biden presidency, which is three times the number of encounters it experienced during Donald Trump's presidency. The average number of monthly encounters under Biden has been roughly 189,000, compared to an average of 51,000 during the Trump administration.

Moreover, as of the end of March 2023, Biden had released more than 2 million of them into the interior of the country. These are not just asylum seekers. The Border Patrol apprehended 169 illegal crossers on the terrorism watchlist in fiscal 2023, compared to only 11 from fiscal 2017 through fiscal 2020.

More illegal crossings are occurring on the northern border, too. One of the northern Border Patrol sectors has apprehended more than 6,100 illegal crossers from 76 countries in the last 11 months, which is more than during the previous 10 years combined.

Biden also has established "legal pathways" that provide an alternative to illegal border crossings for migrants who can't get visas. He has used these initiatives and border practices to parole around 3.6 million migrants into the country in the last three years. The parole status of at least 1.2 million of them has lapsed, and they are still here.

The legal pathways include special processes for paroling up to 30,000 nationals a month into the country from Cuba, Haiti, Nicaragua and Venezuela, and a Family Reunification Parole Process for certain nationals of Colombia, Cuba, Ecuador, El Salvador, Guatemala, Haiti and Honduras.

He also expanded the Customs and Border Patrol One mobile application program that was launched by the Trump administration. It permits migrants without visas to schedule an appointment to present themselves for inspection at a designated port of entry.

Nearly 250,000 migrants without visas have been paroled into the United States through this program through August 2023. From January through Sept. 5, 2023, parole was granted in 99.7 percent of the interviews.

In view of the success Biden has had in using these programs as an alternative to the visa system, I would expect him to maintain or even increase his use of such programs if he is re-elected.

Lax interior enforcement lets them stay.

DHS Secretary Alejandro Mayorkas issued enforcement guidelines in which he says that, "The fact an individual is a removable noncitizen therefore should not alone be the basis of an enforcement action against them." The guidelines focus enforcement efforts instead "on those who pose a threat to national security, public safety, and border security and thus threaten America's well-being."

Unlike the past, the new guidelines shield illegal border crossers from deportation once they have reached the interior of the country, which encourages them to keep trying until they succeed. Such multiple attempts have become common.

Biden can't reverse this without subjecting himself to claims that he has reverted to his predecessor's enforcement policies. Biden and Trump both prioritized the removal of criminal migrants. The main difference is that Biden has exempted migrants who are just deportable for being here unlawfully while Trump didn't exempt any deportable migrants.

The carrot-and-stick solution

Biden tried to reduce illegal crossings with a carrot-and-stick strategy that combines an expansion of legal pathways to the U.S. with adverse consequences for those who still choose to make an illegal entry.

Migrants who enter illegally instead of taking advantage of a legal pathway will be presumed to be ineligible for asylum absent an applicable exception and may be processed in expedited removal proceedings.

Illegal crossings dropped from 183,921 in April 2023 to 99,538 in June, but they rose back to 181,059 in August and were at 218,763 in September (and continued to rise in October to December). The total for fiscal 2023 was 2,045,838!

Backlog crisis

Biden's programs have released so many migrants into the country that they have overwhelmed the immigration court. The court is needed to adjudicate asylum applications and to remove migrants Biden has released into the country who are not able to establish asylum eligibility or any other basis for remaining here.

At the end of 2021, the immigration court backlog had reached 1,596,193—the largest in history. But by the end of fiscal 2023, the backlog was 2,794,629 cases. And progress isn't being made on reducing it. The court received 1,488,110 new cases in fiscal 2023, and only completed 669,011.

Biden has requested funding to hire 150 more judges. But the Congressional Research Service determined that even if the size of the immigration court were to be increased from the 600 judges it has now to 1,349 judges, it would still take 10 years to clear the backlog. And the situation has gotten worse since that calculation was made.

What Happens When the Darien Gap Is Overrun?

Using the Michael Brendan Dougherty "What Happens When the Darien Gap Is Overrun?" alert from the *National Review in* April 2023, he notes:

The most important barrier to illegal entry to the United States from South America was so impassable that only one normal car has ever crossed it. Sixty-two years ago, a Land Rover made the journey. And it took five months to do so, crawling along at just over a tenth of a mile per hour.

This barrier is guarded ferociously day and night, with truly deadly sentries who are indifferent to human life. And it's not even on the American border—it is the no-man's land that exists between Central and South America, the Darien Gap between Panama and Colombia. It is the only place between Prudhoe Bay in Alaska and Ushuaia, Argentina, the world's southernmost city on planet Earth, that cannot be driven over.

The Darien Gap has stopped Colombia's drug-trade dysfunction from spreading north into Panama. It's also been the one thing, including massively tightened visa restrictions into Mexico, stopping a tsunami of potential migration to the United States from South America. And not just South America. After the collapse of Haiti's government in 2021, Haitians began pioneering a route to the southern border of the United States using the Darien Gap.

Since Covid, a number of countries have become drastically more unlivable, and hundreds of thousands of their citizens are now following in those Haitian footsteps, whether from Venezuela, Ecuador, Gambia, or China. And this wave of humanity is starting to tame the jungle by trampling it. Increasingly, drug smugglers and paramilitaries are organizing the gap for migration. It's estimated that as many as 400,000 will cross the Darien Gap in 2023; 90,000 have already done so as of April 2023. People are coming from all over the world as well.

2 – Biden's Border Policies & Ending Title 42 Break All American Illegal Immigration Records

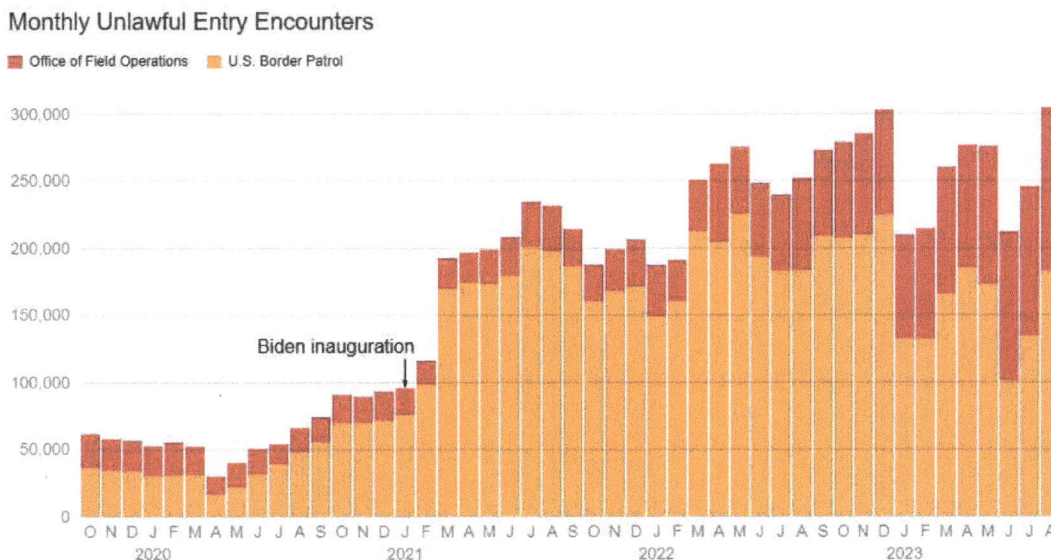

Monthly Unlawful Entry Encounters

■ Office of Field Operations   ■ U.S. Border Patrol

Credit: Heritage Foundation.

From day one of the Biden administration's inauguration on January 21, 2021—the border crisis began as noted in the Simon Hankinson "Congress Should Fund Real Border Security, Not a Worldwide Welfare State" Heritage Foundation November 2023 report as follows:

Fast forward to October 2023, U.S. Customs and Border Protection reports that 240,988 foreigners were "encountered" attempting to enter the U.S. from Mexico, the highest total for that month in our history. That's more than 7,700 per day!

According to former officials in the Obama administration, the standard for a border crisis was 1,000 attempted crossings a day. Who was on the team that set that standard? President Joe Biden—then vice president—and Alejandro Mayorkas, then deputy secretary, and now secretary, of homeland security.

When the Trump administration ended, the U.S. was deporting more people than were illegally coming into the country. In less than a month under Biden's term, the number of people illegally coming into the country is more than 6,000 per day—that's six times the crisis level as set by the Obama team.

For months now, poll after poll has shown that the very different groups of Americans the Census Bureau has collectivized under the terms Hispanic and Latino—in order of numerical size, Mexican Americans, Puerto Ricans, Salvadoran Americans, Cuban Americans and others—are running away from Biden.

The latest poll, by *USA Today* and Suffolk University, out in January 2024, shows Biden actually trailing the leading Republican candidate, Donald Trump, among Hispanics by 5 percentage points, 34% percent to 39%.

The Border-Crisis Numbers the Biden Administration Doesn't Want You to Know About

As per the Mark Green "The Border-Crisis Numbers the Biden Administration Doesn't Want You to Know" *National Review* October 2023 article: The 2023 fiscal year is over—but the Biden border crisis is anything but. If you blinked, you missed it: Early Saturday morning October 26, 2023, the Department of Homeland Security (DHS) quietly released the border-encounter numbers for September.

A look at those numbers, which also closed out fiscal year 2023, demonstrate why DHS secretary Alejandro Mayorkas clearly wanted them released while most Americans had their attention focused elsewhere.

In October 2023, Customs and Border Protection (CBP) documented an astounding 269,735 total encounters of inadmissible aliens at the southwest border, at or between U.S. ports of entry—around 17,000 encounters more than the previous record, also set on Mayorkas's watch. When factoring in encounters along all of America's borders, at or between ports of entry, the total jumped to 341,392—another all-time high.

In FY 2023, CBP recorded more than 2.4 million encounters at the southwest border, a 42 percent increase from fiscal year 2021, Mayorkas's and President Joe Biden's first year in office, and a 4 percent increase from the 2,378,944 encounters in fiscal year 2022. Nationwide, encounters in FY 2023 totaled more than 3.2 million, a 63 percent jump from FY 2021 and a 15 percent increase from FY 2022.

Despite these historic numbers, which have completely overwhelmed Customs and Border Protection and other DHS law-enforcement officials, Mayorkas has continued to double down on his open-borders policies. In his testimony before the House Judiciary Committee in late July 2023, for example, he claimed: "Our approach of expanding lawful pathways for people to reach the border . . . is working. The number has dropped."

Mayorkas isn't telling the whole story. In June 2023, following the end of the Title 42 public-health order, encounters dropped for a few weeks as the cartels pulled back to assess how to respond to the change in policy. As one source told the *New York Post* at the time, "the intel is that they are testing the waters, seeing who's released into the United States and who is getting deported." Even the chief of the Border Patrol at the time, Raul Ortiz, told members of my committee in an official briefing that he expected encounters to soon climb back to what CBP had been seeing for months.

These assessments proved true. In June 2023, Border Patrol agents recorded 99,538 apprehensions along the southwest border. Apprehensions climbed to 132,642 in July, 181,054 in August, and 218,763 in September. Illegal crossings since June have continued to skyrocket, in large part due to Mayorkas's policy of mass "catch and release."

Mayorkas is either ignorant, or he's simply lying about the consequences of his policies.

It's not just illegal crossings between the ports of entry that are driving this crisis, either—it's Mayorkas's expansion of the legally dubious mass-parole programs that allow otherwise inadmissible aliens to enter the United States through official ports of entry.

In October 2022, Customs and Border Patrol (CBP) recorded around 71,000 encounters nationwide at these ports. By March 2023, that number had jumped to more than 94,000, following the implementation of Mayorkas's CBP One app scheme and the new parole program for Cubans, Haitians, Nicaraguans, and Venezuelans. Last month, there were more than 121,000 encounters at U.S. ports—almost double the number from September 2022. In February 2021, Mayorkas's first month in office, the number was fewer than 18,000.

And now we know, based on documents the House Committee on Homeland Security obtained from DHS under threat of subpoena, that just this year Mayorkas's DHS released into the interior almost 96 percent of the 278,431 individuals who made appointments through CBP One.

Those journeying to the southwest border to make use of the CBP One app or other parole programs are still paying the cartels to get to the border, further enriching these criminal organizations. In fact, the cartels have even exploited the app itself in order to make more money off migrants. These inadmissible aliens are still overwhelming the ports of entry. And when they are released by Customs and Border Protection, they put the same strain on resources in communities across this country as those who are apprehended and released by the Border Patrol.

This simply cannot continue. Our country is at a tipping point. On Mayorkas's watch, CBP has recorded more than 6.2 million encounters at our southwest border, and more than 7.5 million nationwide. Millions of these individuals have been released into the United States, and Homeland Security's own reporting shows that if they are not removed within a year, historically they rarely are.

This does not even include the 1.7 million known "gotaways" who have evaded apprehension altogether and entered our country since January 2021, in large part thanks to Border Patrol agents being pulled off the line to process and release those who have been encouraged to cross on Mayorkas's watch.

If September showed anything, it's that this crisis is only getting worse. It's time for the Senate to pass H.R. 2, the Secure the Border Act of 2023, and for Secretary Mayorkas to answer for sparking the worst border crisis in our history.

Biden's Immigration Policies Have Turned a Trump Win Into a Loss

Per the Lora Ries and Carla Sands "Biden's Immigration Policies Have Turned a Win Into a Loss" Heritage Foundation July 2021 article: The Biden administration has systematically abandoned the border security policies and immigration reforms that enabled the Trump administration to turn back the tide of illegal immigration. With the floodgates to illegal immigration wide open once again, drug cartels and human traffickers are cashing in and both American and immigrant lives are at greater risk.

It doesn't have to be this way.

In 2019, when faced with an acute, albeit less severe, border crisis than the one we face today, the Trump administration implored Congress to close loopholes in the immigration system. Then, as now, Congress refused to act.

Rather than let the situation at the border continue to deteriorate, Trump took executive action. He continued to build the border wall, as the Border Patrol requested. He started a never-before-used (but authorized by Congress in 1996) "Remain in Mexico" program requiring asylum seekers from Central America to stay in Mexico during their immigration proceedings. And he reached cooperative agreements with El Salvador, Guatemala, and Honduras requiring those countries to take back any migrants who had sought asylum with the U.S. without first seeking protection in a "safe third country" they had passed through on their way to the U.S.

These changes quickly halted the caravans coming to the U.S. because migrants knew they would no longer be able to enter and disappear into the U.S. simply by claiming fear. By late 2019, our southern border was under control.

A new public health threat emerged in 2020.

Moving early in the COVID pandemic to help contain that danger, the Trump administration authorized border officials to turn back migrants for public health safety ("Title 42").

The Biden administration, however, has snatched defeat from the jaws of victory. It immediately stopped border wall construction, halted the "Remain in Mexico" program, tore up the asylum cooperative agreements, ended most deportations, requested congressional amnesty for the untold millions of illegal aliens in the U.S., decreased use of Title 42 health protections, and repeatedly messaged that no unaccompanied alien child would be turned away.

Predictably, historic numbers of immigrants—from all over the world, not just south of the border—flocked to enter the U.S. illegally. Human smugglers are pocketing $14 million a day, profiting royally from their "services" that often leave women raped in route and children abandoned at journey's end.

Border agents have intercepted known terrorists, gang members and sexual predators, but no doubt others have slipped through. Illegal aliens have been transported throughout the U.S. even after testing positive for COVID.

Knowing that the Border Patrol is being overwhelmed by the sheer volume of illegal entries, drug traffickers have picked up the pace, too. The amount of deadly fentanyl seized by U.S. Customs and Border Protection in the first four months of 2021 exceeds what was seized in all of 2020. How many Americans have to die from these drugs before this administration will implement policies to secure the border?

Biden Signs Executive Orders Ending Trump's Travel Ban, Stopping Border Wall Construction

As noted in the Brittany Bernstein "Biden Signs Executive Orders Ending Trump's Travel Ban, Stopping Border Wall Construction" *National Review* January 2021article:

President Joe Biden in January 2021 signed a series of executive orders on immigration, moving to preserve and fortify the Deferred Action for Childhood Arrivals (DACA) program, to end the so-called "Muslim ban," and to stop construction on the U.S.-Mexico border wall.

Biden's executive orders are in line with campaign promises that he would overturn a number of former President Donald Trump's immigration policies on day one and come as part of a slate of 17 executive orders, memorandums and proclamations the Democrat will issue on his first day.

While the Supreme Court stopped Trump from terminating DACA, Biden's executive order directs the Secretary of Homeland Security to "take all appropriate actions under the law" to "preserve and fortify" the program. It also calls on Congress to enact legislation providing permanent status and a path to citizenship for people who were brought to the U.S. illegally as children.

The president also ordered an end to Trump's travel ban that restricted entry into the U.S. from eight nations: Chad, Iran, Somalia, Libya, North Korea, Syria, Venezuela, and Yemen, a policy that the Biden White House called "rooted in religious animus and xenophobia."

The order "instructs the State Department to restart visa processing for affected countries and to swiftly develop a proposal to restore fairness and remedy the harms caused by the bans, especially for individuals stuck in the waiver process and those who had immigrant visas denied."

"This is an important step in providing relief to individuals and families harmed by this Trump Administration policy that is inconsistent with American values," the White House said in a statement announcing the orders.

It also calls for the review of "other Trump Administration 'extreme vetting' practices" and orders increased information sharing with foreign governments to strengthen screening and vetting of travelers.

Another executive order repeals a Trump executive order that "directed harsh and extreme immigration enforcement."

"This revocation will allow the Department of Homeland Security and other agencies to set civil immigration enforcement policies that best protect the American people and are in line with our values and priorities," the White House said.

Biden also declared an "immediate termination of the national emergency declaration that was used as a pretext to justify some of the funding diversions" for the U.S.-Mexico border wall.

"The proclamation directs an immediate pause in wall construction projects to allow a close review of the legality of the funding and contracting methods used, and to determine the best way to redirect funds that were diverted by the prior Administration to fund wall construction," the announcement reads.

Biden to End Trump Asylum Deals With Three Central American Countries

Furthermore, the Biden administration is ending asylum deals brokered under the Trump administration with three Central American countries just as the number of migrants arriving at the southern border is spiking as reported in the Mairead McArdle "Biden to End Trump Asylum Deals with Three Central American Countries" *National Review* February 2021 article:

"The United States has suspended and initiated the process to terminate the Asylum Cooperative Agreements with the Governments of El Salvador, Guatemala, and Honduras as the first concrete steps on the path to greater partnership and collaboration in the region laid out by President Biden," Secretary of State Antony Blinken announced.

The agreements with El Salvador, Guatemala, and Honduras required many migrants who showed up at the U.S.-Mexico border to seek asylum in one of those countries first. The deals with El Salvador and Honduras were never formally enacted, and the agreement with Guatemala has been effectively on hold since March 2020 due to the coronavirus pandemic.

"To be clear, these actions do not mean that the U.S. border is open. While we are committed to expanding legal pathways for protection and opportunity here and in the region, the United States is a country with borders and laws that must be enforced," Blinken said in the statement.

"We are also committed to providing safe and orderly processing for all who arrive at our border, but those who attempt to migrate irregularly are putting themselves and their families at risk on what can be a very dangerous journey," he added.

President Biden is looking to undo other aspects of the Trump administration's stringent immigration enforcement policies as well.

The Biden administration announced the return of the so-called "catch and release" policy at the southern border, a practice President Trump had issued an order to stop. U.S. Customs and Border Protection is reimplementing the Obama-era policy of releasing newly-apprehended migrants back into U.S. cities along the South Texas border, citing coronavirus concerns at detention facilities as well as the rising numbers of apprehended migrants.

Law, ICE Are "Irrelevant" to Biden Administration

Per the Erin Dwinell "Law, ICE Are 'Irrelevant' to Biden Administration" Heritage Foundation July 2022 article, she notes that from Day One, Biden got to work demoralizing the ICE workforce the *Washington Post* reported in May of 2021:

'It's a weird, frustrating time,' said one ICE official, who is not authorized to speak to reporters, describing a climate of distrust. 'It feels like the administration doesn't have our backs.' Just as quickly, the administration largely defunded ICE, making it next to impossible for the agency to do its job.

And despite a federal court last month vacating Biden and Mayorkas' latest attempt to radically limit lawful immigration enforcement, it's hard to believe the administration will comply and not push back. It has a well-documented track record of ignoring court orders and acting as though it's above the law.

To make matters worse, Biden's DHS is on track to let 1 million deportable illegal immigrants off the hook through "de facto amnesty." This irresponsible direction not only compromises public safety, but also leaves illegal aliens without any sort of official determination of status or directions for how to proceed.

Most recently, Biden's U.S. Citizenship and Immigration Services issued June 24, 2022, policy guidance reinterpreting the law and, in effect, waiving explicit language in the Immigration and Naturalization Act stating that illegal aliens who were previously "unlawfully present" for at least six months are barred from returning to the U.S. for three or 10 years after "departure or removal."

In short, U.S. Citizenship and Immigration Services will approve of prior lengthy illegal presence.

What's more, the Biden administration is sending the message that if deportable illegal aliens have willingly left or been removed from the United States, they can enter again unlawfully and stay in the interior of the U.S. as many days as they wish.

It also opened the door for illegal aliens whose applications were previously denied on these inadmissibility grounds to submit a motion to reopen their case any time before Dec. 27. (Normally, a motion to reopen must be filed within 30 days of a decision.)

One of the highlights in the Citizenship and Immigration Services policy alert states: "a noncitizen's location during the statutory 3-year or 10-year period and the noncitizen's manner of return to the United States during the statutory 3-year or 10-year period are irrelevant (emphasis added) for purposes of determining inadmissibility under INA 212(a)(9)(B)."

You read that right: The written law is "irrelevant" to the Biden administration.

Meanwhile, the administration continues to refuse to release the congressionally required ICE Enforcement and Removal Report for fiscal year 2021.

The most obvious conclusion is that the Biden administration wants to effectively do away with ICE and immigration enforcement, hide the glaring issues that come along with nonenforcement policies, make it appear that all is well at the border, and dodge all responsibility by escaping congressional oversight and the criticism of the American people.

Biden's border policies and directives are some of the clearest examples proving that he bows to the demands of far left, open-borders activists. Day in and day out, this administration's actions reveal nothing but disregard for national security and public safety, and disdain for the enforcement of the rule of law in this country.

Harris Defends Her Absence at the Border: 'I Don't Understand the Point'

As per the Brittany Bernstein "Harris Defends Her Absence at the Border: 'I Don't Understand the Point'" *National Review* June 2021 article: Adding insult to injury, Vice President Kamala Harris was named "Border Czar" and then deflected questions about why she has not yet visited the southern border after being tasked with handling the "root causes" of migration, saying "we've been to the border."

NBC's Lester Holt asked Harris whether she has plans to visit the border, having gone 76 days without a trip there since being named border czar.

"I – at some point – you know – we are going to the border. We've been to the border," Harris said. "So this whole – this whole – this whole thing about the border. We've been to the border. We've been to the border."

Holt pushed back, noting Harris had not been to the border herself while in office.

"I – and I haven't been to Europe. And I mean, I don't – I don't understand the point that you're making," Harris said, adding "I'm not discounting the importance of the border."

"Listen, I care about what's happening at the border," Harris said, adding that she is "in Guatemala because my focus is dealing with the root causes of migration."

"There may be some who think that that is not important, but it is my firm belief that if we care about what's happening at the border, we better care about the root causes and address them," she said. "And so that's what I'm doing."

Here's What You Need to Know About Title 42, the Pandemic-Era Policy That Quickly Sends Migrants to Mexico

From the Uriel J. Garcia "Here's What You Need to Know About Title 42, the Pandemic-Era Policy That Quickly Sends Migrants to Mexico" *The Texas Tribune* MAY 2023 story:

The public health order that quickly expels migrants to Mexico was launched early in the pandemic during the Trump administration. Known as Title 42, it has been the subject of different court rulings, delaying its lifting until the Biden administration ended its use on May 11, 2023.

It was originally set to expire in May 2002, but a federal judge in Louisiana blocked the Biden administration from lifting Title 42, a public health order that immigration officers have used to quickly expel migrants at the southwest border, including asylum-seekers.

For more than three years, the federal government has turned away illegal immigrants at the U.S.-Mexico border, including those who are seeking asylum, using a public emergency health order known as Title 42. It was launched by the Trump administration at the start of the COVID-19 pandemic and continued under the Biden administration.

Here's what you need to know about the law.

What is Title 42?

Title 42 is part of the Public Health Service Act of 1944 aimed at preventing the spread of communicable diseases in the country. According to the law, whenever the U.S. surgeon general determines there is a communicable disease in another country, health officials have the authority, with the approval of the president, to prohibit "the introduction of persons and property from such countries or places" for as long as health officials determine the action is necessary. That authority was transferred from the U.S. surgeon general to the director of the CDC in 1966.

Congress approved a similar law in 1893 during a cholera epidemic that gave the president authority to exclude people from certain countries during a public health emergency. It was used for the first time in 1929 to bar people coming from China and the Philippines during a meningitis outbreak.

Why was it activated?

The Trump administration invoked Title 42 for the first time since its creation in March 2020 as a way to help stop the spread of COVID-19 in immigrant detention centers, where many migrants are placed after they arrive at the U.S.-Mexico border.

According to the *New York Times*, Stephen Miller, a senior adviser to former President Donald Trump, had pushed the idea to invoke Title 42 at the U.S.-Mexico border as early as 2018, long before COVID-19 emerged.

As COVID-19 cases rose in the U.S., then-CDC Director Robert Redfield enacted Title 42 to seal the land borders with Canada and Mexico for migrants seeking asylum on March 20, 2020. The Associated Press reported that then-Vice President Mike Pence ordered Redfield to enact Title 42 over the objections of CDC scientists who said there was no evidence that it would slow the virus' spread in the U.S.

Dr. Anthony Fauci, the nation's top infectious disease expert, has said that immigrants are not driving up the number of COVID-19 cases.

How many migrants have been removed under Title 42?

Since March 2020, immigration officials have used the health order more than 2.7 million times to expel migrants, many of whom have been removed multiple times after making repeated attempts to enter the U.S. at the southern border.

Under Title 42, the recidivism rate—the percentage of people apprehended more than once by a Border Patrol—increased from 7% to as much as 27%.

During the Trump administration, immigration agents expelled all types of migrants; the Biden administration has instructed agents to exempt unaccompanied children from Title 42. When agents apprehend unaccompanied children, they are placed in a federal shelter or a state-run facility until they are reunited with a family member in the U.S. or until they find a sponsor.

While most migrants are sent across the border to Mexico under Title 42, others are returned to their home countries. Immigration officials also have the discretion to allow certain migrants to enter the country if there are "significant law enforcement, officer and public safety, humanitarian, and public health interests."

Is every migrant expelled under Title 42?

No. In order for a migrant to be expelled from the country under Title 42, Mexico or their home country must have previously agreed to accept them. Mexico has accepted migrants from Mexico, Guatemala, Honduras, El Salvador and Venezuela.

If a migrant suspected of crossing the border illegally can't be expelled under Title 42, immigration agents process them under Title 8, the process that Border Patrol agents have historically used.

Under Title 8, undocumented immigrants can be criminally prosecuted for attempting to enter the country illegally—the charge is usually a misdemeanor, but it can be elevated to a felony if they have previously been charged for attempting to enter the country. Migrants are typically deported after serving their sentence.

Border Patrol agents can also move to expedite a migrant's deportation without going to court.

Migrants can request political asylum during this process, and immigration officials have the discretion to allow migrants to remain in the country without being detained as their asylum cases are pending.

Currently, the average wait time to receive a final decision on an asylum case is five years.

What's the status of the legal fights over Title 42?

The public health order has been the subject of lawsuits in federal courts across the country.

In March 2022, U.S. District Judge Mark Pittman in Fort Worth ruled in favor of Texas and ordered the Biden administration to stop exempting unaccompanied children from Title 42 expulsions. That same day, a federal appellate court in Washington, D.C., reaffirmed a lower court's ruling in a separate case that it's illegal to expel asylum-seeking migrant families to countries where they could be persecuted or tortured.

After the CDC announced that it was letting Title 42 expire, Arizona and 21 other states filed a federal lawsuit on April 3, 2022, in the Western District of Louisiana, asking a judge to stop the government from lifting Title 42. Texas filed a separate lawsuit later that month, seeking the same thing.

Both lawsuits argue the Biden administration violated administrative procedural laws and that if Title 42 is lifted as planned, it could lead to chaos at the border.

In May 2022, District Judge Robert R. Summerhays, an appointee of former President Donald Trump, temporarily blocked the Biden administration from winding down the use of Title 42.

Another federal judge, Judge Emmet Sullivan of the U.S. District Court in Washington, D.C., handed down an opposite ruling in November 2022 and blocked the federal government from continuing to use Title 42.

The Arizona-led coalition attempted to intervene in the Washington lawsuit, which brought the case to the U.S. Supreme Court. The court scheduled arguments in the case then canceled them in February without an explanation.

The high court's move came after the Biden administration filed a brief saying the case would be moot because the federal government planned to end the national public health order that allowed it to invoke Title 42.

What happens if Title 42 is ended?

If the administration lifts Title 42 as planned this month (which happened on May 11, 2023), Border Patrol agents are expected to return to using Title 8 to process migrants.

Last year, before the Louisiana judge blocked the Biden administration from ending Title 42, the administration released a six-part plan to transition away from the policy.

As part of that plan, migrants who were in federal custody would be vaccinated for COVID-19, 600 additional U.S. Customs and Border Protection agents would be deployed across the southwest border and the capacity of federal holding centers would be increased from 12,000 to 18,000.

The Biden administration has announced various policy changes in anticipation of Title 42 lifting.

To discourage migrants from rushing across the border to seek asylum, the government since January 2023 has urged them to use CBP One, a cellphone-based application that allows people to request asylum from their home countries—or from Mexico—and schedule an appointment with immigration agents at a U.S. port of entry. The app offers 740 appointments per day across the nearly 2,000-mile southern border.

Two New Polls Show Biden Immigration Approval Further Slipping

As per the Andrew R. Arthur "Two New Polls Show Biden Immigration Approval Further Slipping" Center for Immigration Studies (CIS) August 2023 article:

Two new polls—one from Reuters/Ipsos and one from Fox News—show that Americans' disapproval of the job President Biden is doing on immigration is growing, after he had received a tiny approval bump once an expected surge of post-Title 42 migrants failed to immediately develop. Advance reporting indicates that the wave is bubbling up now, as July 2023 Southwest border apprehension numbers jumped by about a third from the month before. Not surprisingly, the government appears to be sitting on the official border numbers for last month—because that's what this administration does with bad border news.

Title 42 and Its Immediate Aftermath. While Biden quickly ditched nearly all the successful Trump-era immigration-related policies that had brought a modicum of security to the Southwest border, he kept CDC orders—issued under Title 42 of the U.S. Code in response to the Covid-19 pandemic—directing the expulsion of illegal migrants in place, at least for a while.

Biden tried to end Title 42 in late May 2022, but that effort was blocked in the courts, and his DOJ made only half-hearted efforts to overturn that result. Then, in mid-November 2022, a different federal judge told DHS it had to stop expelling aliens by December 20, though the Supreme Court further delayed that end date.

Finally, after the White House issued a notice on January 30, 2023, that it would end to all Covid-19 restrictions on May 11, 2023, Title 42's death warrant was signed, effective on that later date.

The reason why there was so much litigation to keep Title 42 going was a concern that illegal entries would skyrocket once those CDC orders were lifted. In the spring of 2022, DHS had initially warned that up to 18,000 aliens would attempt to enter illegally per day once Title 42 ended, and although that figure kept getting pared back, the consensus was that illegal entries would climb from already record levels.

3 – Betraying America's Sovereignty With Parole, Gotaways, Visas, Amnesty, Asylum, DACA & More

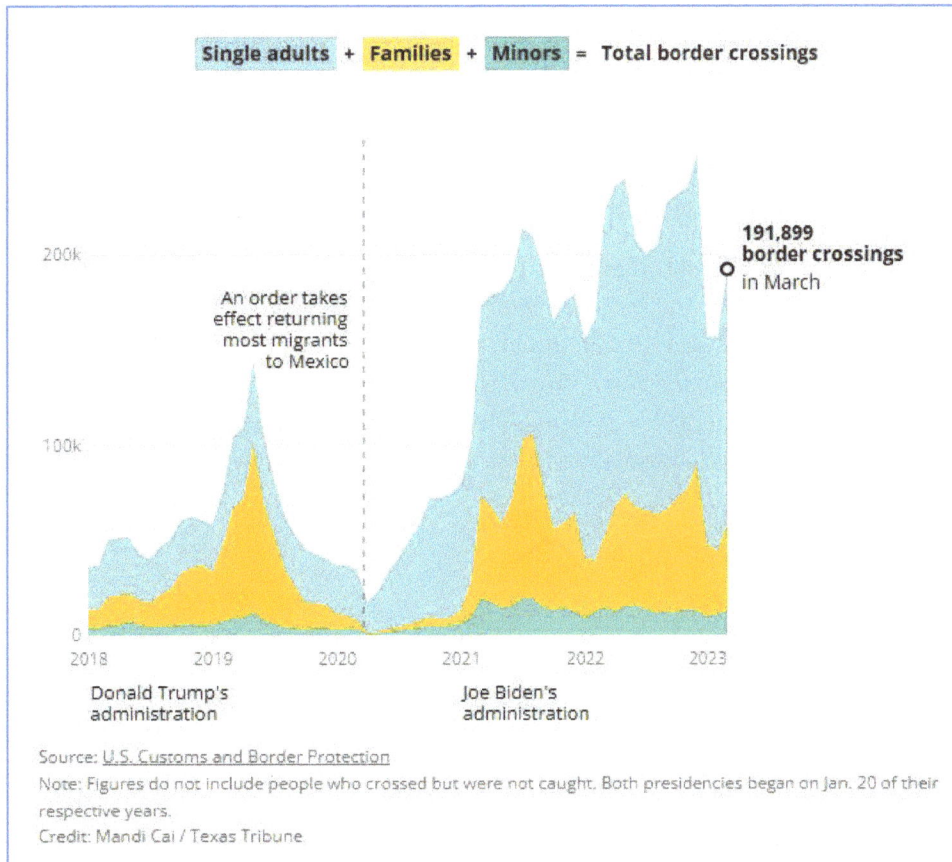

Single adults + Families + Minors = Total border crossings

191,899 border crossings in March

An order takes effect returning most migrants to Mexico

200k

100k

0

2018   2019   2020   2021   2022   2023

Donald Trump's administration

Joe Biden's administration

Source: U.S. Customs and Border Protection
Note: Figures do not include people who crossed but were not caught. Both presidencies began on Jan. 20 of their respective years.
Credit: Mandi Cai / Texas Tribune

Regardless of where you sit on the political and ideological spectrum, there is no denying the catastrophic crisis at our southern border as noted by Mark Morgan in the "The Got-Away Crisis at Our Southern Border" Heritage Foundation September 2022 report: Whether you see it as a humanitarian, national security, or constitutional crisis, or all three rolled into one, it's a colossal failure by any definition.

The Biden administration's open-border policies have drawn seven million illegal aliens from 160 different countries to our borders. The predictable result is a chaotic and deadly southern border where a complex set of threats are pouring into to the U.S. The situation has become so dangerous and untenable that a judge in Kinney County, Texas, formally declared the county was being invaded.

The crux of the crisis is not overly complicated. To deal with the crushing flow of illegal aliens, 80% to 90% of Border Patrol personnel are often pulled off the front lines to care for, process, and release those who have crossed illegally.

Furthermore, per the Lora Ries and Mark Morgan "Biden Encourages Massive Illegal Immigration and Tries To Hide It With Secret Flights" Heritage Foundation January 2022 article:

Biden's Border Patrol has essentially been compelled to abandon much of its core mission to protect the American people. This has left our borders wide-open and facilitated the cartels broadening their operational control over our southern border, making it easier for them to smuggle drugs into the U.S. and expand their human trafficking operation.

It also makes it far simpler for criminal aliens and national security threats to enter the U.S. undetected. You don't have to be a border security expert to understand that as illegal immigration increases, our ability to effectively secure the border deceases.

The Biden administration refuses to acknowledge this basic premise or come clean to the American people about the magnitude of the threats not being interdicted because resources are being diverted to the self-inflicted illegal migration disaster. Intentionally hijacking the Border Patrol's mission, forcing it into an expansive role as a humanitarian agency that must welcome the new generation of illegal alien arrivals, has foreseeably resulted in an exponential increase in "got-aways" illegal aliens who break into our southern border and avoid apprehension.

Why does it matter?

What's another million got-aways on top of the millions of illegal aliens the Biden administration has willfully released into the U.S.? It matters because illegal immigration is not a victimless crime. It has damaging downstream effects across our nation. Unfortunately, in today's environment, emotions, politics, and ideology drive the narrative rather than the truth.

Not everyone entering our country illegally are good, upstanding people. Many have been convicted of or charged with violent offenses. Others are considered dangerous sexual predators. Some are members of some of the most violent transnational gangs in the world. Many have been convicted of driving under the influence. And for those who somehow see drunk driving as "lesser" offense, a threat to be dismissed, I'd to point to the 10,000 drunk-driving fatalities every year in the United States.

Since the Biden administration took the reins, Customs and Border Protection (CBP) has arrested more than 32,000 criminal aliens. Border Patrol alone has apprehended 113 convicted murders and more than 770 illegal aliens convicted of sexual related offenses, including sex with a minor child.

Those numbers represent a 2,000% increase in murderers and a 260% increase in sexual predators, as compared to the Trump administration. Keep in mind—these are only the criminals they've apprehended. Imagine the number of criminals among the million got-aways who now call the U.S. home.

Biden's 'Catch and Release' System for Illegal Border Crossers is a Failure

From the Nolan Rappaport "Biden's 'Catch and Release' System for Illegal Border Crossers is a Failure" *The Hill* September 2023 update:

The inspector general (IG) of the Department of Homeland Security (DHS) recently issued a report finding that the Customs and Border Patrol did not get reliable destination addresses for locating the million illegal border crossers it released into the United States from March 2021 through August 2022.

The IG makes four recommendations for improving DHS's system for obtaining and confirming the accuracy of the destination addresses it gets from illegal border crossers. DHS has rejected all of them.

Would the changes the IG recommended make any difference? The migrants could still give incorrect destination addresses or simply say they don't know where they will be staying. What's more, the average wait for a hearing is four years. Will migrants report changes in their address if they move to a new location while they are waiting?

The Border Patrol released 76 percent of the 1.3 million illegal border crossers it apprehended during the audit period. The release conditions depend primarily on voluntary compliance. Here are some fast facts:

- More than 430,000 were released with a Notice to Appear (NTA), which they were instructed to file with an immigration court to initiate removal proceedings;

- Nearly 95,000 were released with a Notice to Report (NTR) to a U.S. Immigration and Customs Enforcement (ICE) office near their intended destination within 60 days of release, which took less time to issue than an NTA; and

- More than 318,000 were released pursuant to the Parole Plus Alternatives to Detention program. ICE manages this program, which can include electronic devices such as ankle bracelets and smartphones to ensure compliance with release conditions, appearances at court hearings and compliance with final orders of removal.

ICE must be able to locate these migrants to issue NTAs to those who were released without one. Eighty percent (790,090) of the 981,671 recorded addresses were used at least twice; 780 were used more than 20 times. Moreover, the addresses in more than 177,000 migrant records were either missing, invalid or not legitimate residential locations.

The IG made the following recommendations:

- The Border Patrol and ICE should create and implement a plan of action to coordinate requirements and processes when migrants do not have a valid U.S. address for release;

- ICE should establish a policy for validating migrant addresses and elevating address concerns, such as recurring or invalid migrant release addresses recorded into Border Patrol and ICE record-keeping systems;

- ICE's Enforcement and Removal Operations office should analyze address data on a recurring basis to identify trends, such as recurring and uninhabitable addresses, and share known address concerns with U.S. Border Patrol; and

- ICE should evaluate resources and address results for officers overseeing the addresses.

Migrants who think they are eligible for asylum can be expected to attend their hearings, but migrants without a genuine persecution claim have little, if any, reason to appear at a hearing. In any case, for enforcement purposes, it doesn't matter whether they appear. The significant question is whether they will leave the United States if an immigration judge denies their asylum requests and doesn't grant them any other form of relief from deportation.

The DHS Fiscal Year 2020 Enforcement Lifecycle Report indicates that this is not a realistic expectation.

The Lifecycle Report provides statistical data on the end-to-end enforcement lifecycle of 2.8 million migrants who were apprehended after making illegal crossings between ports of entry along the Southwest Border from fiscal 2014 through fiscal 2019, and 725,000 migrants who were released into the country after being found inadmissible at Southwest border port of entry.

Overall, 42 percent of the migrants in this study remained continuously in DHS custody between their initial encounter and a final enforcement outcome (or had no final-outcome but were still in custody as of March 31, 2020). These migrants were repatriated 98 percent of the time, with 0.5 percent receiving relief or other protection from removal and 1.5 percent remaining unresolved as of March 31, 2020.

In contrast, migrants who were never detained were repatriated only 30 percent of the time. In this group, 15 percent were granted relief, 11 percent were subject to unexecuted removal orders, and 55 percent were unresolved.

Only 3 percent of the migrants who were detained initially and then released prior to a final enforcement outcome were repatriated. Eighty-five percent of these cases were unresolved, including 18 percent with unexecuted removal orders.

Frankly, there may not be a good solution to this problem. But continuing to release 76 percent of the illegal crossers the Border Patrol apprehends will only make it worse.

Effective Immigration Enforcement Can't Rely on Honor System

This content is from the Tom Homan Heritage Foundation March 2022 article "Effective Immigration Enforcement Can't Rely on Honor System":

The Department of Homeland Security's own data shows that when individuals were only briefly detained, they were more likely to disappear into the interior of the country—3% of those people were actually repatriated, while 12% were granted relief.

Cases involving the rest—a whopping 85%—were left unresolved. Those seeking to end ICE's ability to detain know that it significantly lowers the chances of deportation, a goal of open-borders advocates.

As part of the Biden administration's new vision for ICE enforcement—one that aligns with the goals of open-borders activists—DHS is not only avoiding detention, but also gutting effective alternative programs, and turning to "community" outreach programs that amount to "catch and release."

This troublesome development signals that the Biden administration may be looking to replace existing programs that have been successfully implemented for nearly two decades with community support services that would require little more than a phone call every three months to monitor migrants' whereabouts after illegally crossing the border.

The current program, called the Intensive Supervision Appearance Program, utilizes a blend of technology solutions and case-management protocols to help ensure compliance with court dates and hearings. It has a pretty good record of ensuring that migrants appear throughout their immigration proceedings.

However, the most effective way of ensuring an alien is removed after receiving a final order of removal is detention. Since detention funds have a limit, the use of programs such as Intensive Supervision are a necessary element to use along with detention.

The Intensive Supervision Appearance Program already covers the population covered by the new request for proposal, so this new case-management program appears to be a redundant waste of taxpayer money that will eliminate any possibility of ensuring individuals actually adhere to the requirements of their immigration proceedings.

Put another way, the administration seems to be launching a program to "catch and release." Further, it's reasonable to wonder whether this program is designed to benefit Biden administration cronies through sweetheart deals, as seen last year in the case of the contractor Family Endeavors.

Biden Administration is Playing Deceitful Shell Game to Claim Fewer Illegal Border Crossings

Per the Erin Dwinell "Biden Administration Is Playing Deceitful Shell Game to Claim Fewer Illegal Border Crossings" Heritage Foundation January 2023 article:

The Biden administration is getting ready to claim that its new immigration "parole" process is a success—drastically cutting down the number of immigrants illegally crossing the southern border between ports of entry. What it won't tell you is that it's playing a crooked shell game—simply taking the same illegal aliens and shifting the processing burden to different locations while still releasing the same number or more into the U.S.

And contrary to the administration's claims, there is no expanded deterrence mechanism to curtail illegal immigration under this parole program. In fact, the program doesn't make the process more safe, orderly, or humane; it continually floods the system, keeping aliens vulnerable to abuse, trafficking, and exploitation.

Earlier this month, President Joe Biden announced his administration's plan to expand the new parole process from just Venezuelans to Cubans, Nicaraguans, and Haitians.

Under this process, a total of 30,000 aliens every month from these four countries will be allowed to make an appointment at a port of entry on Customs and Border Protection's CBP One online app, jump the line ahead of millions waiting their turn in our legal immigration system, be paroled into the U.S., and obtain work authorizations.

What the administration is not telling the American public—at the same time, the Department of Homeland Security touts lower illegal crossing numbers in January (a week before January even ended)—is that it is cooking the books.

This parole program takes the same aliens—those looking for work and filing fraudulent asylum claims so they can be quickly released into the U.S.—and just shifts the processing burden to different locations and personnel.

In addition to being deceitful, this new parole program is unlawful and far from the case-by-case parole process outlined by our lawmakers in the Immigration and Nationality Act. Twenty states have already sued the administration over this unconstitutional program.

The consequence of mass parole and fraudulent asylum claims is that a large majority of those who lose their claims in immigration court will never actually be removed from the United States, thanks to the administration's anti-detention policy.

Because the administration refuses to detain most illegal immigrants while they're awaiting their court hearings, they are released into the U.S. on parole and become difficult to find when their claims are denied.

How difficult? From 2013 to the end of 2021, only 7.7% of illegal aliens who were never detained and who should have been removed from the country were actually removed. That compares to a removal rate of 97% for those who were continuously detained after being caught.

We have already seen the gotaways number skyrocket after the administration started its "successful" parole program for Venezuelans. Now, it will use that as a model for the Cuban-Haitian-Nicaraguan parole program.

For the sake of transparency, the Department of Homeland Security must publish the CBP One app numbers for both "asylum seekers" and parolees each month. If DHS does not publish this information, Congress must demand it during oversight hearings and through legislation.

Put bluntly, the new parole program is an attempt at a crisis cover-up, and expanding it to other countries will only make the crisis worse. Unsurprisingly, it fits in perfectly with the administration's plan to get more aliens into the interior of the U.S. and gut interior immigration enforcement, granting mass de facto amnesty.

The administration's goal is to facilitate the border crisis more quickly and efficiently with reckless disregard and disdain for our nation's security, safety, and laws. Shamefully, Biden and Homeland Security Secretary Alejandro Mayorkas deliberately caused this crisis and continue to shirk all responsibility, always quietly furthering their open-borders agenda.

Robbing Pavel to Pay Pedro: The Biden White House's New Refugee Plan

The Biden administration recently sent Congress a proposal to admit a total of 125,000 refugees in the fiscal year that begins next month.

If recent years are any guide, though, President Joe Biden won't get anywhere near that target. In fiscal year 2021, the U.S. Refugee Admissions Program let in only 11,411 refugees out of an authorized ceiling of 62,500, and in fiscal year 2022, which ends Sept. 30, the program estimates that it admitted up to 25,000 of an authorized 125,000 refugees per the Simon Hankinson "Robbing Pavel to Pay Pedro: The Biden White House's New Refugee Plan" Heritage Foundation September 2022 article:

The Biden administration would like to blame its failure to reach ambitious refugee targets on COVID-19 or the Trump administration rather than on the true cause: a wholesale loss of control at the southern border that has exacerbated massive backlogs in both the legal immigration system and the asylum process.

"Refugees" mostly are recommended to the U.S. by the United Nations High Commissioner for Refugees or other partners in foreign countries. Based on U.S. priorities, the State Department and other U.S. agencies interview applicants and screen them for criminal history and health issues. If they are approved as refugees, the government pays private organizations to transport them to the U.S. and integrate them into our society.

"Asylum," on the other hand, is something that illegal immigrants ask for at the border or after already entering the U.S. without permission. Their claims are handled domestically by U.S. Citizenship and Immigration Services or the Justice Department's immigration courts.

Imagine someone hosting a fancy party at his mansion. He lets the guests in at the front door, checking their tickets to confirm they were invited. Meanwhile, around the back, the kitchen staff is letting in 15 times as many people, with no tickets, no reliable identification, and no background checks.

That, in a nutshell, is the Biden administration's refugee policy versus its policy for asylum-seekers.

Ambitious and Slapdash

Biden's new target numbers for the Refugee Admissions Program are contained in a State Department document, "President's Report to Congress on Proposed Refugee Admissions for Fiscal Year 2023." The ceiling of 125,000 refugees proposed for the new fiscal year "would address the growing needs generated by humanitarian crises around the globe," according to the report submitted to Congress on Sept. 9.

Compounding the morass at the border has been the Biden administration's slapdash effort to admit nearly 80,000 Afghans following the panicked American evacuation from Afghanistan in August 2021.

A chart of U.S. refugee admissions shows that 125,000 would be ambitious even if the border disaster wasn't sucking up all available resources, and if we weren't expecting tens of thousands more Afghan refugees. The only times in the past 40 years that we've come anywhere close to the refugee cap was 1980 (the Mariel boatlift) and a couple of years in the 1990s.

The Obama administration tried shifting resources to refugee processing, but only at the cost of massively increasing delays in the cases of asylum-seekers. Resources to handle the border and subsequent immigration cases are finite: The government has to rob Peter to pay Paul—or more likely, delay an application by Pavel the Ukrainian overseas to admit Pedro the Venezuelan at the border.

For all its flaws, the Refugee Admissions Program is time-tested, organized, and methodical. In comparison, the Afghan and southern border streams are about as orderly as the U.S. evacuation from Saigon in 1975.

For Biden Administration, Self-Reliance is Not an American Value

As noted in the Joe Edlow "For Biden Administration, Self-Reliance Is Not an American Value" Heritage Foundation February 2022 article:

The Biden administration continues to take America down the unsustainable path of open borders and a welfare state for noncitizens. It has proposed a new "public charge" rule that greatly expands the types of government assistance immigrant applicants may receive without becoming a public charge. The administration is breathing new life into the old adage of never letting a good crisis go to waste.

With unprecedented numbers of illegal border crossers being allowed to remain in the United States, the Department of Homeland Security's proposed rule will ensure that most never face scrutiny as public charges, regardless of how many public benefits they receive.

Yet again, Homeland Security Secretary Alejandro Mayorkas says this policy change is consistent with our nation's values. Apparently, the Biden administration no longer values self-reliance.

Self-sufficiency has long been a basic precept of American immigration law and policy. Since the late 19th century, the United States prohibited entry to those deemed to be public charges. While Congress has taken actions consistent with that principle in almost every major piece of immigration legislation, the unwillingness to concretely define "public charge" has caused unresolved tumult and provided a gray area for those that administer our immigration laws. The Biden administration views this as an opportunity to now render it useless.

Critics of Trump-era immigration policies often focused on the public charge rule, a regulation aimed at finally providing some stability and clarity to the issue. While the rule was ultimately undone through well-funded and coordinated litigation efforts, President Joe Biden's Department of Homeland Security has recently announced its intention to publish its own version of the public charge rule.

Unlike the previous administration, this new public charge rule appears to largely codify the gap-filling guidance issued in the late '90s—a measure proven wholly ineffective for over 20 years.

Under the guise of being "fair and humane," the new rule purports to define public charge as "significant reliance on government support." While appearing to be broad and sufficiently encompassing in scope, the definition is, at best, misleading.

In the opinion of Biden's DHS, only cash benefits for income maintenance purposes or long-term institutionalization, when at government expense, meet that standard. Focusing on the former, this definition relegates public charge determinations to only those aliens receiving supplemental Social Security income, cash assistance under Temporary Assistance for Needy Families, or other state, local, or tribal cash programs.

With the focus on cash benefits, DHS seemingly forgets that many in the United States receive and significantly rely on non-cash public benefits. A recipient of federal or state housing assistance is significantly reliant on the government and so are recipients of Medicaid or other state low- or no-cost medical benefits.

Yet, under this proposed rule, neither of those public benefits, nor any other benefit that does not directly provide cash to a recipient, could be considered in determining whether an alien is a public charge. Either DHS is outright ignoring these and other significant benefits or it is drawing an artificial distinction between income deriving cash benefits and other significant non-cash benefits.

Assuming DHS is distinguishing cash and non-cash benefits, DHS is relying on a flawed premise that, for public charge purposes, the analysis should rest on how the benefit is used by the individual. Instead, DHS should generally only look to whether an individual is, in fact, relying on a public benefit at all.

Additionally, the federal government alone spends billions of dollars on federal housing subsidies and Medicaid each year. If the goal is to ensure that aliens are not reliant on the government, the focus should be on how much the government spends on the benefit, not simply whether the benefit is income-deriving.

This proposed rule seems to ignore that reliance on the public benefits comes at a sharp cost to the public. The semantic distinctions never alter the bottom line that everyone who relies on public benefits relies on public tax dollars to fund those benefits.

Self-sufficiency is an American value, but just as critical a value is stewardship of public funds. This rule and its faux distinctions violate the spirit of the law and flies in the face of our American values at great cost to our values and our wallets.

Congress Should Reject Biden Administration's Asylum Rule and Ruin

As per the Lora Ries "Congress Should Reject Biden Administration's Asylum Rule and Ruin" Heritage Foundation August 2022 report: The Biden administration has opened our southern border to an unlimited number of illegal immigrants from all parts of the globe—and has no intention of changing course.

Rather than act to secure our border, it has implemented a three-point border plan:

- Quickly process illegal immigrants into the country, using NGOs that receive FEMA and HHS grants to transport them to the U.S. interior.

- Grant these immigrants parole (albeit in violation of the parole law).

- Use its new rule to expedite applications for asylum for hundreds of thousands of illegal aliens (most of whom are not eligible for asylum).

The administration is actively ruining our asylum system by encouraging this fraud. Congress has the obligation to disapprove of the rule and bring meaning and integrity back to asylum.

Other than naturalization, asylum is the most important immigration benefit we, as a nation, bestow on aliens. Asylum provides protection to those who have been persecuted, or have a well-founded fear of persecution, by a government on account of their race, religion, nationality, political opinion or membership in a particular social group.

By law, anyone who knowingly files a frivolous asylum application is to be permanently barred from all immigration benefits. Asylum is not a benefit that should be abused, nor should the eligibility standards be watered down to "grant" asylum to more aliens in feel-good gestures. Yet those are exactly the approaches the Biden administration is pursuing.

Countless illegal immigrants approaching our southern border admit to journalists and agents that they are coming to the U.S. to work.

They are economic migrants, not victims of persecution. Yet NGOs coach them to claim a fear of returning home as the tactic to get them processed into the U.S.

Meanwhile, the Left misleadingly paints the masses coming here illegally all as "asylum seekers." Exploiting the vagueness of the "membership in a particular social group" catch-all ground for asylum, they expand it to include broad categories of circumstances, such as domestic abuse, general crime, gang activity and, of course, climate change.

Moreover, with its new asylum rule, the administration seeks to remove the adversarial process and cut other procedural corners to accelerate getting to grants of asylum. The net effect of all of this is to encourage more immigrants to submit fraudulent asylum applications.

The administration claims that the rule will reduce the asylum backlog in the immigration courts. In fact, it would simply shift the backlog to Homeland Security's U.S. Citizenship and Immigration Services (USCIS).

The immigration courts currently have a backlog of more than 1.8 million cases. USCIS dwarfs that backlog with more than 8.5 million cases, including more than 468,000 pending asylum cases. By taking on credible fear asylum applications, USCIS will make non-asylum applicants wait even longer for their applications to be decided. Members of Congress need to realize that illegal immigration and asylum fraud hurt legal immigration applicants.

It is also important to note that the administration refuses to charge a fee for asylum applications, even though USCIS is a fee-funded agency. The cost to adjudicate asylum applications is paid through higher fees placed on other applicants seeking different types of benefits.

Because those fees have increased significantly over the years, DHS has now developed the habit of asking Congress for appropriations to cover the asylum adjudication costs instead of charging applicants even a nominal fee. This defies congressional intent that applicants, not U.S. taxpayers, pay for their applications.

Further, charging no fee encourages aliens to file fraudulent asylum claims. There is no downside for them. Indeed, filing a free asylum application makes an illegal immigrant eligible for a work authorization document and buys them much more time in the U.S.—exactly what they want—while they wait for their applications to be adjudicated.

Fourteen states have joined to sue the administration over this asylum rule. Regardless of the court outcome, Congress needs to retake control over asylum, starting with rejecting the new rule. The Left has taken asylum far afield from Congress' original intent. Congress should defund any administrative effort that encourages asylum fraud or waters down the standards for the important benefit.

Indeed, due to the serious national security threats our country faces from Biden's open border policies, this is just the beginning of what Congress needs to do to secure our border. We are running out of time.

Why Amnesty is a Bad Idea

In the context of immigration, amnesty is usually understood as the granting of legal status to a foreign national who illegally entered the United States or illegally overstayed their work or travel visa. Amnesty is a problem for many reasons, most notably because it undermines the rule of law by condoning unlawful behavior and encouraging more aliens to attempt to break the law. The granting of amnesty inevitably fosters the hopes of illegal immigrants that they can attain a future amnesty.

From the "Why Amnesty Is A Bad Idea" FAIR article on their website in December 2023: History has shown the perils of granting amnesty. In 1986, President Ronald Reagan signed the Simpson-Mazzoli Act, which granted amnesty to nearly 3 million illegal aliens. It opened a door that politicians since then have failed to close. The evidence is that the number of illegal aliens in the United States has continued to grow, reaching approximately 14.3 million in 2019.

Most recently, lawmakers in states and at the federal level have introduced successive reincarnations (2001 and 2013) of the DREAM Act, which would grant amnesty to the children of illegal aliens and eventually to their parents. Unable to achieve their legislative aims or to garner public support, activists persuaded President Obama to foist a smaller, deferred semi-amnesty (DACA) upon the country in 2012. DACA remains controversial and is a subject of current examination by the Supreme Court.

We can be reasonably sure that the ever-persistent open-borders, pro-mass-migration lobby will undoubtedly push more amnesties in the future. Federation for American Immigration Reform (FAIR) is here to match their determination and help oppose and defeat such harmful proposals.

Deferred Action for Childhood Arrivals (DACA)

From the Heritage Foundation team of Charles D. Stimson, Hans A. von Spakovsky, and Lora Ries "Assessing the Trump Administration's Immigration Policies" June 2020 report: In April 2001, United States Senators Dick Durbin (D-Illinois) and Orrin Hatch (R-Utah) first introduced the DREAM Act bill in the Senate as S. 1291, but it did not pass. The proposal has since been reintroduced several times, but has not been approved by majorities in either house of the United States Congress.

Obama Administration

In response to the failure of the DREAM Act legislation to pass both houses of Congress, President Obama initiated the immigration policy known as the Deferred Action for Childhood Arrivals (DACA) and was created on June 15, 2012, without legal authority under any immigration statute or the approval of Congress, by then-Secretary of Homeland Security Janet Napolitano.

DACA provided a temporary promise—deferred action—that the DHS would not deport illegal aliens who arrived in the U.S. before their sixteenth birthday, had resided continuously in the U.S. since June 15, 2007, and were under the age of 31 as of June 2012. This administrative amnesty was for two years, although it could be renewed. It also provided government benefits such as work authorizations. The DACA program covered a staggering 700,000 illegal aliens.

The Obama Administration tried to expand the program in 2014 by adjusting the original entry date back to January 1, 2010, and removing the age maximum of 31. At the same time, the Administration tried to establish a new, similar administrative amnesty, the Deferred Action for Parents of Americans and Lawful Permanent Residents (DAPA).

DAPA would have provided the same types of benefits as DACA for illegal aliens who were the parents of minors who were U.S. citizens or lawful permanent residents. However, Texas and 25 other states sued to stop DAPA and the expansion of the DACA and obtained a nationwide injunction that stopped both the implementation of the DAPA program and the DACA expansion.

As the Fifth Circuit Court of Appeals said, federal immigration law establishes an "intricate system of immigration classifications and employment eligibility" and "does not grant the Secretary [of Homeland Security] discretion to grant deferred action and lawful presence on a class-wide basis to 4.3 million otherwise removable aliens." The court also noted that Congress had repeatedly declined to enact legislation "closely resembling DACA and DAPA."

Trump Administration

After the Trump Administration announced that it was ending DACA, numerous lawsuits were filed and the plaintiffs were successful in obtaining preliminary nationwide injunctions keeping the program in place. The Trump Administration filed interlocutory appeals and that consolidated litigation ended up before the U.S. Supreme Court.

The Solicitor General, on behalf of the United States, argued that the rescission of DACA was not reviewable by the courts under the Administrative Procedure Act (APA), which governs rulemaking by federal agencies, because decisions on whether to enforce federal law—here, federal immigration law—is committed to agency discretion. In any event, the government argued that the rescission was lawful because it was beyond the authority of the executive branch to decline on this scale to enforce a law adopted by Congress, and the DHS could not impose such a general amnesty with government benefits without "express statutory authorization."

As the government summarized:

These cases concern the Executive Branch's authority to revoke a discretionary policy of nonenforcement that is sanctioning an ongoing violation of federal immigration law by nearly 700,000 aliens. At best, DACA is legally questionable; at worst, it is illegal. Either way, DACA is similar to, if not materially indistinguishable from, the policies—including an expansion of DACA itself— that the Fifth Circuit previously held were contrary to federal immigration law in a decision that this Court affirmed by an equally divided vote. In the face of those decisions, DHS reasonably determined—based on both legal concerns and enforcement priorities—that it no longer wished to retain DACA.

On June 18, 2020, however, in a legally unsound decision, a five-justice majority held that the DHS's decision to end the program was "arbitrary and capricious" under the Administrative Procedure Act because the DHS did not give "adequate" reasons for its actions. Spirited dissents were filed, including by Justices Samuel Alito and Clarence Thomas, disagreeing that any further justification needed to be provided by the DHS.

Alito said that DACA was "unlawful from the start, and that alone is sufficient to justify its termination." Thomas wrote that this litigation "could—and should—have ended with a determination that [former Attorney General Jeff Sessions'] legal conclusion [that DACA was unconstitutional] was correct." The Court remanded the case to the lower courts to give DHS an opportunity to further explain its reasons for terminating the program.

The Trump Administration's decision to end DACA was the correct decision since President Obama did not have the constitutional or statutory authority to implement a general amnesty program or to provide government benefits to illegal aliens. Providing such an amnesty simply attracts even more illegal immigration—and does not solve the myriad enforcement problems we have along our borders and in the interior of the country.

Moreover, we should not be rewarding law breaking, incentivizing criminal behavior, or providing benefits and preferential treatment to illegal aliens ahead of legal immigrants who have followed the rules to come to the United States and become citizens.

The Other Half of Our Immigration Crisis

Per the Dave Seminara "The Other Half of Our Immigration Crisis" *City Journal* May 2023 article: By now, you've likely heard plenty about the crisis on our southern border. In Fiscal Year 2022, border patrol officers had nearly 2.4 million encounters with migrants from around the world. They're on pace to break those record numbers in 2023, and that tally doesn't include so-called got-aways or those evading detection entirely.

But all this is only half of our illegal immigration problem. There's another surge, this one unfolding at embassies and consulates—and it begins with visas placed in foreign passports. Visa abuse, which begins as legal entry, doesn't get nearly as much attention as illegal border crossings.

As I've been detailing since 2008, roughly half of all illegal immigrants come to the U.S. legally on various non-immigrant visas (NIV)—typically tourist visas (B1/B2)—and overstay them. But the breadth and scope of NIV abuse is likely much worse than that.

We still don't have a firm grasp on NIV overstay rates because many ports of entry don't stamp travelers out of the country when they leave. We do know, however, that last year consular officers approved 80 percent of tourist visa applicants worldwide. That includes, for example, 70 percent of applicants from China, 85 percent from Brazil, 46 percent from Iran, 74 percent from Russia, and an astonishing 94 percent from India.

Customs and Border Protection (CBP) officers authorize most foreign tourists who arrive with B1/B2 visas for a six-month stay, and some can legally extend their stays for up to 18 months. They can't work legally, but many work anyway. (Ironically, CBP officers typically give travelers from rich visa-waiver countries only 90 days, while those from less well-off countries that require visas get twice as much time.)

Foreigners can arrive here on tourist visas and then legally adjust their visa status if they marry an American. It's also legal for foreign "tourists" to come here and interview for jobs. If they find one, their employer can file an adjustment-of-visa-status request for them. The bottom line is that the U.S. is likely the only Western country where one can arrive as a tourist and never go home—all legally.

Many companies, particularly those that can't capture as many H-1B visas as they want, send employees here with B1/B2 visas, claiming that they're here for training when in fact they work here. The government doesn't have the manpower to investigate what foreign employees on B1/B2 visas actually do when they set foot in offices.

During the pandemic, NIV visa numbers plunged as embassies and consulates halted visa processing for spells, but now a new surge of applicants is overwhelming posts in many parts of the world. In March, NIV issuances exceeded 1 million in a single month for the first time since the State Department began releasing monthly NIV data in 2017. The more than 1.1 million NIVs issued in March represent a 41 percent increase over March 2019 figures. Prior months also saw robust increases compared with 2019.

4 – 'Illegal' Aliens Who Break the Rules—Cheat the 'Legal' Immigrants Who Play by Them

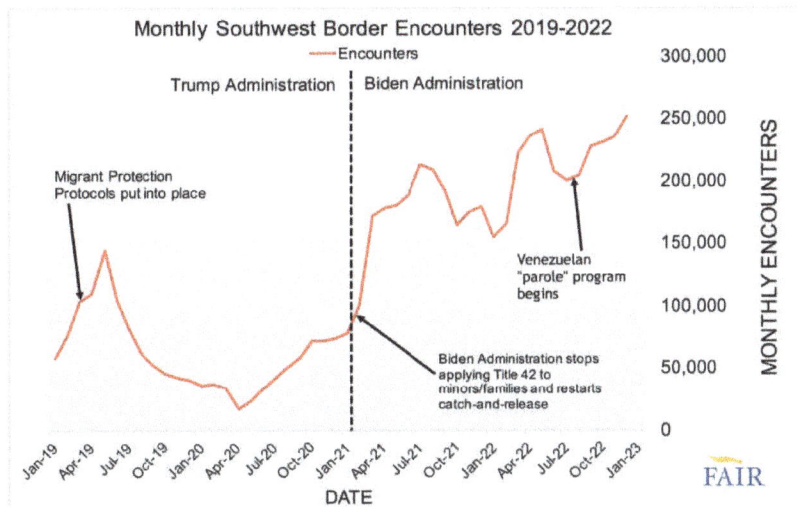

Monthly Southwest Border Encounters 2019-2022

Although the U.S. has experienced three straight record-setting years of illegal alien apprehensions, the Biden Administration has refused to acknowledge this situation as a crisis as shown in the Robert Law and Kristen Ziccarelli "The Biden Administration's Day One Immigration Proposal: Mass Amnesty and No Border Security" America First Policy Institute February 2023 article:

This three-year period corresponded with the 117th Congress, which was controlled by the president's own political party. Now, with a new House majority in the 118th Congress, the Biden Administration has pivoted from denying the existence of a border crisis to blaming conservative policies for what is now taking place.

On January 5, 2023, President Biden unveiled his administration's new border strategy. When doing so, he explained that on his first day in office, he had "sent Congress a comprehensive piece of legislation that would completely overhaul what has been a broken immigration system for a long time."

President Biden argued that this legislation would help the country by "cracking down on illegal immigration; strengthening legal immigration; and protecting DREAMers, those with temporary protected status, and farmworkers, who all are part of the fabric of our Nation." However, he faulted conservatives for refusing to consider this legislation and said, "the failure to pass and fund this comprehensive plan has increased the challenges that we're seeing at our southwest border."

The Biden Administration's U.S. Citizenship Acts of 2021 & 2023

The administration's signature immigration proposal, the U.S. Citizenship Acts of 2021 and 2023, are the most radical and nonsensical pieces of legislation ever proposed for our Nation's borders, as noted in detail by the America First Policy Institute.

On President Joe Biden's first day in office, he proposed the **U.S. Citizenship Act of 2021**, which immediately sparked uproar over provisions like pathways to citizenship for some 11 million illegal immigrants. The measure, introduced in the House of Representatives but died with the end of the 117th Congress, was revived in a somewhat modified form in May 2023 as the **U.S. Citizenship Act of 2023**, which remains stuck in Committee.

The first bill, the **U.S. Citizenship Act of 2021**, was introduced in the House of Representatives by Rep. Linda Sanchez (CA-38) as H.R. 1177 and in the Senate by Sen. Bob Menendez (D-NJ) as S. 348. Its main provisions include giving those in the U.S. "lawful prospective immigrant" status, which would provide work authorization and a Social Security Number. This status would also provide green cards to all Deferred Action for Childhood Arrivals (DACA) recipients and those under Temporary Protected Status (TPS) or Deferred Enforced Departure.

Both prior and current versions of President Biden's immigration reform bill propose pathways to citizenship for millions of illegal immigrants, including DREAMers and farm workers.

Furthermore, the legislation would require the State Department to advertise new rules welcoming illegal aliens deported during the Trump Administration back to the U.S. and would eliminate one-year filing deadlines for asylum applications. On the whole, this bill offers large-scale amnesty for illegal aliens and—unlike previous amnesty legislation—contains no meaningful enforcement provisions either at the border or for criminal aliens detained in American communities. Despite what the administration may try to suggest, amnesty does not equate to border security.

The U.S. Citizenship Act did not gain any traction in Congress, but the Left's fallback legislation was H.R. 6, the **American Dream and Promise Act (ADPA) of 2021**. This was a smaller amnesty package that similarly contained no law enforcement mechanisms. H.R. 6, which would have certainly worsened our Nation's border crisis, passed in the House but hit a bottleneck in the Democrat-controlled Senate Judiciary Committee and was ultimately not brought to the floor.

Both H.R. 6 and H.R. 1177 demonstrated that the Biden Administration is not really interested in border security and that their only policy proposal regarding immigration is amnesty. Still, it is important for all Americans to understand the devastating effects these bills would have had on our Nation.

Here are the top five ways the Biden Administration's day one signature immigration bill, the U.S. Citizenship Act of 2021, would have exacerbated the humanitarian crisis at the southern border, further enriched the cartels, and fueled more human trafficking of vulnerable populations:

It would have granted amnesty to nearly every illegal alien in the country.

The U.S. Citizenship Act of 2021 is the largest amnesty proposal ever introduced. The bill would immediately provide "temporary legal status" (amnesty) to nearly every illegal alien unlawfully in the country as of January 1, 2021, and the ability to then obtain lawful permanent resident status (a green card) and become a naturalized U.S. citizen. Illegal aliens who claim to have entered the country under the age of 18, hold TPS, or worked unlawfully in agriculture are immediately eligible for a green card. Though the bill requires illegal aliens to pass background checks, numerous waivers for a wide range of qualifications are available.

Furthermore, the Biden Administration has a track record of failing to vet aliens thoroughly. In total, more than 11 million illegal aliens would be expected to benefit from amnesty under this bill—more than three times the population that received amnesty in 1986. Granting amnesty to these people would have effectively legalized a group the size of the entire state of Georgia or more than twice the population of Los Angeles.

It contains no mechanisms to secure the border.

Legalizing aliens already in the country will do nothing to stop future flows of illegal immigration. In fact, amnesty fuels more illegal immigration, as demonstrated by the illegal alien population exploding from an estimated 3 million to at least 11 million since the Reagan administration's amnesty bill in 1986. That bill paired amnesty with new enforcement measures, but while the amnesty happened immediately, the enforcement provisions never materialized.

Recent failed attempts to pass a large-scale amnesty bill in 2006, 2007, and 2013 took the same structural approach of pairing amnesty with at least the pretext of border security. In stark contrast, the U.S. Citizenship Act of 2021 contains no provisions to secure the border or enforce the law against illegal aliens in American communities.

Instead, this bill functioned as a lucrative marketing tool for the cartels and traffickers to entice vulnerable aliens to take the dangerous journey north on the prospect of benefiting from amnesty in the future. Increasing such "giveaways" for the illegal alien population serves as a significant pull factor for prospective illegal migrants who are not deterred from coming because there are no consequences for their illegal behavior.

It would have taken jobs away from American citizens.

Granting amnesty to 11 million illegal aliens would flood the labor market and could harm the job prospects and wages of similarly skilled Americans. For example, some research shows that newly legalized people may act as a source of competition with less educated Americans for jobs. These Americans are already subject to long-term declines in labor participation from the past two decades, and the legislation would likely present even greater challenges for them.

As demonstrated by the aftermath of the 1986 amnesty legislation, legalized alien farmworkers would probably leave demanding agricultural work and fill non-agricultural positions within the workforce, which could crowd out Americans from filling these jobs. This is a key example of a policy that puts Americans last and slights many people who immigrated to the U.S. and obtained legal status so they could work legally.

It gives criminals a free pass.

Another harmful component of the bill is its provisions regarding criminal aliens. Though the bill does include stipulations preventing criminal aliens from receiving green card benefits, it contains many exceptions to these rules, including a provision that basically allows anyone who claims their criminal conduct was done in self-defense to qualify for amnesty. Additionally, if an alien is denied an application, he can appeal two different times and may also have felony behavior waived for "humanitarian purposes, family unity or if otherwise in the public interest." One misdemeanor offense may also be waived if the most recent one occurred more than five years before an application.

These rules do nothing but reward criminal behavior because violent offenders will suffer no consequences for their actions, and innocent people will continue to be victimized without justice. The bill also includes requirements for paid lawyers to be provided for illegal alien gang members and other illegal aliens who are public-safety risks, even if they already have one or cannot afford one.

It misleads and wastes money on "root causes."

The Biden Administration's classic catchphrase on immigration is that the "root causes" of illegal immigration must be addressed to solve the crisis at the border. The bill's investment in programs that will allegedly fuel economic growth and enhance workforce productivity in Central American countries acknowledges that migrants are illegally immigrating to the U.S. for economic reasons, which are not grounds for asylum or eventual legal status.

These investments are also meant to address the challenges of hurricanes, drought, and COVID-19, even though weather-related events and pandemics are not grounds for asylum either. Investing millions of dollars in vague initiatives for humanitarian work abroad is not an effective immigration strategy.

Massive barriers to fixing the economic instability in many Central American countries still exist, including decades of government corruption and weak institutions. The bill embraces the "throw money at the problem" approach that has been tried before and has failed. Most importantly, it fails the American taxpayer, whose money is funding a failed strategy, instead of being spent wisely on initiatives that protect them and their way of life.

The border problems afflicting our Nation today are a testament to the bad outcomes of putting politics over practical solution-building. Touting radical mass amnesty as the only viable immigration solution, then blaming those who refuse to accept it while failing to acknowledge the present border crisis, is exactly why the American people have lost confidence in the government's ability to fix these problems.

Before the Biden Administration, innovative policies such as Remain in Mexico, the Asylum Cooperative Agreements, expanded expedited removal, and imposing visa sanctions maintained the integrity of our Nation's borders. We need to implement the successful playbook of America First policies that will secure the border, end human trafficking, and defeat the cartels.

Amnesty Is Unfair to Legal Immigrants Like Me

From the Bill Wong "Amnesty Is Unfair to Legal Immigrants Like Me" *National Review* September 2021 story:

Back in 2021, Democrat lawmakers in Congress were trying to use their $3.5 trillion spending bill to grant amnesty to millions of illegal aliens—even after the Senate parliamentarian ruled that their initial proposal was ineligible for inclusion, due to the complex rules surrounding the filibuster-proof budget "reconciliation" process that Democrats are using to pass their agenda on a strict party-line vote.

Their latest strategy involves updating a registry to allow illegal aliens who arrived after 1972—the current registry cutoff—to seek green cards. Depending on the new date they set, this change could grant legal status, work permits, and ultimately citizenship to millions of people. And if the parliamentarian also rules against this "Plan B," senators such as Dick Durbin (D., Ill.) have already promised to try plans "C and D."

As explained by Bill Wong, a naturalized citizen who jumped through the legal immigration system's many hoops: I find their efforts—and their persistence—deeply offensive. Amnesty would send the wrong message to millions of people trying to immigrate the right way. And it'd also burden our safety-net programs and harm our working class.

I came to America from Hong Kong, which is now, sadly, controlled by the Chinese Communist Party, and lived here for 13 years before beginning the naturalization process. I'm now a proud U.S. citizen, and part of that pride comes from knowing I did it the proper, legal way.

But evidently, it was all unnecessary. If Congress passes this amnesty, people who waltzed across the border would receive the same benefits as legal immigrants like me who patiently followed the rules.

That'll only incentivize more illegal immigration, as people conclude—not unreasonably—that they're better off violating our laws now and waiting for a future amnesty.

Amnestying millions of illegal aliens would also burden already-strained social programs.

Take Social Security and Medicare Part A, which covers hospital stays.

The average illegal alien granted amnesty would cost those retirement and insurance programs about $129,000 more than he contributes via payroll taxes over his lifetime. Multiply that by the 8 million people possibly included in this amnesty, and taxpayers will be on the hook for roughly $1 trillion in additional liabilities.

It's clear that amnesty would effectively bankrupt our beleaguered entitlements.

Amnesty represents a looming disaster for American workers too, especially those on the lower rungs of the socioeconomic ladder. A myth persists that illegal aliens do the jobs that nobody else will.

Yet in reality, illegal aliens constitute a minority of every single occupational category identified by the Department of Labor, even in stereotypically immigrant-heavy occupations such as agricultural field workers and manicurists.

There is simply no job that native-born workers and naturalized citizens won't do. But if they're forced to compete with millions of newly amnestied workers, it'll be harder for citizens to bargain for better wages and benefits.

It's basic supply and demand. Over a dozen credible, peer-reviewed studies have all found that an influx of foreign workers drives down wages. And perversely, less-skilled and minority workers—including many naturalized citizens—tend to suffer the most drastic wage effects.

It's disgraceful that Congress is even considering an amnesty.

Letting lawbreakers cut in front of people who are still patiently waiting to immigrate to this great country would incentivize more criminal behavior, harm American workers of all ethnicities and national origins, and tear holes in our social safety net.

California Offers 700,000 Illegal Immigrants Free Healthcare as Deficit Soars and Population Shrinks

Per the Sarah Rumpf-Whitten "California to Offer 700,000 Illegal Immigrants Free Healthcare as Deficit Soars and Population Shrinks" Fox Business December 2023 news report: California is ushering in 2024 with free healthcare for more than 700,000 migrants living illegally in the Golden State as the state is faced with a looming $68 billion deficit.

The program, which was announced in May 2023 by Gov. Gavin Newsom, will provide health insurance for approximately 700,000 illegal immigrant residents aged 26-49. California has been providing free health insurance to illegal immigrants who are under 26-years-old since 2019. The program began on Jan. 1, 2024 and will provide more illegal immigrants with health insurance under the state's Medi-Cal coverage.

When he proposed the bill two years ago, Newsom called the expansion "a transformative step towards strengthening the healthcare system for all Californians." California's Health and Human Services Secretary Dr. Mark Ghaly called the bill the future "national model" for "expanding access, reducing costs, improving services, and closing equity gaps."

"No other state in the country has done more in the space of health care access and affordability than the state of California," Dr. Ghaly said. "I am proud of this Administration's work to pioneer a comprehensive health care system that will become a national model for expanding access, reducing costs, improving services, and closing equity gaps."

In a statement to Fox News Digital, Gov. Newsom's office said that they believe that everyone deserves access to health care. "In California, we believe everyone deserves access to quality, affordable health care coverage – regardless of income or immigration status," Newsom's office said. "Through this expansion, we're making sure families and communities across California are healthier, stronger, and able to get the care they need when they need it."

The Cost

According to state Sen. María Durazo, D-Calif., the Medi-Cal expansion to include all illegal immigrants is expected to cost $2.6 billion annually. The added cost comes as California is faced with a major budget crisis due to a "severe revenue decline."

According to California's non-partisan Legislative Analyst's Office (LAO) report released, the state's budget deficit has grown exponentially in just a few months' time, up more than $54 billion from just $14.3 billion in June.

Public Benefits for Noncitizen Residents in California Regardless of Status

From the "Public Benefits for Noncitizen Residents in California Regardless of Status" Immigrant Legal Resource Center September 2022 report:

In California, there are many state and local programs that help low-income families, including immigrants, meet their basic needs. Some are limited to lawful permanent residents (green card holders) and people who hold certain types of visas or immigration status while others are available to all people regardless of their immigration status, including those who are undocumented. Here is an overview of some of the benefits available to noncitizens in California. Note that some of these benefits require applicants to also meet income and additional eligibility criteria to qualify.

In-state tuition and financial aid

California allows students who qualify as California residents to pay instate tuition at the University of California, California State Universities, and California Community Colleges. Immigrants who are California residents may qualify for in-state tuition if they have certain types of immigration status. If they are undocumented, they may still qualify for in-state tuition, as allowed under California Assembly Bill 540. If you have any questions about in-state tuition for a specific institution, schools' websites often offer information and resources specifically for undocumented students. The campus admissions office may be able to offer more insights, too.

California also allows certain undocumented students to apply for and receive state based financial aid and institutional scholarships at California colleges and universities. Additionally, California Community College and California State University students can get FREE immigration legal services and fee support that covers the cost of filing DACA or naturalization applications.

Medi-Cal (California's Medicaid program)

In California, emergency Medi-Cal coverage is available to all individuals regardless of immigration status. Undocumented pregnant and postpartum noncitizens are eligible for prenatal Medi-Cal coverage and pregnancy-related coverage for up to a year.

Additionally, undocumented children, individuals age 50 or older, human trafficking survivors, U visa applicants, and U visa holders in California can qualify for full-scope MediCal. California plans to expand full-scope Medi-Cal coverage to undocumented adults ages 26 through 49 by

2024. Full-scope Medi-Cal includes primary, behavioral health, long-term, dental and vision care to those who meet certain eligibility guidelines such as household income based on the federal poverty level.

Other Health Programs

Undocumented Californians may also be eligible for In Home Support Services, Early Breast Cancer Detection and Breast and Cervical Cancer Treatment, Family PACT comprehensive family planning services, and Improving Access Counseling and Treatment for Californians with Prostate Cancer (IMPACT) Food and Nutrition Assistance Undocumented immigrants are eligible for the Women with Infants and Children program (WIC) as well as free or reduced school meals. People who have children with U.S. citizenship or lawful status may apply for CalFresh food assistance on behalf of their children and do not need to provide any information about their own immigration status.

Under the federal government's current definition of public charge, many of the programs listed above will not trigger the public charge rule. For example, use Medi-Cal, CalFresh, housing programs, WIC, emergency and disaster relief, Head Start, free and reduced-cost school meals, stimulus checks, tax credits, and many other benefits are not part of the public charge test.

Other California Laws That Benefit Illegal Aliens:

- Senate Bill No. 1159 (SB 1159): Allows undocumented individuals to apply for professional state licenses (e.g., nursing, barbering, auto repair) using an ITIN instead of a Social Security Number (SSN). Access a list of California state licenses.

- TRUST Act (AB 4): A state-level sanctuary policy that limits local law enforcement's cooperation with Immigration and Customs Enforcement (ICE) unless the arrestee has already been convicted of serious crimes.

- AB 60 Driver Licenses: Allows undocumented individuals to obtain a California state driver license, if certain requirements are met.

- Senate Bill 75 (SB 75): Allows undocumented children and teens under the age of 19 to fully access Medi-Cal benefits.

- Senate Bill 104 (SB 104): This 2019 law allows undocumented immigrants under the age of 26 to be eligible for Medi-Cal.

- Medi-Cal & DACA: In California (under PRUCOL category), DACA recipients can receive full coverage Medi-Cal if they meet the income threshold.

- California Values Act (SB 54): Does not allow state and local resources to be used for mass deportation and separation of families.

- Safe Schools for Immigrants (AB 699): Establishes guidelines for ICE's school visits and provides protections for immigrant students and their parents.

- Immigration Worker Protection (AB 450): Prohibits employers from releasing employee records to ICE agents and prohibits their entry to their place of business. It also requires employers to provide proper notification to employees of upcoming ICE inspection.

- Dignity Not Detention (SB 29): Prohibits new privately funded immigration detention centers to be built in the state of California. It also outlaws cities from rewriting or modifying already existing contracts with private immigration detention centers.

California, of all the large states, has the highest proportion of its immigrant population consisting of illegal aliens, compared to the rest, and this high proportion of illegal immigrants are primarily Hispanic from Mexico and Central America. It's also these groups that have the highest percentage of illegal vs. legal immigrants proportions than other immigrant groups as quantified in "Chapter 5 – How Many Illegal Aliens are in America, Country of Origin, Cross Comparisons & More."

Despite all the many benefits California offers to illegal immigrants compared to other states—could there be a cause and effect relationship, and a relevant correlation, with their inability to assimilate and achieve the American Dream—compared to other states and immigrant populations? Could these many benefits be having the opposite effect? See "Chapter 10 – Mexifornia: California's Largest Ethnic Group is Falling Behind the Others: Why?" that explains the reasons why this inverse relationship could be plausible.

However plausible this relationship may be, it requires more research to determine if there is a strong correlation regarding this perplexing outcome that should concern all Americans, not just Californians.

Migrant Millionaires?

As reported in Dave Seminara's "Migrant Millionaires?" *City Journal* November 2021 article:

In late October 2021, the *Wall Street Journal* reported that the Biden administration was preparing to offer settlements to migrant families that were separated at the border during the Trump administration. The payouts, it said, would total $450,000 each, or $1.8 million for a family of four, possibly costing $1 billion in total.

No one in the administration disputed the story for six days, until Fox News's Peter Doocy asked Biden if such a policy might encourage illegal immigration. Biden responded, "If you guys keep sending that garbage out, yeah, but it's not true." "So this is a garbage report?" Doocy asked. "Yeah, $450,000 per person, is that what you said? That's not gonna happen," Biden said.

But the next day, White House deputy press secretary Karine Jean-Pierre walked back Biden's reaction, insisting that the president is "perfectly comfortable" settling with the migrants—just not for the figure reported. And two days later, the president changed tack, citing the "outrageous behavior" of the Trump administration. "Whether [the border crossing] was legal or illegal, and you lost your child," Biden scolded, his voice raising to a shout. "You lost your child, it's gone—you deserve some kind of compensation, no matter what the circumstance."

It sounds like the president has been out of the loop on the settlement talks. He's attempting to flip the script by talking about children who died during the implementation of Trump's family-separation policy—but that number is likely in the single digits, and it's unclear whether the deaths were caused by the policy or by the dangerous trip over the southern border. In any case, Biden now claims that the $450,000 figure is too high, but even if he's "perfectly comfortable" settling for, say, half that amount, that's still close to $1 million for a family of four.

The potential settlement is just the latest component of an immigration policy that—intentionally or not—encourages illegal immigration. A new NBC News poll gave Republicans a 27-point advantage over Democrats on border security, and a new Harvard-Harris poll shows respondents moving in a hawkish direction. But the president's record suggests that he has little regard for public opinion on the issue.

Still, this latest incentive beggars belief. The child separation policy was a mistake, but the Trump administration was trying to address asylum abuse and the trafficking of children. Aware that families are treated more leniently at the border, smugglers have long matched minors up with their clients to exploit American laws. They also hire teenage boys to move migrants across the border because the U.S. doesn't prosecute minors.

According to the *Washington Post*, some child smugglers have been apprehended more than 100 times. The *Washington Examiner* reported in 2019 that approximately 30 percent of rapid DNA tests in a pilot program revealed no blood relationship between migrant adults and the children they were traveling with.

The *Examiner* reported this spring that border patrol agents performed far fewer DNA tests since Biden's inauguration. And some "minors" released at the border aren't really minors: Yery Noel Medina Ulloa, a 24-year-old Honduran migrant who was released months ago at the border after claiming to be 17, was recently charged with murder in Jacksonville, Florida, after stabbing to death a father of four who had taken him in.

According to the *Journal's* reporting, the migrant lawsuits allege that "some of the children suffered from a range of ailments, including heat exhaustion and malnutrition, and were kept in freezing cold rooms and provided little medical attention." Migrants' attorneys are seeking an average payout of $3.4 million. For context, the per capita GDP in Guatemala, from which 60 percent of the separated migrants hail, is $3,263. In Honduras, the country that produced the second-highest number of migrants, it's $2,010. Gold Star Families who lose a child in combat get $100,000.

Biden Administration to Grant Legal Status to Nearly Half-a-Million Venezuelan Immigrants

From the Caroline Downey "Biden Administration to Grant Legal Status to Nearly Half-a-Million Venezuelan Immigrants" *National Review* September 2023 article: The Biden administration announced in September 2022 that it will grant temporary legal status to nearly half-a-million illegal immigrants from Venezuela so they can pursue work, citing political instability in their home country.

The Homeland Security Department announced the extension and redesignation of Venezuela for Temporary Protected Status (TPS) for 18 months, allowing 472,000 migrants who had arrived in the country as of July 31, 2023, to remain legally and work. The move was greenlighted by Homeland Security Secretary Alejandro Mayorkas.

Venezuelan migrants have accounted for a large portion of those who have crossed the border from Latin America in recent years.

"Temporary protected status provides individuals already present in the United States with protection from removal when the conditions in their home country prevent their safe return," Mayorkas said in a statement. "That is the situation that Venezuelans who arrived here on or before July 31 of this year find themselves in. We are accordingly granting them the protection that the law provides."

About 242,700 Venezuelans were covered under the TPS designation before the update, which could make another 472,000 migrants eligible. The redesignation protects the migrants from deportation and gives them employment authorization. It's unclear how the government will select which migrants will be granted TPS.

Biden Admin Wants Free Medical, Housing for 5.7M Migrants

The Biden administration wants to provide 5.7 million migrants with free medical services, food, and housing, according to government documents per the Charlie McCarthy "Biden Admin Wants Free Medical, Housing for 5.7M Migrants" *Newsmax* October 2023 article:

Immigration and Customs Enforcement (ICE) currently oversees the record number of migrants in the U.S. The total number is 2.4 million more than before President Joe Biden took office—something that was buried in paperwork detailing its "Release and Reporting Management" (RRM) program, the *New York Post* reported.

ICE's plan is for private companies to help in monitoring migrants through ankle monitors, phone apps, and in-person check-ins.

The administration's aim to provide free medical services, food, and housing would cost "billions" and effectively be a "welfare" program for non-detained migrants awaiting court dates, former ICE Director Tom Homan told the *Post*.

"The RRM is just a push by the open border advocates to provide welfare benefits to 6 million people," Homan said. RRM will "replace all of ICE's nondetained programs" and would "apply to the entire nondetained docket," an ICE question-and-answer form published in September read.

Migrants held in ICE detention for processing at the border or in facilities awaiting deportation are not included in the 5.7 million number.

A request for information (RFI) form published Aug. 17, 2023, said RRM participants would receive "legal assistance; psychosocial services; therapeutic services; medical services; food and clothing banks; housing; public transportation information; parental information; education information; and repatriation and reintegration services."

"These services are designed to increase participant compliance with immigration obligations through information, stabilization, and support. Services will be individualized to each participant's needs and may range from basic referrals to intensive direct assistance," the RFI form read.

"They're going to give legal assistance to illegal aliens at the taxpayers' expense to fight the government," Homan told the *Post*. He added that all the services combined are a "massive giveaway that are going to cost billions of dollars."

RRM remains in the planning phase. The Biden administration plans to send out a "Request for Proposal" to vendors in fiscal year 2024, the ICE Q&A form reads.

The RFI form said RRM is intended to replace Alternatives to Detention (ATD), which was released in 2004. The new Biden initiative would "require additional funding" beyond what is currently allocated for ATD, the Q&A form says.

5 – How Many Illegal Aliens in America, Country of Origin, Cross Comparisons & Tracking

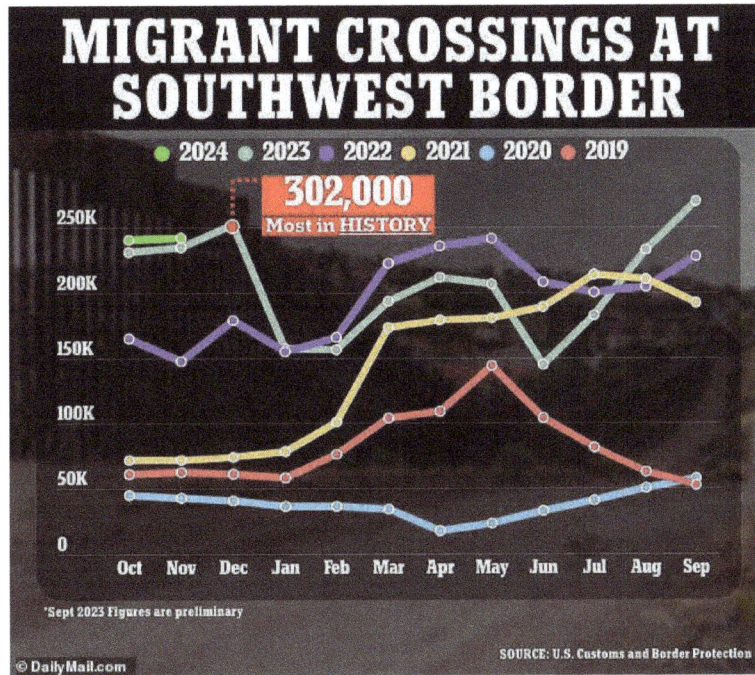

Contrary to the popular narrative that America has always been a nation of mass immigration ("a nation of immigrants"), U.S. immigration policy has, in reality, alternated between more permissive and more restrictive schemes. As a result, America has experienced both "great waves" of immigrants and "great lulls," with very little immigration.

From the Population Growth and the Environment website page of FAIR:

New immigrants and their U.S.-born children currently make up 75 to 80 percent of our annual population growth. Our country's population is estimated to increase by approximately 77 million people – from 327 million in 2019 to 404 million in 2060 – in only four decades.

Immigration has long been integral to America's national identity, but our citizenry has also historically been united by what Abraham Lincoln called "the political religion of the nation"—a shared reverence for our Constitution and laws. Indeed, while Americans tend to support immigration as an ideal, many intuitively sense that something has gone badly awry with an immigration system overrun with illegality. And the facts support that intuition.

Denying Reality on Immigration

Per the Jeffrey H. Anderson "Denying Reality on Immigration" *City Journal* July 2022 article: According to Census Bureau statistics, immigrants' share of the U.S. population rose more from 1990 to 2010 than during any other 20-year period since these figures were first recorded in 1850—from 7.9 percent to 12.9 percent (up 5 percentage points).

This broke the previous record set from 1850 to 1870, when it rose from 9.7 percent to 14.4 percent (up 4.7 percentage points). In other words, immigration reshaped the composition of the population more significantly from 1990 to 2010 than over any prior 20-year period since at least 1850, including during the great waves of immigration of the late nineteenth century.

While the Census Bureau couldn't collect reliable statistics on immigrants' share of the U.S. population during the most recent decennial census—largely because it adopted Covid policies that kept it from going door-to-door during much of 2020—its (generally less reliable) annual surveys indicate that immigrants' share of the U.S. population continued to rise from 2010 to 2020, though not by as much as over the previous few decades.

Under President Biden, border crossings have accelerated at an extraordinary clip. Under the Trump administration, the Department of Homeland Security (DHS) called the "Remain in Mexico" policy (officially, the Migrant Protection Protocols) "an indispensable tool in addressing the ongoing crisis at the southern border and restoring integrity to the immigration system."

Yet, as Andrew Arthur of the Center for Immigration Studies (CIS) writes, "the Biden administration suspended enrollments in the program the day after taking office." Arthur adds that the Biden administration has now proposed a rule that would "allow DHS to release any illegal migrant it cannot detain into the United States, while at the same time Biden is asking Congress to cut immigration detention in his proposed FY 2022 budget."

As most Americans intuitively glean, strange things are afoot when it comes to immigration. Its sheer quantity, its frequent illegality, and the de-emphasis of assimilation are all profound departures from our country's traditional norms. As with other issues, it is not every day Americans but elites who are denying reality.

Foreign-Born US Population of 49.5M Highest in History

As noted in the Mark Swanson "Foreign-Born US Population of 49.5M Highest in History" *Newsmax* November 2023 article: Illegal immigration has fueled the U.S. foreign-born population to 49.5 million, a number that accounts for 15% of the population in the country, according to analysis by the Center for Immigration Studies (CIS).

Foreign-born estimates earlier provided by the Census Bureau showed the U.S. wouldn't hit 15% until 2033, according to CIS.

CIS showed that the foreign-born population has increased by 137,000 per month since President Joe Biden took office, a number CIS called "unprecedented." By comparison, the foreign-born population grew 42,000 per month under former President Donald Trump. The count under Biden dwarfs that of former two-term Democrat President Barack Obama (68,000 per month).

The 4.5 million increase of foreign-born since January 2021 also includes 2.5 million in illegal immigrants, according to the CIS analysis.

Key to CIS' findings is that the 4.5 million represents a net change, meaning, "significantly more than 4.5 million people had to have arrived from abroad for it to grow this much." CIS said the actual number of arrivals was likely closer to 5.6 million from January 2021 through last month, though that's at a 90% confidence level.

The influx has strained border states and metropolitan areas that have Democrat mayors and governors losing patience with the Biden administration's immigration policy of allowing asylum-seekers to venture anywhere they wish while they wait for hearings that are backlogged.

The 4.5 million in arrivals is larger than the individual populations of 25 U.S. states.

Also, a net figure is the 2.5 million rise in illegal individuals. CIS says the number is possibly as high as 2.7 million since Biden took office. Biden's campaign promise of curtailing "immigration enforcement" has "helped spur more illegal immigration," CIS said.

According to CIS estimates, at this current rate the foreign-born population would likely hit 59 million—17.3% of the U.S. population—at the end of a would-be Biden second term in 2028.

"Adding so many people to the country so fast may please employers and immigration advocacy groups, but any serious discussion of immigration policy has to grapple with these numbers and the implications they have for American society," CIS wrote.

CIS provided its analysis based on the Census Bureau's Current Population Report, or household survey, that was published Nov. 9. 2023.

How a Half-Million Migrants Moved North

As per the Mary Anastasia O'Grady "How a Half-Million Migrants Moved North" *Wall Street Journal* November 2023 article:

An estimated half-million people are expected to enter Panama from Colombia through the Darién Gap in 2023. Let that sink in. It's a big number for a trail through dense jungle that only three years ago was traversed by about 20,000 souls annually.

Many who have made the trek this year are Venezuelans. There are also Africans, Cubans, Ecuadoreans, Middle Easterners and Chinese, among others. Most are heading north to the U.S. border. But they aren't making the dangerous Darién journey on their own. Local officials in Colombia are helping them enter Panama illegally.

The smuggling of humans through the Darién starts on the south side of the Gulf of Urubá. In a video published at the end of September by CNN en Español, migrants are seen being brought across the water in large, modern boats to the town of Acandi.

Colombia's ministry of defense has blamed the operation on the narcotrafficking cartel known as Clan del Golfo. Yet the business is run in broad daylight—with the enthusiastic assistance of the local government. In the video, the governor of the Colombian department of Chocó explains how his team is "working with all the institutions, NGOs and law enforcement" to help the migrants on their way. He calls them "citizens of the world." You connect the dots.

How Many Illegal Aliens Are in the United States? 2023 Update

As shown in the "How Many Illegal Aliens Are in the United States? 2023 Update" FAIR June 2023 report:

As of June 2023, Federation for American Immigration Reform (FAIR) estimates that approximately 16.8 million illegal aliens reside in the United States. This is significantly higher than our January 2022 illegal alien population estimate of 15.5 million. This estimate is also a 2.3 million increase from our end-of-2020 estimate, meaning the illegal alien population increased 16 percent nationwide during just the first two years of Joe Biden's presidency.

FAIR's most recent comprehensive fiscal cost study showed that illegal aliens and their U.S.-born children impose a net annual cost of $150.6 billion on American taxpayers as of the beginning of 2023. According to the previous (2017) cost study, the annual net cost of illegal migration was approximately $116 billion.

This means that in the short span of 5 years, the annual cost to American taxpayers has increased by nearly $35 billion. When further adjusted for the increased illegal alien population growth demonstrated by this report, taxpayers are being set up for annual spending to the tune of $163 billion and counting. This burden will only continue to grow as a result of the Biden administration's open-borders policies.

Who is an Illegal Alien? An illegal alien is simply any alien who is present in the United States without legal status, like a valid visa or lawful permanent residence.

It is important to note that "legal status" is not the same as "lawful presence." For example, recipients of deferred action, deferred enforced departure, Temporary Protected Status (TPS), or parole do not have legal status. These programs (some of which are authorized by statute, some are not) do not give illegal aliens visas or green cards. They merely defer deportation for a period of time.

Nevertheless, these aliens are still described as "lawfully present" or as having "lawful presence." That is because "lawful presence" is a term of art under immigration law designed to clarify that although an alien has no legal status, he or she is not accruing unlawful presence under Immigration and Nationality Act (INA) Section 212(a)(9) for purposes of the three and ten-year bars.

Under INA Section 212(a)(9), an alien who has no legal status will start to accrue days of unlawful presence. If the alien accrues more than 180 of unlawful presence and is then deported or otherwise leaves, the alien is barred from admission for three years. If the alien accrues 365 or more days (one year) of unlawful presence and is then deported or otherwise leaves, s/he is barred from admission for ten years.

Unsurprisingly, most illegal aliens tend to live near the United States' border with Mexico or in states with "sanctuary" policies that purport to offer welcoming environments and protection from immigration enforcement. The ten states with the largest estimated illegal alien populations account for just under three-fourths (70.6%) of the national illegal alien total.

However, this does not mean that states which hold a comparatively small share of the illegal alien population are unaffected by its negative impact. In fact, as FEDERATION FOR AMERICAN IMMIGRATION REFORM (FAIR) has pointed out in other studies, illegal immigration often hits these states the hardest, as it is more difficult for low-population areas to absorb the impacts of illegal immigration.

States With the Highest Percentage of Illegal Immigrants

As per the "States with the Highest Percentage of Illegal Immigrants" Yahoo! Finance July 2023 report:

It is challenging to calculate the exact impact of undocumented immigration on the US economy. However, independent non-governmental organizations frequently publish studies that estimate these costs. Federation for American Immigration Reform (FAIR) - a nonprofit and anti-immigration organization, recently published a study that estimates the cost of illegal immigration to be $150.7 billion per year. According to the study, the total federal expenditure on illegal aliens is $66.4 billion. It also claims that this expenditure has increased by 45 percent since 2017. The study also claims that illegal aliens contribute about $31 billion in taxes.

While the figures above are alarming, organizations that favor undocumented immigrants believe that citizenship for them would boost US economic growth. The Center for American Progress (CAP), a public policy research and advocacy organization, conducted a study to assess the impact of the legalization of illegal immigrants on the US economy. It claims that legal citizenship of all undocumented immigrants would boost US GDP by $1.7 trillion over 10 years. It also claims that such a measure would create 438,800 new jobs in the same period.

Whether pathways for legal citizenship for illegal immigrants would be created or not, remains to be seen. What is clear for now, however, is that their existence would remain significant in states like California, which has the highest percentage of illegal immigrants. Another point of clarity is regarding the nature of jobs illegal immigrants generally pursue, as the majority is restricted to precarious job opportunities.

What is the profile of illegal immigrants in the United States?

Mexicans traditionally represented the majority of illegal immigrants in the United States. However, their share is declining. By 2017, they declined to less than half of the US illegal immigrant population. So what does the illegal immigrant population of the United States now look like?

As of 2019, the total illegal immigrant population of the United States was estimated to be around 11 million by Migration Policy. Mexicans represented 48 percent of this population. Illegal migrants from El Salvador and Guatemala constituted 7 percent each. Indians represented 5 percent of the total illegal immigrant population of the United States in 2019.

The age group 35-44 represented the highest fraction of this population at about 28 percent. 16 years and under age group constituted the smallest fraction at about 5 percent. 46 percent of the illegal immigrants were women.

The highest fraction (21 percent) of illegal immigrants worked in the construction industry. 16 percent worked in accommodation and food services, arts, entertainment, and recreation. It is worth noting that only 4 percent of illegal immigrants participating in the labor force were unemployed. Despite a considerable employment rate of the participating labor force, 43 percent of illegal immigrants remained below 200% of the poverty level.

Which state has the highest number of illegal immigrants?

California has the highest number of illegal immigrants. According to our estimates, more than 3 million illegal immigrants live in California. They have a considerable impact on California's labor market, as they make up one in ten workers in California.

15 Washington -- Illegal immigrants percentage: 3.68%.

14 Connecticut -- Illegal immigrants percentage: 3.90%.

13 Virginia -- Illegal immigrants percentage: 3.90%.

12 Hawaii -- Illegal immigrants percentage: 3.98%.

11 Georgia -- Illegal immigrants percentage: 3.98%.

10 Illinois -- Illegal immigrants percentage: 4.15%.

9 New Mexico -- Illegal immigrants percentage: 4.32%.

8 Florida -- Illegal immigrants percentage: 4.52%.

7 Maryland -- Illegal immigrants percentage: 4.71%.

6 New York -- Illegal immigrants percentage: 4.87%.

5 Arizona -- Illegal immigrants percentage: 4.99%.

4 New Jersey -- Illegal immigrants percentage: 6.26%.

3 Texas -- Illegal immigrants percentage: 6.77%.

2 Nevada -- Illegal immigrants percentage: 7.4%.

1 California -- Illegal immigrants percentage: 7.63%.

Frequently Requested Statistics on Immigrants and Immigration in the United States

From using the detailed Nicole Ward and Jeanne Batalova "Frequently Requested Statistics on Immigrants and Immigration in the United States" Migration Policy Institute (MPI) March 2023 report we can see:

Worldwide, the United States is home to more international migrants than any other country, and more than the next four countries—Germany, Saudi Arabia, Russia, and the United Kingdom—combined, according to the UN Population Division's mid-2020 data. While the U.S. population represents about 5 percent of the total world population, close to 20 percent of all global migrants reside in the United States.

In this section, **"Foreign born" and "immigrant"** are used interchangeably and refer to persons with no U.S. citizenship at birth. This population includes naturalized citizens, lawful permanent residents, refugees and asylees, persons on certain temporary visas, and unauthorized immigrants.

Immigrants Now and Historically

How many immigrants reside in the United States?

Nearly 45.3 million immigrants lived in the United States in 2021, the most since census records have been kept. In 2021, immigrants comprised 13.6 percent of the total U.S. population, a figure that remains short of the record high of 14.8 percent in 1890 and slightly below the 13.7 percent share they comprised in 2019.

How have the number and share of immigrants changed over time?

In 1850, the first year the United States began collecting nativity data through the census, the country had 2.2 million immigrants, representing nearly 10 percent of the total population.

Between 1860 and 1920, immigrants' share of the population fluctuated between 13 percent and 15 percent, peaking at 14.8 percent in 1890 amid high levels of immigration from Europe. Restrictive immigration laws in 1921 and 1924 limited permanent immigration almost exclusively to those from Northern and Western Europe. Combined with the Great Depression and onset of World War II, this led to a sharp drop in new arrivals from the Eastern Hemisphere. The foreign-born share steadily declined, hitting a record low of 4.7 percent (or 9.6 million immigrants) in 1970 (see figure below).

Size and Share of the Foreign-Born Population in the United States, 1850-2021

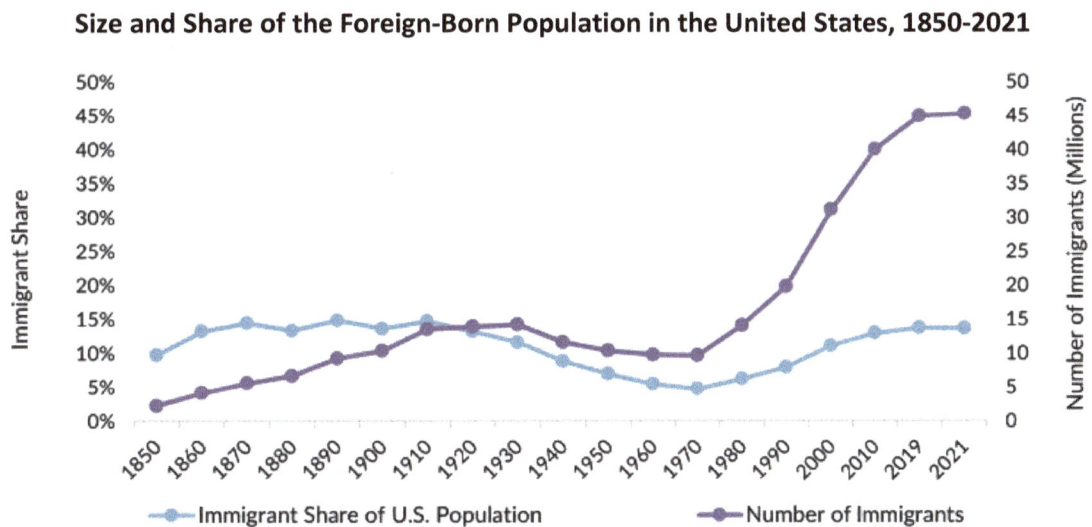

Sources: Migration Policy Institute (MPI) tabulation of data from U.S. Census Bureau, 2010-21 American Community Surveys (ACS), and 1970, 1990, and 2000 decennial census. All other data are from Campbell J. Gibson and Emily Lennon, "Historical Census Statistics on the Foreign-Born Population of the United States: 1850 to 1990" (Working Paper no. 29, U.S. Census Bureau, Washington, DC, 1999).

Since 1970, the share and number of immigrants had increased rapidly, mainly because of increased immigration from Latin America and Asia following important shifts in U.S. immigration law such as the Immigration and Nationality Act of 1965, which abolished national-origin admission quotas.

Where are most immigrants from originally?

Mexicans are the largest group of U.S. immigrants, comprising 24 percent of the total immigrant population in 2021, which is a decline from 30 percent in 2000. India and China (including Hong Kong and Macao but not Taiwan) were the next two largest sending countries, accounting for approximately 6 and 5 percent, respectively, of the overall foreign-born population. Other top countries of origin include the Philippines (4 percent); El Salvador, Vietnam, Cuba, and the Dominican Republic (each 3 percent); and Guatemala and Korea (each 2 percent).

Together, these ten countries accounted for 56 percent of all immigrants in the United States in 2021.

How long have current immigrants resided in the United States?

Forty-eight percent of all immigrants in the United States in 2021 arrived prior to 2000 (28 percent entered before 1990 and 20 percent between 1990 and 1999), 24 percent entered between 2000 and 2009, and 28 percent have come since 2010.

How many U.S. residents are from immigrant families?

Immigrants and their U.S.-born children number approximately 87.7 million people, or close to 27 percent of the U.S. population in the 2022 CPS, an increase of approximately 14.7 million (or 20 percent) from 2010.

Demographic, Educational, and Linguistic Characteristics

Before we proceed we need to clarify that the demographic category of "Hispanic" is not a race, it's an ethnic category, united by language and culture—as opposed to the categories of white, black, or Asian—which are racial categories.

Race as used by the U.S. Census Bureau reflects the race or races with which individuals most closely self-identify. Race categories include both racial and national-origin groups.

Hispanic and Latino are ethnic, not racial, categories. They include individuals who classified themselves in one of the specific Spanish, Hispanic, or Latino categories listed on the decennial census and American Community Survey questionnaire—"Mexican, Mexican Am., Chicano," "Puerto Rican," or "Cuban"—as well as those who indicate that they are "other Spanish/Hispanic/Latino origin." Persons who indicated that they are "other Spanish/Hispanic/Latino" include those whose origins are from Spain, the Spanish-speaking countries of Central or South America, the Dominican Republic, or people who self-identify more generally as Spanish, Spanish-American, Hispanic, Hispano, Latino, and so on.

What is the median age for immigrants?

The immigrant population's median age in 2021 was 47 years, making it older than the U.S.-born population, which had a median age of 37 years. One reason for this difference is that immigrants arrive largely as adults, whereas immigrants' children born in the United States contribute to the younger median age of the native-born population.

What is the racial makeup of immigrants?

In 2021, 27 percent as Asian of immigrants reported their race as single-race Asian, 21 percent as White, 9 percent as Black, and 20 percent as some other race. About 22 percent reported having two or more races.

Note: These statistics reflect changes in how the Census Bureau asks about race that have been made since the 2020 decennial census.

How many immigrants are Hispanic or Latino?

In 2021, 44 percent of U.S. immigrants (19.9 million people) reported having Hispanic or Latino ethnic origins.

How many Hispanics in the United States are immigrants?

Most U.S. Hispanics are U.S. born. Of the 62.5 million people in 2021 who self-identified as Hispanic or Latino, 32 percent (19.9 million) were immigrants and 68 percent (42.6 million) were native born.

Which languages are most frequently spoken at home?

Not including English, Spanish was the most common language spoken at home in all but three states: Hawaii (Ilocano) and Maine and Vermont (French). Not including English or Spanish, Chinese, German, French and Vietnamese were among the commonly spoken languages.

	Number	Share of All Speakers of Foreign Languages
TOTAL	67,754,000	100.0%
Spanish	41,255,000	60.9%
Chinese (incl. Mandarin and Cantonese)	3,405,000	5.0%
Tagalog (incl. Filipino)	1,715,000	2.5%
Vietnamese	1,523,000	2.2%
Arabic	1,391,000	2.1%
French (incl. Cajun)	1,175,000	1.7%
Korean	1,073,000	1.6%
Russian	1,045,000	1.5%
Portuguese	937,000	1.4%
Haitian	895,000	1.3%
Hindi	865,000	1.3%
German	857,000	1.3%
Yoruba, Twi, Igbo, other languages of Western Africa	640,000	0.9%
Amharic, Somali, other Afro-Asiatic languages	596,000	0.9%
Yiddish, Pennsylvania Dutch, other West Germanic languages	574,000	0.8%
Polish	533,000	0.8%
Italian	513,000	0.8%
Urdu	508,000	0.7%

Source: Migration Policy Institute (MPI) tabulation of data from the U.S. Census Bureau 2021 ACS.

Regardless of nativity, in 2021 approximately 78 percent (245.5 million) of all 313.2 million U.S. residents ages 5 and older reported speaking only English at home. The remaining 22 percent (67.8 million) reported speaking a language other than English at home.

Among those who reported speaking a language other than English at home, 61 percent spoke Spanish. Other top languages were Chinese (including Mandarin and Cantonese, 5 percent); Tagalog (almost 3 percent); and Vietnamese, Arabic, French (including Cajun), and Korean (about 2 percent each).

How many immigrants are Limited English Proficient (LEP)?

In 2021, approximately 46 percent (20.8 million) of the 45 million immigrants ages 5 and older were Limited English Proficient (LEP). Immigrants accounted for 80 percent of the country's 25.9 million LEP individuals.

Note: The term "Limited English Proficient" refers to persons ages 5 and older who indicated on the ACS questionnaire that they spoke English less than "very well."

What share of the immigrant population has a college education?

In 2021, 34 percent (13.6 million) of the 40.2 million immigrants ages 25 and older had a bachelor's degree or higher, a rate similar to that of U.S.-born adults. However, newer arrivals tend to be better educated; 47 percent of immigrants who entered the country between 2017 and 2021 held at least a bachelor's degree and these educational attainment levels vary by immigrants' countries of origin.

Approximately 80 percent of immigrant adults from India had a bachelor's degree or more in 2021, more than any other origin country. Other top countries were the United Arab Emirates (78 percent), Saudi Arabia (77 percent), Taiwan (73 percent), Bulgaria, France, and Singapore (67 percent each). Among immigrants who arrived between 2017 and 2021, the share who were college graduates was the highest among Indians (86 percent), followed by those from France, Taiwan, and Spain (between 81 percent and 82 percent). The college-educated share is also high among Venezuelans, who represent the fastest growing U.S. immigrant group. Fifty-seven percent of all Venezuelan immigrant adults and 62 percent of recent arrivals have at least a bachelor's degree.

Immigrant Destinations

Which U.S. states have the largest numbers of immigrants?

The U.S. states with the most immigrants in 2021 were California (10.5 million), Texas (5.1 million), Florida (4.6 million), New York (4.4 million), and New Jersey (2.1 million).

As a percentage of the total population, immigrants made up the largest shares in California (27 percent), New Jersey (23 percent), New York (22 percent), Florida (21 percent), Hawaii (19 percent), and Nevada (18 percent).

How many immigrants are in the U.S. civilian labor force?

Immigrants constituted 17 percent (28.6 million people) of the civilian labor force (166.9 million) in 2021, which comprises both employed and unemployed people. Immigrants' share of the labor force has more than tripled since 1970, when they accounted for approximately 5 percent of the civilian labor force.

Income and Poverty

Immigrants tend to have very similar incomes to the native born. Immigrant households in 2021 had a median income of $69,622, compared to $69,734 for native-born households.

Fourteen percent of immigrants were poor (that is, with family incomes below the official poverty threshold of $27,500 for a family of four with two children in 2021), compared to 13 percent of the U.S. born.

Health Insurance Coverage

What share of immigrants have health insurance?

Approximately 57 percent of immigrants had private health insurance in 2021 (compared to 69 percent of the U.S. born), and 32 percent had public health insurance coverage (compared to 38 percent of the U.S. born). Meanwhile, 19 percent lacked health insurance (compared to 7 percent of the U.S. born).

Children of Immigrants

In the context of immigration law, children are legally defined as follows:

- **First-generation immigrant children** are any foreign-born children with at least one foreign-born parent.

- **Second-generation immigrant children** are any U.S.-born children with at least one foreign-born parent.

- **Children with immigrant parents** are both first- and second-generation immigrant children.

How many U.S. children live with immigrant parents?

Approximately 18 million U.S. children under age 18 lived with at least one immigrant parent in 2021. They accounted for 26 percent of the 69.7 million children under age 18 in the United States, up from 19 percent in 2000 and 13 percent in 1990.

Most of these children are native born. Second-generation immigrant children born in the United States to at least one foreign-born parent accounted for 88 percent (15.8 million) of all children with immigrant parents. The remaining 12 percent (2.2 million) were born outside the United States.

Permanent Immigration

How many immigrants obtain lawful permanent residence (also known as getting a green card)?

In fiscal year (FY) 2021, 740,000 immigrants became lawful permanent residents (LPRs), also known as green-card holders). This was a 5 percent increase over the 707,000 new green cards issued in FY 2020, which covered the end of the Trump administration and the first few months of the COVID-19 pandemic and marked the lowest number since 2003 and the first time the figure dropped below 1 million since 2013, when 991,000 people obtained green cards. The number of new LPRs in FY 2021 represented a decrease of 444,000 (37 percent) from the recent high of almost 1.2 million in FY 2016.

Under which categories are permanent immigrants admitted?

There are four main pathways to obtain a green card: through a family relationship, employment sponsorship, humanitarian protection (for refugees and asylees), and the Diversity Visa (DV) lottery (also known as the green-card lottery). Some categories within these pathways are capped at the number of new green cards that can be issued each year.

Of the 740,000 immigrants receiving green cards in FY 2021, 52 percent were immediate relatives of U.S. citizens (an uncapped visa category), followed by 9 percent who were family-related immigrants (whose admission is limited by visa and country caps). About 26 percent of new LPRs were sponsored by their employers or self-petitioned, including investors who create jobs, a jump from 21 percent of new LPRs in FY 2020 and 14 percent in FY 2019. Meanwhile, 8 percent adjusted from refugee or asylee status and approximately 2 percent were diversity lottery winners.

What are the most common countries of origin for new permanent immigrants?

The top six countries of birth for new LPRs in FY 2021 were Mexico (14 percent), India (13 percent), mainland China (7 percent), the Philippines (4 percent), and the Dominican Republic and Cuba (3 percent apiece). Together, these countries represented about 44 percent of all new green-card recipients in FY 2021.

Temporary Visas

Non-immigrants are citizens of other countries who come to the United States temporarily for a specific purpose, such as education or tourism. There are more than 80 classes of non-immigrant visas, including temporary workers and trainees, religious workers, intracompany transferees, foreign students, visitors for business or for pleasure, international representatives, and foreign government officials. Most classes of non-immigrants must have a permanent home abroad and most can be accompanied by a spouse and minor children. Non-immigrants are restricted to the activities allowed by their visa while in the United States.

How many non-immigrant visas does the State Department issue each year?

The 6.8 million non-immigrant visas issued by the State Department in FY 2022—which include tourists and other short-term visitors—represented a non-surprising, post-pandemic rapid increase of 144 percent from the 2.8 million issued in FY 2021, the lowest number since 1996.

Sixty-six percent of non-immigrant visas issued in FY 2022 were temporary business and tourist visas (B and BCC visas). The next largest visa class was for academic students and exchange visitors and their family members (F and J visa categories) and temporary workers and trainees and their family members (H visa categories), which each comprised about 11 percent.

How many temporary employment-based visas does the State Department issue each year?

Roughly 1 million foreign nationals (along with their immediate family members) receive employment-based temporary visas each year. In FY 2022, the Department of State issued a total of 1.1 million such visas in multiple categories, up from 965,000 in FY 2019. Among these were approximately 298,000 H-2A seasonal agriculture workers visas, 208,000 H-1B specialty occupation worker visas, 125,000 H-2B seasonal nonagricultural worker, and 73,000 L-1 intracompany transferee visas.

How many non-immigrant admissions does DHS grant each year?

Foreign nationals were admitted into the United States for non-immigrant purposes 35.3 million times in FY 2021—a 59 percent decrease from the 86.1 million in FY 2020 and an 81 percent decrease from the 186.2 million in FY 2019. Of the 35.3 million admissions, 21.7 million were admissions of Canadians and Mexicans traveling for business or pleasure, who are exempt from completing the I-94 arrival/departure form at the port of entry; DHS does not provide characteristics for this group.

The remaining 13.6 million temporary admissions of non-immigrants who filled out the I-94 form were 63 percent fewer than the 37.2 million admissions a year earlier and 83 percent fewer than the 81.6 million in 2019.

Most of the I-94 admissions in FY 2021 were those of tourists (66 percent) or temporary workers and their families (14 percent), followed by business travelers (10 percent; see table below for all types).

Category of Temporary Admission	Number of Admissions	Share of Total
TOTAL	13,623,000	100.0%
Tourists	9,055,000	66.5%
Temporary workers and families	1,844,000	13.5%
Temporary visitors for business	1,346,000	9.9%
Students and families	799,000	5.9%
Exchange visitors	174,000	1.3%
Transit admissions	211,000	1.6%
Diplomats and other representatives	161,000	1.2%
Fiancé(e) and child admissions	19,000	0.1%
Other	13,000	0.1%

Refugees and Asylum Seekers

What is the difference between a refugee and an asylee? In the United States, the main difference is the person's location at the time of application. Refugees are nearly always outside the United States when they are considered for resettlement, whereas asylum seekers submit their applications while physically present in or at a port of entry to the United States.

Asylum seekers can submit an asylum request either affirmatively or defensively. The affirmative asylum process applies to people who initially file an asylum application with U.S. Citizenship and Immigration Services (USCIS) as well as those who subsequently have their application referred by USCIS to the Executive Office for Immigration Review (EOIR). The defensive asylum process applies to people in removal proceedings who appear before EOIR and people who apply for asylum at U.S. borders and points of entry.

How many refugees enter the United States each year, and where were they from?

Every year, the president in consultation with Congress sets the annual refugee admissions ceiling and allocations by region of origin. The Biden administration set the ceiling at 125,000 each for FY 2022 and FY 2023, an increase from the revised FY 2021 limit of 62,500 (the Trump administration had originally set the FY 2021 ceiling at 15,000, but the Biden administration modified it after entering office). The lowest limit since the resettlement program was formally created in 1980 was set by the Trump administration for FY 2020, at 18,000.

This number is a ceiling, and the number of resettled refugees does not always reach this limit. Due to the reduced capacity of the resettlement program and COVID-19-related logistic challenges, slightly fewer than 25,500 refugees were resettled in the United States in FY 2022, amounting to 20 percent of the 125,000 allocated spaces for the year. For the first five months of FY 2023 (October 2022 through February 2023), 12,300 refugees arrived in the United States, which is 10 percent of the number of available spaces.

What is the sex ratio and median age of the admitted refugee population?

About 49 percent of refugees admitted into the United States in FY 2021 were female. The median age of all FY 2021 arrivals was 22 years old.

What are the most common religions of admitted refugees?

Refugees who identified as Christian made up 57 percent of all admitted refugees in FY 2022. Muslim refugees comprised 39 percent of admitted refugees. The remainder included Buddhists (2 percent), Hindus and Jews (less than 0.2 percent combined), and those who reported no religious affiliation or being atheists (about 2 percent).

How many asylum applications are filed each year?

In FY 2022, nearly 198,000 affirmative applications were filed with U.S. Citizenship and Immigration Services (USCIS), representing a 224 percent increase from FY 2021 and the highest number of affirmative applications filed since FY 2017.

Meanwhile, 226,000 defensive asylum applications were filed with the Executive Office for Immigration Review (EOIR) in FY 2022. This was the most on record and marks a significant increase from FY 2021, when 65,000 applications were filed.

What is the asylum approval rate?

The approval rate in FY 2022 for asylum applications filed with USCIS was 34 percent, an increase from 28 percent in FY 2021. Approval rates from applications filed through EOIR also increased, to 47 percent in FY 2022 up from 34 percent in FY 2021.

What is the current asylum application backlog?

Due to the large application volume and limited resources, both the affirmative and defensive asylum systems have extensive backlogs. Based on USCIS data, the backlog in September 2022 was 605,000 cases, up from nearly 413,000 at the end of FY 2021. In FY 2022, the total backlog for EOIR (including affirmative and defensive claims) was 703,000, down from 714,000 in FY 2021.

How many people receive asylum status?

In FY 2021, 17,700 individuals were granted asylum after seeking protection upon or after arrival in the United States, including principal applicants, their spouses, and unmarried children under age 21. This represented a 43 percent decrease from the almost 31,000 grants in FY 2020 and a 61 drop from the 46,000 people granted asylum in FY 2019. In FY 2021, an additional 2,150 individuals received derivative asylum status in the United States as immediate family members of principal applicants and 2,170 were approved for derivative status outside the United States.

Fifty-eight percent of asylum grants came affirmatively through USCIS (rather than defensively through the immigration courts), of which there were 10,300 in FY 2021, down 37 percent from 16,400 in FY 2020 and 62 percent from 27,000 in FY 2019, the highest since FY 2003.

Where are most asylum seekers from?

Venezuela was the top country of origin for those receiving asylum in FY 2021, with 2,100 people (or 12 percent of total asylum grants), followed closely by China, with close to 2,000 individuals (11 percent). Other top countries of origin were El Salvador (with 1,500 individuals), Guatemala (1,300), and Turkey (1,100). Together, nationals of these five countries made up 45 percent of those receiving asylum in FY 2021.

Unauthorized Immigrants

How many unauthorized immigrants are in the United States?

The Migration Policy Institute (MPI) estimates there were about 11 million unauthorized immigrants in the United States in 2019, accounting for 23 percent of the U.S. immigrant population. The unauthorized population was largely stable in size from 2007 to 2019. While more recent data are yet not available, the population has likely increased since 2019, due to the large number of border arrivals in recent years.

Almost half of the 11 million unauthorized immigrants resided in three states as of 2019: California (25 percent), Texas (16 percent), and New York (8 percent). The vast majority (81 percent) lived in 176 counties with 10,000 or more unauthorized immigrants each, of which the top five—Los Angeles County, California; Harris County, Texas; Dallas County, Texas; Cook County, Illinois; and Orange County, California—accounted for 20 percent of all unauthorized immigrants.

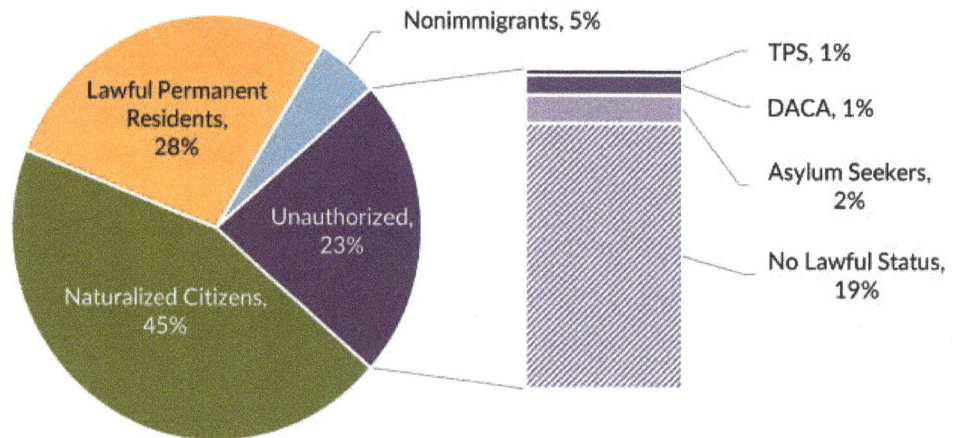

Credit: Migration Policy Institute (MPI).

What are unauthorized immigrants' countries of birth?

Mexicans and Central Americans accounted for roughly two-thirds (67 percent, or 7.4 million) of U.S. unauthorized immigrants in 2019, according to MPI estimates. About 1.7 million (15 percent) were from Asia; 907,000 (8 percent) from South America; 440,000 (4 percent) from Europe, Canada, or Oceania; 327,000 (3 percent) from the Caribbean; and 295,000 (3 percent) from Africa.

Unauthorized immigrants' top countries of birth were Mexico (48 percent), El Salvador and Guatemala (7 percent each), India (5 percent), and Honduras (4 percent).

How many people currently have DACA status?

USCIS reports that 589,660 individuals had active DACA status as of September 30, 2022.

The top states of residence for active DACA participants were California (29 percent), Texas (16 percent), and Illinois (5 percent), followed by New York, Florida, North Carolina, and Arizona (about 4 percent each).

Active DACA program participants' top countries of origin of were Mexico (81 percent), El Salvador (4 percent), Guatemala (3 percent), Honduras (2 percent), and Peru, South Korea, Brazil, Ecuador, and Colombia (about 1 percent each).

Immigration Enforcement

How many times are unauthorized immigrants stopped at the border each year?

U.S. Customs and Border Protection (CBP) reported nearly 2.8 million combined enforcement encounters at the southern and northern borders in FY 2022, a major increase from 2 million in FY 2021 and 647,000 in FY 2020, when the pandemic suppressed movement around the world.

The vast majority of these FY 2022 encounters (2.4 million) were at the U.S.-Mexico border. This is the highest number of encounters on record, beating the previous high of 1.6 million in FY 2000. Enforcement encounters at the Southwest border increased significantly starting in March 2021.

Motivations for migrants seeking protection in the United States vary, but overall the rapid increase in arrivals reflects uneven economic impacts of the COVID-19 pandemic; crises in the Americas, including major displacement from Cuba Haiti, Nicaragua, and Venezuela, as well as ongoing violence in Central America; political persecution and other factors driving emigration from China, India, Russia, and Turkey; the change in U.S. presidential administrations and perception of a unique window of opportunity; ever more sophisticated smuggling networks; and other factors.

Notably, data on encounters refer to individual actions, not the number of people who attempted to cross the border without authorization. The Title 42 order to immediately expel migrants during the COVID-19 pandemic, which remained in place at least until mid-May 2023, has changed the consequences for individuals crossing the border, and many have responded by repeating attempts on multiple occasions, contributing to higher numbers of encounters.

How many families and unaccompanied children have been detained at the U.S.-Mexico border?

In FY 2022, authorities recorded 561,000 encounters of family units (children and adults travelling as families) at the border, up from 480,000 in FY 2021. There were also 152,000 encounters of unaccompanied minors at the border in FY 2022, up from 147,000 the previous year.

Family units made up 24 percent of encounters at the U.S.-Mexico border in FY 2022, unaccompanied minors comprised 6 percent, and single adults accounted for 70 percent) of all encounters. In FY 2022 the largest number of family units came from Honduras, while the plurality of unaccompanied minors were from Guatemala.

Note: The term "family unit" refers to individuals—either a child under 18 years old, parent, or legal guardian—apprehended with a family member by the U.S. Border Patrol.

How many people are arrested by U.S. Immigration and Customs Enforcement (ICE) within the United States each year?

ICE made 142,800 administrative arrests in FY 2022, up from 74,100 the year before. The increase in administrative arrests was largely in the "other immigration violation" category, which ICE attributes to the increase in Southwest border apprehensions and the ICE's assistance to CBP in processing those arrivals.

How many people are deported per year?

In FY 2022 ICE conducted nearly 72,200 removals and 117,200 Title 42 expulsions.

Naturalization Trends

How many immigrants are naturalized citizens?

More than 24 million immigrants were naturalized U.S. citizens in 2021, accounting for approximately 53 percent of all 45.3 million immigrants and 7 percent of the total U.S. population (331.9 million).

Of these naturalized citizens, 37 percent were naturalized between 2010 and 2021, 27 percent between 2000 and 2009, and 36 percent prior to 2000.

How many immigrants become U.S. citizens annually?

USCIS naturalized about 814,0000 green-card holders in FY 2021, a 30 percent increase from the 628,000 people who became citizens in FY 2020. There were 789,100 petitions for naturalization filed in FY 2021, a decrease of 18 percent from a year earlier (968,000). At the same time, the number of denied petitions decreased by 6 percent, from 80,600 in FY 2020 to 85,200 in FY 2021.

The amount of time USCIS takes to process naturalization applications increased from an average of 5.6 months in FY 2016 to 11.5 months in FY 2021, but has since declined to 6.7 months as of the end of January 2023.

From a historical perspective, the number of annual naturalizations has increased dramatically in recent decades. On average, fewer than 120,000 LPRs became citizens each year between FY 1950 and FY 1969, 150,000 in the 1970s, 210,000 in the 1980s, 500,000 in the 1990s, 680,000 during the 2000s, and 721,000 between 2010 and 2020.

Naturalizations reached an all-time high in FY 2008, increasing 59 percent from 660,000 the prior year to 1,047,000. This came as a result of impending application fee increases and the promotion of U.S. citizenship in advance of the 2008 presidential election.

Where are newly naturalized citizens from?

Of the new U.S. citizens in FY 2021, 14 percent were born in Mexico, 7 percent in India, and 6 percent each in the Philippines and Cuba. Immigrants from these four countries, together with those from China, the Dominican Republic, Vietnam, Jamaica, El Salvador, and Colombia accounted for 50 percent of the 814,000 immigrants who naturalized that year.

Country	Naturalized Persons	Share of Total
TOTAL	**814,000**	**100.0%**
Mexico	113,000	13.9%
India	57,000	7.0%
Philippines	48,000	6.0%
Cuba	48,000	5.9%
China, People's Republic	29,000	3.6%
Dominican Republic	28,000	3.5%
Vietnam	24,000	3.0%
Jamaica	21,000	2.5%
El Salvador	18,000	2.3%
Colombia	18,000	2.2%

Source: DHS Office of Immigration Statistics, *2021 Yearbook of Immigration Statistics.*

Where in the United States do newly naturalized citizens live?

Nearly 60 percent of people naturalized as U.S. citizens in FY 2021 lived in one of five states: California (21 percent, or 171,900 individuals); Florida (13 percent, or 109,200); New York (11 percent, or 90,000); Texas (9 percent, or 77,000); and New Jersey (5 percent, or 40,000).

The top metropolitan areas with the largest number of new naturalizations were the greater New York (116,200), Los Angeles (80,700), Miami (68,900), Washington, DC (30,100), and Dallas (26,200) metropolitan areas. These five metro areas were the home to 40 percent of all newly naturalized citizens in FY 2021.

How many green-card holders are eligible to naturalize?

According to the latest available DHS estimates, about 9.2 million of the 12.9 million green-card holders residing in the United States on January 1, 2022 were eligible to become naturalized citizens based on how long they had held LPR status. The top five nationalities of LPRs eligible to naturalize were Mexico (2.5 million), China (490,000), the Philippines (360,000), Cuba (340,000), and the Dominican Republic (330,000).

Visa Backlogs

How many visa applications for permanent immigration (green cards) are backlogged?

Because of limits on certain visa categories and per-country caps, the U.S. government in some cases is still processing applications that are more than two decades old. In March 2023, the State Department was processing some family-sponsored visa applications dating to November 1997, and employment-related visa applications from June 2012.

Nearly 4.1 million applicants (including spouses and minor children) were on the State Department's immigrant visa waiting list as of November 1, 2022, a 1 percent decline from the more than 4.1 million applicants in the backlog a year previous.

The overwhelming majority of backlogs were among family-sponsored applicants (more than 3.9 million, including principal applicants and their immediate family members). About 168,000 backlogged applicants were for employment-sponsored channels and their families.

Of the overall 4.1 million applicants, the largest number (1.2 million) were citizens of Mexico, followed by those from the Philippines (296,000), India (294,000), the Dominican Republic (284,000), and Vietnam (229,000). Family- and employment-based prospective immigrants already within the United States who are waiting to adjust their status are not included in the State Department estimates.

6 – The Evils of Illegal Immigration: More Crime, Drugs, Deaths, Rapes & Human Trafficking

Select encounter type:

Assault/Battery/Domestic Violence

CRIMINAL ALIEN ENCOUNTERS

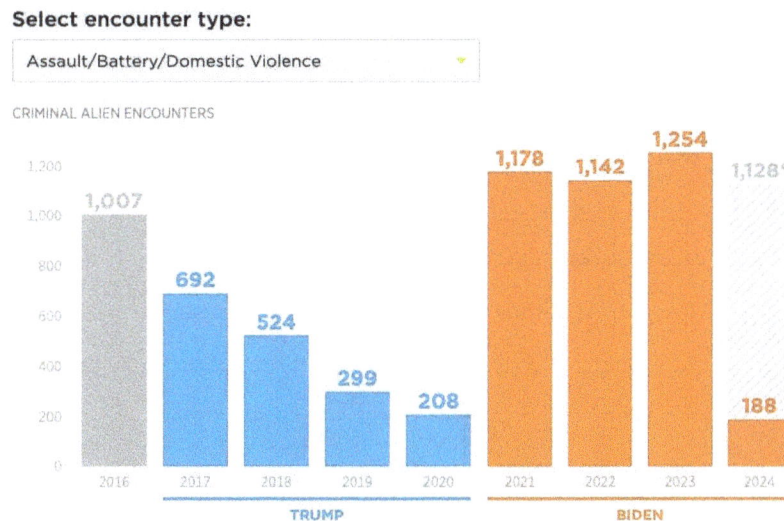

Credit: Heritage Foundation.

As noted in the Diana Glebova "Majority of Americans Think Cartels Have More Control Over Border than U.S. Government: Poll" *National Review* September 2022 article:

A majority of Americans believe cartels have more control over the southern border than the U.S. government, according to a poll published by RMG Research. Sixty-one percent of registered voters surveyed said that cartels had greater control of the border, compared to 19 percent who said the government has more control. Twenty percent of respondents were "not sure."

The poll surveyed 1,200 registered voters from September 20 to 21, 2022, and was conducted online by Scott Rasmussen. The margin of error is +/- 2.8 percent. The majority of voters surveyed, 54 percent, responded that the federal government is not "seriously trying to secure the border and reduce illegal immigration."

Vice President Kamala Harris claimed the border is "secure" in September, despite a record-breaking 2 million arrests at the southern border this fiscal year.

However, the Texas Department of Public Safety (DPS) announced in 2021 that in the prior year alone they seized enough fentanyl crossing the border to kill 200 million people. The drug seizures are part of Operation Lone Star—a Texas initiative to curb entry of human traffickers and drug runners into the state per the Timothy H.J. Nerozzi Fox News December

2021 news story "Texas Seized Enough Fentanyl to Kill 200 Million People This Year Alone, Officials Say":

According to new data provided by the Texas DPS, Operation Lone Star has seized 160 pounds of fentanyl within its targeted area. Other drugs seized within that area include marijuana (13,494 pounds), cocaine (2,430 pounds), meth (1,647 pounds), and heroin (37 pounds).

Combining activity inside and outside of Operation Lone Star's area of interest, the Texas DPS has seized 886 pounds of fentanyl—approximately 200,790,522 lethal doses, according to data provided by the DPS in a slide presentation.

"They try and sell it as 'synthetic heroin' in order to increase their profits," DPS seized drug system trainer Jennifer Hatch said. "But what ends up happening with a lot of these is they end up leading to death because people don't know these are in the drugs they're ingesting."

"Most recently it's been found in ecstasy tablets," she later added.

America's Fentanyl Crisis Begins at the Southern Border

From the Vince Bielskil "America's Fentanyl Crisis Begins at the Southern Border" *National Review* December 2021 article:

The cartels are taking advantage of law-enforcement weaknesses and policy failures to smuggle record amounts of the lethal drug into the United States, according to interviews with half a dozen current and former drug and immigration agents. While a lack of screening technology to find contraband at ports of entry and an inept U.S.-Mexico campaign to cripple the cartels are longstanding issues, there's also a new one: the flood of migrants across the border that the Biden administration has done little to stop.

Former law-enforcement officials say the cartels are behind the surge, overwhelming the capacity of agents to pursue drug smugglers. They can freely enter Texas, New Mexico, Arizona, and California carrying fentanyl while agents are diverted to apprehending and processing migrants.

Frustrated border agents and their union have been calling on Congress to send reinforcements. But help is not on the way. The administration's upcoming budget request doesn't include funding for more Customs and Border Protection agents.

Instead, the administration is embracing a public-health approach to the fentanyl crisis. It has proposed spending $11.2 billion—a huge increase over last year—to expand substance-abuse prevention, treatment, and recovery services. But curbing opioid addiction is very challenging. Most substance abusers avoid treatment, according to researchers, and only about one-third of those receiving long-term medical care fully recover.

Cartels have turned to fentanyl because the super-potent powder is cheap to produce, making it more profitable than heroin, says Eric Triana, an assistant special agent in charge at the DEA division in New York. Fentanyl's potency—at 50 times the strength of heroin—is what makes it so deadly. DEA analysis found that 40 percent of the seized pills had a potentially deadly dose.

"I saw the devastation that heroin brought to Baltimore as a young police officer," Triana says. "But fentanyl is a more potent deadly threat. It's frightening."

But President Andres Manuel Lopez Obrador ended Mexico's military campaign against cartel leaders two years ago. The populist president is pushing an agenda to reduce poverty in the hope that it will curb the appeal of drug smuggling. Meanwhile, the cartels face little resistance.

"The cartels control Mexico. All of it," says Victor Avila, the former ICE agent who survived gunshot wounds in an ambush with a cartel. "They are running a parallel government."

Vanda Felbab-Brown, a scholar focusing on nonstate armed actors at the Brookings Institution, has called on the administration to "get tough" with Mexico, urging it to use financial support as leverage to compel Mexico to target mid-level cartel operatives and their corrupt government protectors. But the State Department is taking a conciliatory position, essentially backing Lopez Obrador's economic-development strategy in an agreement between the two countries announced in early October.

In the meantime, more fentanyl smuggled into the U.S. means more deaths. Triana, the DEA special agent, estimates that the number of overdose fatalities this year will either be on par with or exceed last year's.

Biden's Border Policies Are Taking Us Back To Pre-9/11 Homeland Security

From the Lora Ries "Biden's Border Policies Are Taking Us Back To Pre-9/11 Homeland Security" *The Federalist* September 2022 article: It was a generation ago when the 9/11 terrorist attacks killed nearly 3,000 Americans. How many of the post-9/11 generation know what happened that day? And how many of us who lived through it know what allowed that tragedy to happen?

Homeland security is no less at-risk today than it was 21 years ago. To avoid yet another catastrophe, we would do well to revisit some key findings from the 9/11 Commission.

The commission found four failures across the government: imagination, policies, capabilities, and management. With respect to imagination, the commission found that political leaders did not understand the gravity of the terrorist threat posed by Al Qaeda. It was barely discussed among the public, media, or Congress.

The current administration's open border policies, combined with that same lack of imagination, are actively undermining our national security.

In the last two years, Customs and Border Protection has apprehended 81 known and suspected terrorists illegally crossing our southern border. During that time, another 900,000 "gotaways" have successfully evaded the Border Patrol. It doesn't take any imagination to assume foreign terrorists have been among them. This should be the overriding national security concern for the U.S. government.

Yet according to the commission, one critical factor leading to the 9/11 terrorist attack was "permeable borders and immigration controls." It noted agencies did not discover false statements on visa applications, recognize fraudulent passports, or take adequate steps to find two of the hijackers residing illegally in the United States.

The 9/11 terrorists made false statements to border officials to gain entry into the United States and violated immigration laws while in the United States. The commission concluded that "protecting borders was not a national security issue before 9/11."

Today, we have an open border and few immigration controls. The Biden administration has directed ICE not to arrest, detain, prosecute or deport the majority of categories that make an alien removable. It effectively grants a provisional status of "asylum-seeker" to any immigrant claiming to live in fear in their native lands. It cuts corners in vetting applicants and adjudicating applications to grant more benefits more quickly.

All of this encourages more illegal immigration and makes it easy for terrorists and other bad actors to enter our country. The Biden regime has returned us to a pre-9/11 posture.

Fighting Human Trafficking and Battling Biden's Open Border

Revealed in the Hannah Davis "Fighting Human Trafficking and Battling Biden's Open Border" Heritage Foundation March 2023 article:

President Biden has professed a commitment to fight this multifaceted criminal enterprise, yet his immigration policies have only exacerbated the problem. Human trafficking increased massively in the last fiscal year. Arrests rose 50%; convictions soared by 80%. The vast majority, 72%, of those trafficked in the U.S. are immigrants. Most of them are here illegally.

Many are women and children who are highly vulnerable to being smuggled and eventually trafficked. A study from the Coalition Against Trafficking In Women estimated that 60% of unaccompanied alien children, or UACs, are caught by cartels and exploited through child pornography and drug trafficking.

To put this into perspective, more than 150,000 UACs crossed into our country last year. The Biden administration responded by declaring January "National Human Trafficking Prevention Month." This, of course, did nothing to curb the problem.

That month, 5,882 UACs crossed the border—an increase of more than 80% over the number logged by the Trump administration in January 2020. The dramatic increase can be traced directly to the Biden administration's open border policies. On average, over 12,000 UACs are entering the nation monthly in 2023.

Since taking office, the Biden administration has reported over 300,000 alien minor encounters. The Department of Health and Human Services reports that between Jan. 20, 2021, and Feb. 7, 2022, it placed nearly 150,000 unaccompanied children with sponsors in the U.S. It has been estimated that this influx of students will cost school districts an extra $4.6 billion annually.

Rather than attempting to lower these large numbers, the Biden administration has embraced the Trafficking Victims Protection Reauthorization Act in a way calculated to increase them. Section 235 of the act, misleadingly titled "Enhancing Efforts to Combat the Trafficking of Children," grants UACs special accommodations, such as expedited processing and benefits.

"Not surprisingly, after Congress passed that provision, the number of UACs from non-contiguous countries soared, as parents (and more importantly smugglers) realized that section 235 ... all but guaranteed that any such child who could make it illegally into the United States would be released into this country," said Andrew Arthur of the Center for Immigration Studies.

Section 235, coupled with Homeland Security Secretary Alejandro Mayorkas' public statements that "we are not expelling unaccompanied children," has only enticed more minors into making life-threatening decisions.

The increased flow of UACs increased the demand for "sponsors"—i.e., people willing to house and care for the children so they can be processed out of Health and Human Services housing. To "remedy" this, the administration lowered the standards for sponsors, slashing the vetting process times to meet the deadlines set to meet Mr. Biden's self-induced emergency.

According to an HHS whistleblower, the lowered standards led to more of these children falling into the hands of cartels, pedophiles and pimps. Many were claimed by "family members" they had never met and then subjected to horrendous conditions.

To curtail human trafficking, especially of children, the Trump administration allowed Immigration and Customs Enforcement to run DNA tests on immigrants claiming to be traveling in "familial units." This program detected more than 6,000 fraudulent families. But even though the program was effective, Mr. Biden ended it.

The absence of border security, in conjunction with nonexistent interior enforcement, has made the U.S. a fertile breeding ground for human trafficking.

The Biden administration's National Action Plan to Combat Human Trafficking proudly proclaims "pillars," principles and priority actions but makes no mention of securing the southern border. It does, however, dutifully present ideas regarding equity, inclusion and gender.

The administration persistently presses leftist talking points yet fails to recognize an obvious truth: Human trafficking—and the misery it causes—will continue to soar as long as there is no operational control of the southern border.

Congress must act to repeal Section 235 of the Trafficking Victims Protection Reauthorization Act. Otherwise, UACs will continue to head for our southern border, with many encountering human trafficking cartels along the way and others falling prey to insufficiently vetted sponsors or "family members" they do not know.

The Biden administration's refusal to enforce humane, effective immigration laws tempts people into risking their lives daily. Until the administration makes commonsense policy changes and starts enforcing the rule of law, the cartels will continue to control the border and the people who attempt to cross it.

The Progressive Call for Compassion at the Border is a Political Prop

As shown in the Pedro L. Gonzalez "The Progressive Call for Compassion at the Border Is a Political Prop: Opinion" *Chronicles: A Magazine of American Culture* March 2021 article:

In early 2016, the Permanent Subcommittee on Investigations published a report about children released by the Office of Refugee Resettlement. In the 13 documented cases, children were handed over to human traffickers masquerading as sponsors. The report noted more than a dozen other cases possibly linked to human trafficking. Among the most prominent incidents, eight minors were trafficked and forced to work 12-hour days for little pay under substandard living and working conditions at an Ohio egg farm.

This is slavery begotten by cries for "compassionate" immigration policy. And it's guaranteed to occur again because there is no easy way to stop it or even monitor the children once they're in the country. "According to ORR officials," a Government Accountability Office report found, "the agency is generally not required by law to track or monitor the well-being of these children once they are released to sponsors."

The horrified progressive rallying cry against "kids in cages" serves mainly as a political prop for the media and Democratic Party. Once these children are released, nobody seems to care what happens to them, an indifference and unseriousness with a terrible social cost for citizens and foreign nationals alike.

In the absence of a family—of social, cultural, and familial bonds—criminality fills the vacuum; the areas in the United States most afflicted by MS-13 gang violence correspond with locations that received the bulk of the 130,027 children from Central America that the government resettled in the U.S. between October 2014 and December 2017.

Where is the compassion? How is it humane to allow children into a country where they are likely to encounter the very gangs they fled? As researcher Heather Mac Donald has pointed out, participation in gangs and drug culture is rising in the second and third generation of Latino immigrants.

The United States immigration system is essentially creating a social bomb by inviting masses of people we cannot properly care for, feed, or educate. Nearly 2 million Latino households in California alone cannot afford the cost of basic needs such as housing, food, health care, childcare, and transportation.

What have we gained by allowing children into this country if they are going to live in poverty here, too? How is this humane or compassionate? And how is it fair to the millions of Americans who are struggling in a cage of destitution, yet are instructed to care about even more desperate people?

More Than 100,000 DACA Applicants Have Been Arrested—Murder, Rape, DUI

Per the "More Than 100,000 DACA Applicants Have Been Arrested—Murder, Rape, DUI" *Judicial Watch* November 2019 report:

More than 100,000 illegal immigrants who requested a special Obama-era amnesty for adults who came to the U.S. as children have criminal histories, according to an alarming report released this month by the government. Offenses committed by the illegal aliens seeking protection, benefits and rights under the policy known as Deferred Action for Childhood Arrivals (DACA) include murder, rape, weapon and assault charges.

DACA has shielded nearly 800,000 illegal aliens under the age of 31 from deportation and allowed them to obtain work permits and drivers licenses. Obama launched the outrageous measure through executive order in 2012 to help children who came to the U.S. "through no fault of their own." The Trump administration tried to end DACA in 2017 but open borders groups sued to keep it going and now the Supreme Court is set to decide the matter.

Regardless of how the high court may rule, the fact remains that a big chunk of DACA applicants have arrest records, according to the figures released by U.S. Citizenship and Immigration Services (USCIS), the Homeland Security agency that administers the nation's lawful immigration system. The stats show that nearly 110,000 DACA requestors out of nearly 889,000 had arrest records, accounting for 12% of applicants. "Offenses in these arrest records include assault, battery, rape, murder and driving under the influence," USCIS writes in a statement announcing the report.

Here's another disturbing fact; of approved DACA requestors with an arrest, a whopping 85% (67,861) were arrested right before the U.S. granted them amnesty. Nearly 25,000 DACA recipients with arrests had multiple arrests and 218 had more than 10 arrests. Incredibly, around one-fourth of the illegal immigrants with more than 10 arrests were approved by the government as of last month. In all, the government reveals that it has approved 79,398 DACA requestors with arrest records. Not all the delinquents are approved, the figures show. More than 100,000 with criminal arrests were denied or terminated.

Most of the arrested DACA approvals involve driving infractions and immigration related civil and criminal offenses, but thousands were granted amnesty after committing serious crimes. Nearly 8,000 illegal immigrants granted protection under DACA committed theft or larceny, the records show, and nearly 7,000 drug-related offenses. More than 4,000 were apprehended for driving under the influence, 3,421 for battery and 3,308 for assault. Thousands of others rewarded with DACA committed vandalism, burglary, offenses against children and weapons crimes.

Hundreds of others were approved for DACA despite arrests for sexual abuse and rape, kidnapping or trafficking, hit and run, embezzlement and a variety of other serious offenses. Fifteen illegal aliens with murder charges got DACA as well as 15 street gang members and two arrested for child pornography. Most of the DACA candidates were arrested between the age of 19 and 22 though tens of thousands were also arrested between 23 and 26, well into adulthood. Mexicans account for the overwhelming majority of DACA recipients arrested (91,272) followed by El Salvador (4,998), Honduras (4,597) and Guatemala (4,304).

"This agency is obligated to continue accepting DACA requests from illegal aliens as a direct result of the previous administration's decision to circumvent the laws as passed by Congress," according to USCIS Acting Director Ken Cuccinelli. "We hope this data provides a better sense of the reality of those granted the privilege of a temporary deferral of removal action and work authorization under DACA."

USCIS figures released last year show that the biggest concentration of illegal aliens protected by DACA are in California (197,900) and Texas (113,000), though states such as Illinois (35,600), New York (32,900), Florida (27,000) and Arizona (25,500) also have significant numbers.

Majority of Federal Arrestees are Foreigners, Thousands of "Unknown Citizenship"

From the "Majority of Federal Arrestees are Foreigners, Thousands of 'Unknown Citizenship'" *Judicial Watch* August 2019 report: Months after the U.S. Sentencing Commission revealed most federal crimes are executed by Hispanics and involve immigrants and drugs, the Department of Justice (DOJ) reports that foreigners accounted for the vast majority of federal arrests last year.

Furthermore, apprehensions in the five judicial districts along the Mexican border, home to a quarter of all drug cases in 2018, have nearly doubled in the last decade. It doesn't end there; the number of Central Americans captured by federal authorities in the five border districts tripled in one year alone and has risen 30-fold in the last two decades. During the same period, the apprehension of Mexican citizens also increased significantly.

The disturbing figures were released in August 2019 by the DOJ's Bureau of Justice Statistics, the government agency responsible for collecting crime data. In a 25-page report the agency outlines a distressing trend of criminal activity involving foreign nationals, revealing that non-U.S. citizens accounted for 64% of all federal arrests in 2018. "From 1998 to 2018, the share of all federal arrests by country of citizenship rose from 28% to 40% for Mexican citizens, rose from 1% to 20% for citizens of Central American countries, and fell from 63% to 36% for U.S. citizens," the DOJ report states. The document uses tables and graphs to show an alarming increase in immigration crimes, from 20,942 back in 1998 to 58,031 in 2017 and an astonishing jump to 108,667 by 2018, marking a breathtaking 418.9% increase in two decades.

The five judicial districts along the Mexican border—California, Arizona, New Mexico and western and southern Texas—have experienced an eye-popping 539.6% in immigration-related arrests in the last two decades. Thousands are of "unknown citizenship," according to the federal statistics, which show a spike of 202 aliens from unknown countries to 6,657 in a few years.

Besides immigration violations, drug offenses appear to be the most popular crimes committed by non-U.S. citizens, followed by fraud, alien smuggling and misuse of visas. The overwhelming majority of perpetrators are young men like the ones marching north in the Central American caravan.

Judicial Watch traveled to the Guatemala-Honduras border last fall and reported that the caravan mostly included young men. Guatemalan authorities confirmed that human smugglers, violent gang members and other criminal elements are incorporated in the highly organized caravans and the federal statistics indicate it's a problem that predates the latest convoy.

The updated figures from the DOJ come just a few months after a separate government report disclosed that most federal crimes are executed by Hispanics, involve immigrants and drugs. In that equally alarming document, the U.S. Sentencing Commission disclosed that nearly half of all federal crimes in the United States are perpetrated by foreigners who are not American citizens and that immigration cases account for the largest single type of offense.

Non-U.S. Citizens Committed 42.7% of all Federal Crimes in 2018

Non-U.S. citizens committed 42.7% of all federal crimes in 2018, according to the independent agency created by Congress decades ago to reduce sentencing disparities and promote transparency and proportionality in sentencing. In its report the agency discloses that 54.3% of the 69,425 federal offenders last year were Hispanic.

"Immigration cases accounted for the largest single group of offenses in fiscal year 2018, comprising 34.4% of all reported cases," the commission writes in its annual report to Congress. "Cases involving drugs, firearms, and fraud were the next most common types of offenses after immigration cases. Together these four types of offenses accounted for 82.9 percent of all cases reported to the commission in fiscal year 2018."

The second largest offense category, drugs, accounted for 28.1% of federal crimes last year and most cases involved methamphetamine. *Judicial Watch* has reported for years on the enormous amounts of meth that enter the U.S. through Mexico.

A few years ago the Department of Homeland Security (DHS) reported a startling 300% increase in meth seizures coming from Mexico in one border state alone. The Sentencing Commission found that in 2018 Hispanics committed 9,020 federal drug trafficking crimes, nearly twice as many as those perpetrated by blacks (4,670) and more than double the drug trafficking offenses carried out by whites (4,499). Hispanics were also charged with more drug possession crimes (389) last year than any other group.

Not surprisingly, Hispanics also committed the overwhelming amount of immigration related crimes, according to the federal statistics made public in May 2019. Of the 23,656 immigration offenses recorded last year, Hispanics accounted for 22,782. They also committed the most money laundering crimes (504) compared to whites (444) and blacks (236), the Sentencing Commission document shows. Unlike the arrest records provided this month by the DOJ, the commission figures only include convicts that actually got sentenced.

Illegal Aliens Released From Local Custody Commit More Crimes–One Freed 10 Times

Per the "Illegal Aliens Released From Local Custody Commit More Crimes – One Freed 10 Times" *Judicial Watch* July 2019 report:

Following a *Judicial Watch* lawsuit, the Department of Homeland Security (DHS) has reinstated a reporting system that informs the public about illegal immigrants who commit crimes after being released from state or local custody. The offenders are shielded by sanctuary policies that ban local law enforcement from honoring Immigration and Customs Enforcement (ICE) detainers placed on illegal aliens who have been arrested on local criminal charges.

If the detainer is honored ICE takes custody and deports the criminal rather than release him or her back into the community. When law enforcement agencies fail to honor immigration detainers and release serious criminal offenders, it undermines the federal government's duty to protect public safety.

To pressure municipalities that protect illegal aliens, the Trump administration published weekly Declined Detainer Outcome Reports highlighting state and local governments that did not comply with ICE's detainer program. The troublesome logs included details of illegal aliens who committed all sorts of atrocious crimes after local authorities let them go and identified the law enforcement agency that released them.

Published on ICE's website, the reports ignited outrage among open borders groups and their mainstream media allies, who complained that the information was controversial and discriminatory. One mainstream media outlet actually reported that "immigration advocates also criticized the list for singling out the criminals among undocumented immigrants without acknowledging the contributions of the broader population to their communities."

DHS caved into the pressure and temporarily suspended the informative weekly Declined Detainer Outcome Reports. *Judicial Watch* immediately launched an investigation, requesting records from the agency under the Freedom of Information Act (FOIA) and subsequently suing for the information. Sanctuary cities violate federal law and put the public at risk.

In the last decade *Judicial Watch* has also gone to court to fight sanctuary policies nationwide, including in Arizona, California, Illinois, the District of Columbia and Texas, to name a few. In California alone, *Judicial Watch* has sued several municipalities for protecting illegal immigrant criminals. Among them are San Francisco, Los Angeles and Pasadena, though practically the entire state shields illegal immigrants from the feds, including serious criminals.

In fact, the reinstatement of the Declined Detainer Report includes a small sample from just the Golden State. ICE recently announced the report's comeback and revealed it will be issued on a quarterly basis. "In order to increase transparency surrounding the immigration enforcement process, ICE will produce the Declined Detainer Report on a quarterly basis, beginning in the second quarter of Fiscal Year (FY) 2018," the agency announced recently.

"The report will highlight cases where ICE issued a detainer, the detainer was declined, and the alien subsequently committed a crime after being released from state or local custody.

Because ICE is often not alerted by uncooperative jurisdictions when a detainer has been declined, and because ICE may only learn of the detainer having been declined after an alien is arrested for a subsequent offense, the cases contained in this report are examples of a broader public safety issue and are not exhaustive."

The comeback report offers alarming details involving 16 illegal immigrants who committed crimes after being released by various California law enforcement agencies during a three-month period. Some were arrested and released multiple times by the same local law enforcement agency after committing felonies.

In all of the cases, ICE issued detainers but local police ignored the federal agency to protect the illegal alien from deportation, instead freeing the perpetrator back into the community. Offenders include Mexican, Honduran and Salvadoran nationals charged with murder, rape, assault with a deadly weapon, spousal abuse, driving under the influence of alcohol, possession of illegal drugs and other serious crimes.

One 23-year-old Honduran man was booked and released in San Francisco ten times in less than a year for crimes ranging from burglary, vehicle theft and driving without a license. In each of the arrests, ICE issued a detainer but the San Francisco Police Department disregarded it and let the man go.

Chris Crane, a veteran ICE agent who serves as president of the union that represents some 7,600 officers, reminds that this is only a tiny snippet of a national public safety crisis because the agency doesn't have the manpower to track everyone released. "If I was working in a sanctuary city, my released criminal aliens that would reoffend would be more than five a year," Crane said.

Federal Report Shows Open Borders Bring Increased Crimes and Costs for Taxpayers

From the Hans A. von Spakovsky "Federal Report Shows Open Borders Bring Increased Crimes and Costs for Taxpayers" Heritage Foundation December 2021 report:

According to a new report from the U.S. Justice Department, almost half of all of the criminals prosecuted in federal courts in 2018 were aliens, charged with crimes ranging from drug trafficking to murder to kidnapping. While a small number of those over 41,000 criminals were in this country legally, the vast majority—38,000—were illegal aliens. Compare this to 1998, when there were only a little over 18,000 aliens prosecuted in federal courts.

In addition to the horrendous human costs of their crimes, when you consider the costs of law enforcement related to their arrest, prosecution, and incarceration, these aliens are also costing U.S. taxpayers a tremendous amount of money. According to the government, the incarceration cost alone for criminals serving time in federal prisons—such as these aliens—is between $35,000 and $40,000 per year per inmate. At the end of 2018, 19 percent of the prisoners in the Federal Bureau of Prisons—30,848—were aliens, costing the American taxpayer between one billion and 1.2 billion dollars a year just to house them.

The special report, "Non-U.S. Citizens in the Federal Criminal Justice System, 1998-2018," goes to extraordinary lengths to avoid using the politically incorrect (but legally correct) term "aliens" in the report. Instead, illegal aliens are referred to as "undocumented non-U.S. citizens."

Political correctness aside, the report cannot disguise the dangers and costs represented by the raw numbers. In many instances, illegal aliens are repeat offenders. For instance, of the illegal aliens prosecuted in 2018, 12.5 percent had at least one prior federal or state criminal conviction, 18.5 percent had two to four prior convictions, and over 10 percent had five or more convictions. Hispanics dominate the criminal prosecutions, representing 74 percent of the criminal illegal aliens.

The crimes committed by these aliens ranged from drug trafficking to "violent offenses" including murder, sexual assault, robbery, and kidnapping. In fact, 24 percent of all federal prosecutions for drug offenses were of aliens. And we are not talking about simple possession. As the report states, "drug offenses" are defined as the "manufacture, import, export, distribution, and dispensing" of dangerous drugs like methamphetamine. So, aliens are a major source of the debilitating drug problem that is a scourge on our society.

While these numbers are distressing, what's even more distressing is that they only represent the proverbial tip of the iceberg. The vast majority of crimes committed in this country are prosecuted at the local level, not the federal level.

These federal numbers are only a fraction of the crimes committed by criminal aliens.

The latest report from the state of Texas alone, for example, reports that between June 1, 2011, and Nov. 30, 2021, 356,000 criminal aliens were booked into Texas jails, of which over 243,000 were identified as being in the country illegally.

Those illegal aliens were charged with more than 401,000 criminal offenses, including 742 murders, 47,737 assaults, 7,524 burglaries, over 11,000 sexual assaults and other sex crimes, and numerous kidnappings, thefts, robberies, and drug and weapons charges.

Many criminal aliens were convicted of federal immigration offenses, including "smuggling of persons," a relatively benign-sounding term for human trafficking, a cruel practice that often results in the exploitation, abuse, and sometimes rape or death of its victims.

Eighty percent of aliens were charged with illegal reentry—something that would not be happening if we were actually securing our border.

The report also shows the difference between the laissez-faire attitude of the Obama administration versus the "enforce the law" attitude of the Trump administration. From fiscal year 2012, when Obama was re-elected, to fiscal year 2018, the number of aliens prosecuted in the federal courts declined nine percent on average each year. But in the first year of the Trump administration (from 2017 to 2018), the number of prosecutions jumped by 12 percent.

Now, with the Biden administration's reckless open border policies, the United States is facing one of the worst national security, immigration, and public safety crises in its history, and the government's own numbers prove it.

Biden's Border Crisis—Crime Problem in Texas a Bad Omen for Rest of U.S.

As noted in the Hans A. von Spakovsky "Biden's Border Crisis—Crime Problem in Texas a Bad Omen for Rest of U.S." Heritage Foundation August 2021 article:

Supporters of illegal immigration like to portray all of the aliens now flooding across the southern border as benign individuals simply seeking a better life. Many no doubt are, but the latest report from the Texas Department of Public Safety shows just how dangerous some of them are.

That report outlines more than 573,000 criminal offenses committed by illegal aliens "over the course of their entire Texas criminal careers." And that's surely just the tip of the iceberg, as the report only covers state offenses, not federal crimes, not crimes committed in other states, and not crimes committed by aliens in the country legally.

But what a shocking catalogue of victimization of Texas residents it is. The report by the famous Texas Rangers shows that over 344,000 criminal aliens were booked into local Texas jails between June 1, 2011, and June 30, 2021, of which over 235,000 were classified as illegal aliens. The criminal offenses with which they were charged included:

- 1,245 homicides
- 66,924 assaults
- 17,456 burglaries
- 72,835 drug charges
- 980 kidnappings
- 33,335 thefts
- 4,155 robberies
- 7.076 sexual assaults
- 8,332 sexual offenses
- 49,408 obstructing police charges
- 8,317 weapons charges

Keep in mind, as the Texas report says, that these figures "represent the minimum number of crimes associated with criminal illegal aliens" (emphasis added). Why? Because Texas is counting as illegal aliens only those who "previously had an encounter" with the Department of Homeland Security that "resulted in their fingerprints being entered into the DHS IDENT database."

Except in a relatively small number of cases, aliens who enter the country illegally but "avoid detection by DHS" are not going to be identified as being in the country illegally when they are arrested for committing a crime in Texas.

There are two important points here. First, given the huge number of illegal aliens getting into the country without detection, the number of crimes committed by these aliens in Texas (and other states) is probably much higher than these already-unacceptable numbers.

Second, why were these 235,000 illegal aliens—who were identified because they had been previously detained by DHS—still in Texas, still present in this country, and thus able to commit their crimes? This is the consequence of the "catch and release" policy favored by liberal administrations, including the Biden administration, which the Trump administration tried to end.

The bottom line here is that, using just one of the appalling numbers highlighted by the Texas report, there are 1,245 Texans who would likely still be alive today if we were securing our border and vigorously enforcing our immigration laws by quickly and effectively deporting aliens whose first act is to enter the country illegally, and whose second act is to assault, kidnap, rob and murder our citizens.

As the Texas Department of Public Safety starkly says, this report, "identifies thousands of crimes that should not have occurred and thousands of victims that should not have been victimized because the perpetrator should not be here."

No truer words have been spoken about the illegal alien problem and the reckless open-border policy of the Biden administration.

7 – Impeaching Mayorkas for Reckless & Irresponsible Abuse of Power & Malfeasance

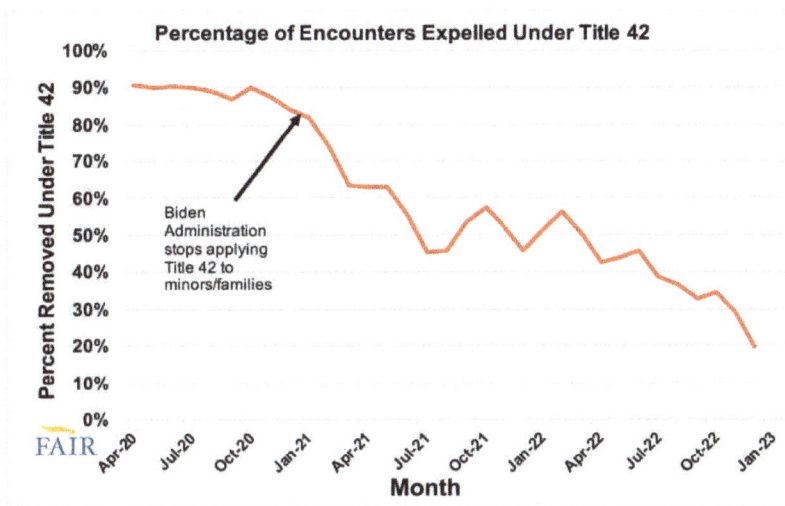

As reported in the Jennie Taer "Heritage Foundation Sues Biden Administration for Failing to Share Details on Limiting Deportations" Heritage Foundation August 2022 article:

The Heritage Foundation filed a lawsuit in August 2022 against the Department of Homeland Security, seeking the names of those the Biden administration consulted in deciding to limit immigration enforcement, according to a copy of the lawsuit obtained exclusively by the Daily Caller News Foundation.

The lawsuit follows a Freedom of Information Act request in January 2022 in which the think tank's Oversight Project sought relevant information about stakeholders involved in the administration's decision and any communications they may have had with Homeland Security Secretary Alejandro Mayorkas. In the lawsuit, Heritage argues that DHS failed to comply with "statutory timelines" in providing the requested information.

"Unfortunately, Secretary Mayorkas has conspired with open-borders advocates within the Biden administration, as well as radical groups in the private sector, to open the border and severely limit ICE agents' ability to do their job," said Tom Homan, a visiting fellow at Heritage who headed Immigration and Customs Enforcement during the Trump administration. [The Daily Signal is Heritage's multimedia news organization.]

Homan added of Mayorkas:

He has effectively abolished ICE, and that's why we just saw the lowest deportation number in ICE's history, and more than 14,000 criminal illegal aliens released into our communities. This lawsuit will hopefully shine a light on how we got here, and who else is responsible.

On President Joe Biden's first day in office, then-acting Homeland Security Secretary David Pekoske issued a memo ordering a 100-day moratorium on deportations and a review of immigration enforcement policies after Biden requested a revision.

Mayorkas' New Policies Effectively Abolish ICE

As per the Preston Huennekens Immigration Reform.com October 2021 post "Mayorkas' New Policies Effectively Abolish ICE":

During the Trump administration, progressive politicians and activists made abolishing Immigration and Customs Enforcement (ICE) a top campaign issue. Representatives Alexandria Ocasio-Cortez (D-N.Y.), Mark Pocan (D-Wis.), Pramila Jayapal (D-Wash.) and Senators Elizabeth Warren (D-Mass.), Bernie Sanders (I-Vt.), and Kirsten Gillibrand (D-N.Y.) all called on Congress to support legislation abolishing or otherwise reorganizing the responsibilities of ICE.

That was all before Joe Biden became president in January 2021. It turns out that the progressives did not need Congress to act at all. Through the use of two memoranda, Department of Homeland Security (DHS) Secretary Alejandro Mayorkas used his power to abolish ICE.

The memos do not abolish ICE in the literal sense—the agency is still an existing component of DHS. But the memos are a broadside against ICE's purpose, and mark a total abandonment of immigration enforcement.

Mayorkas released the first memorandum on September 30, 2021. Titled "Guidelines for the Enforcement of Civil Immigration Law," the document outlines new guidance to ICE officers for the apprehension and removal of illegal aliens. Relying on the doctrine of prosecutorial discretion, Mayorkas lays out the case for refusing to prosecute and remove most illegal aliens present in the United States.

Mayorkas writes that "We do not have the resources to apprehend and seek the removal of every one of these noncitizens... In exercising our discretion, we are guided by the fact that the majority of undocumented noncitizens who could be subject to removal have been contributing members of our communities for years."

Mayorkas declares that ICE will prioritize for removal only aliens who are a threat to national security, public safety, and border security. Threats to national security include those suspected of terrorism and espionage.

The second category addresses threats to public safety, but includes exceptions if these violent criminals are of "advanced or tender age," have lived in the United States for a "lengthy" period of time, have a mental illness that led to their criminal conduct, or whose removal would leave dependents behind.

This is remarkable. This policy will shield criminal aliens if they are elderly, have lived here for a long time, or who have children. Anyone who can claim some form of mental illness can remain, regardless of the lives their crimes shattered. Ignoring any sense that criminal aliens pose threats to U.S. citizens, Mayorkas ends by defending his actions by saying that: "The gravity of an apprehension and removal on a noncitizen's life, and potentially the life of family members and the community, warrants the dedication of investigative and evaluative effort."

Secretary Mayorkas is Very Concerned About the Well-Being of Criminal Aliens and Their Families

The final catch-all, "threats to border security," include any illegal aliens apprehended in the U.S. who entered after November 1, 2020. This renders safe any illegal alien who happened to arrive before November 1, 2020. This is the equivalent of Mayorkas ordering DHS and its immigration enforcement components to throw in the towel. It is difficult to prove time-of-entry and the Biden administration already made it clear they intend to remove as few illegal aliens as possible. This third point is nothing more than a paper tiger.

Mayorkas released the second memorandum on October 12, 2021. The document, "Worksite Enforcement: The Strategy to Protect the American Labor Market, the Conditions of the American Worksite, and the Dignity of the Individual" bars ICE from conducting worksite enforcement. This is a crucial aspect of ICE's work, and reverses gains made under the Trump administration.

Worksite enforcement is a crucial tool that ICE used to detain large numbers of illegal aliens at once while also holding accountable the unscrupulous employers who choose to hire them instead of Americans. Illegal aliens come to the U.S. for one reason—to work and make money. In an ideal world, worksite enforcement would be the preferred way to identify and remove illegal aliens while cracking down on the employers who hire them.

Addressing the memorandum, FAIR's president Dan Stein stated that:

The 1986 Immigration Reform and Control Act (IRCA), which then-Senator Joe Biden voted for, explicitly prohibits the employment of illegal aliens. The stated intent of the law was to cut off the magnet of jobs that draws illegal aliens to the U.S., and protect the jobs and wages of American workers. As president, Joe Biden's policy is precisely the opposite: to draw as many illegal aliens as possible to the United States, no matter the cost to national security, public health, burdens to taxpayers, or the jobs and wages of American workers.

This policy does just that. It encourages additional illegal immigration by promising that ICE will not investigate or prosecute the employment of illegal aliens. Instead of allowing ICE to do its job and prosecute employers and illegal aliens, this memo empowers employers who run afoul of existing law and shields illegal aliens from deportation.

Taken together, these two memos destroy ICE's capability to enforce our immigration laws in the interior of the country. Ask yourself—what can ICE do with these policies in place? They cannot prosecute employers who hire illegal aliens. They cannot conduct worksite enforcement investigations to detain illegal aliens working in the U.S. without authorization.

They can detain only the most extreme of criminal aliens, and even then there are carve-outs. Are there any illegal aliens in the United States not shielded by these two policies, aside from terrorists?

With the stroke of a pen, President Biden's DHS secretary—Alejandro Mayorkas—all but abolished the effectiveness of ICE.

Mayorkas' "6 Pillars" Border Security Plan is Delusional

This article is from the Simon Hankinson Heritage Foundation May 2022 article "Mayorkas' '6 Pillars' Border Security Plan Is Delusional":

As May 23, 2022 neared, when border agents' Title 42 public health authority to quickly expel illegal aliens was due to expire, U.S. Customs and Border Protection already had seen predicted increased numbers of illegal aliens. Even the Biden administration admitted that "migration levels will increase."

Homeland Security Secretary Alejandro Mayorkas issued a 20-page memo April 26 detailing his agency's plan for coping with the expected surge of illegal immigration after the lifting of Title 42. Title 42 authority has been used more than 2 million times since March 2020 to expel illegal entrants at the border, in a process much quicker than the normal Title 8 process.

The termination of Title 42 was set to go into effect on May 23, but a federal court in Louisiana blocked the Biden administration from doing so. As of the time of publication, Title 42 remains in effect following that court order.

Mayorkas' six-pillar "Plan for Southwest Border Security and Preparedness" is a continuation of the Biden administration's approach to those illegally crossing the border; namely, quickly process them into the U.S., release them under parole, and grant them asylum.

The plan is lightly sweetened with optimistic, underfunded measures to mitigate the collateral damage on local communities. For example, DHS' Southwest Border Coordination Center and Customs and Border Protection leaders would engage in regular coordination, which "includes a focus on noncitizen transport and capacity planning, resolving logistical challenges, and addressing community concerns through shared solutions."

In the very first lines of his plan, Mayorkas gaslights Americans by blaming the previous administration for handing DHS "a broken and dismantled immigration system," but still claims credit for managing "an unprecedented number of [illegal aliens] seeking to enter the United States" and higher numbers of drug and smuggling interdictions.

Rather than admit the powerful pull factor of the Biden administration's lax policies generally, and proposing to end Title 42 specifically, for the expected surge in illegal entries, Mayorkas blames larger global trends, such as violence, hunger, severe poverty, corruption, climate change, the COVID-19 pandemic, and dire economic conditions.

None of those is grounds for asylum, yet the administration's plan is for all those illegally crossing our border to be able to seek asylum, in most cases under fraudulent pretexts, then expecting to be released into the interior.

Pillar 1 of the plan is a small increase in Customs and Border Protection staff and enlarged or new facilities to increase its capacity to hold aliens up to 18,000 at a time, from 13,000 currently. DHS has also doubled its ability to transport illegal aliens, mostly by bus, away from processing centers once they have been given paperwork to pursue asylum.

This is the essence of the plan: Get the illegal entrants out of detention and into the asylum pipeline as fast as possible, all to avoid media scrutiny and political outrage.

Pillar 2 describes a pilot program using "Enhanced Central Processing Centers," combining Customs and Border Protection, Immigration and Customs Enforcement, unspecified nongovernmental organizations, and "possibly other entities" to more efficiently get illegal aliens out of custody.

The first joint center was scheduled to go online April 29 in Laredo, Texas, and more are planned. Non-governmental organizations will be present to provide legal orientation services and "onward transportation" for the vast majority of the illegal aliens who will be released into the country.

Pillar 3 is where Mayorkas disingenuously promises "consequences for unlawful entry, including removal, detention, and prosecution," and that "[c]ore to this plan is our commitment to continue to strictly enforce our immigration laws."

In reality, he has already issued multiple memos to prohibit most ICE arrests, detentions, and prosecutions. Mayorkas is also well aware that immigration court cases take years due to the 1.7 million-case backlog and an abusive number of continuances, motions, and appeals—all of which buy illegal aliens more time in the U.S. and make their ultimate removal increasingly unlikely.

When immigration judges do issue final orders of removal, Mayorkas has prohibited ICE from detaining and removing such aliens, so they will remain in the U.S.

Pillar 4 reveals the growing administration reliance on non-governmental organizations to perform government functions and provides a mere glimpse into the money going to these groups.

Mayorkas' plan states that these groups will "receive" illegal aliens, who will be released directly into the community and provide them with "onward travel" out of sight and mind. The DHS offers $150 million in taxpayer-funded Federal Emergency Management Agency (FEMA) grants to non-governmental organizations "to help alleviate" the population and fiscal "pressures" that communities experience from "increased migration levels."

States should note this admission when they sue the Biden administration for the expenses they incur due to its refusal to secure the border or enforce immigration laws.

DHS is exploring additional ways to give money to communities to resettle illegal alien populations and will do so by giving more taxpayer money to community organizations. The Biden administration is thus both rewarding its ideologically aligned non-governmental organizations and attempting to buy off community leaders to accept the illegal aliens the administration is encouraging and processing into this country.

Pillar 5 targets "transnational criminal organizations and smugglers who take advantage of and profit from vulnerable migrants and who seek to traffic drugs into our country."

The Biden administration's open-border policies have caused the smuggling of humans and drugs to thrive, and yet Mayorkas has the audacity to pat himself on the back for increased drug and smuggling arrests.

What would really disrupt the cartels would be preventing illegal immigration in the first place and cutting off their revenue source. This plan will only further enrich the cartels and smugglers, kill more Americans with more drugs and crime, and endanger more migrants.

Pillar 6 is a pie-in-the-sky search for a magical deal with Latin American countries that will somehow stem flows of illegal migration with causes far beyond the control of foreign governments.

It contains the forlorn hope that sending a counter-message through media and diplomacy that "the termination of the Title 42 public health order does not mean that the U.S. border is open" will fool anyone.

Mayorkas touts recently struck deals with Panama and Costa Rica, but the deals have few practical applications yet.

He boasts of "close cooperation with Mexico," but the illegal immigration numbers are increasing, not decreasing. As the memo states, "In the past three weeks, [Customs and Border Protection] has encountered an average of over 7,800 migrants per day across the Southwest Border ... compared to a historical average of 1,600 per day in the pre-pandemic years (2014-2019)."

In short, Mayorkas' "Plan for Southwest Border Security and Preparedness" is a 20-page, six-pillar delusion. There's nothing safe, orderly, or humane about the border currently. As a result, neither our national security nor our public safety is protected.

Mayorkas concludes that DHS has been "able to manage increased encounters because of prudent planning and execution." Yet, privately, he has told his agents that the border numbers are unsustainable.

The bottom line is this: Mayorkas' public statements cannot be taken seriously, and his policies have put Americans in daily danger.

Alejandro Mayorkas Isn't Incompetent—He's a Man on a Nefarious Mission

Per the "Alejandro Mayorkas Isn't Incompetent. He's A Man On A Nefarious Mission" FAIR August 2023 report:

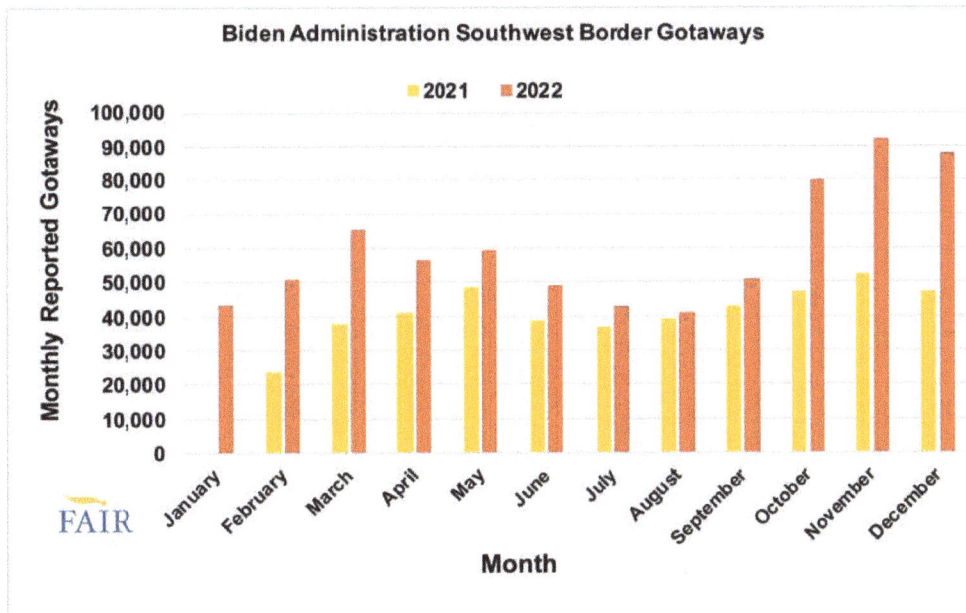

Biden Administration Southwest Border Gotaways

Homeland Security Secretary Alejandro Mayorkas spent more than five hours before the House Judiciary Committee answering questions about his department's management of the border and its seeming lack of interest in enforcing U.S. immigration laws.

It was not the first time Secretary Mayorkas has given testimony before a congressional committee on these matters. In the Republican-led House of Representatives, several committees are looking into the Biden administration's handling of immigration matters, and one is specifically examining whether the secretary himself is in dereliction of his duty to secure our borders and faithfully enforce federal laws.

In advance of the hearing, Secretary Mayorkas was notified in writing about the specific information the oversight committee was looking for. This was information he had been asked to provide on several previous occasions, but has yet to produce. These issues included:

- All policies and data related to encounters, gotaways, paroles, and releases at the southern border since January 20, 2021.

- All policies and data regarding arrests, removals, releases, and detentions since January 20, 2021.

- All policies and data regarding the Department's adjudication of immigration benefits since January 20, 2021.

Repeatedly throughout his appearance last week, Secretary Mayorkas expressed his pride in leading a federal agency with more than 260,000 employees and a nearly $100 billion annual budget. Yet with all these resources, and despite repeated requests (dating back months) for some of the most basic and important information that his agency should be collecting as a matter of course, Mayorkas could not or would not provide answers.

Since President Biden has taken office, more than 7 million migrants have been encountered at our borders. More than 2 million migrants who crossed the border illegally have been released into the United States pending hearings on their claims to remain here, at some distant future date. An additional 1.4 million have been allowed to enter under the administration's massive abuse of parole authority. Another 1.5 million are known to have entered the country illegally, but evaded inspection by the Border Patrol.

In fact, Mayorkas could not even reassure the committee that his department has in custody, or is closely monitoring a small subset of migrants who, by definition, pose a threat to the security of the nation. He could not, or would not, provide status reports on 238 apprehended migrants who are on the terrorist watch list (much less those who might be among the 1.5 million "gotaways'), or the 14,000 drug smugglers who have been arrested at the border this year alone.

Mayorkas is neither stupid nor incompetent. He is, in fact, the very shrewd architect of the Biden administration's open border policies and their efforts to circumvent almost every statutory restriction on the number of people who are allowed to enter the United States and the means by which they get here. His performance at last week's Judiciary Committee hearing only reinforces the notion that, when it comes to immigration policy, he and the administration are deliberately withholding vital information from Congress and the American people.

Mayorkas is deliberately hiding information because there is virtually no public support for this administration's unchecked immigration policies. And, they are being abetted by a largely compliant media that has turned a blind eye to the administration's actions and the crisis on our soil. Mayorkas and his minions are not keeping track of the millions of people they are allowing to enter the country because they have no intention of ever removing them and want to ensure that no subsequent administration will be able to.

Mayorkas' repeated stonewalling of congressional oversight committees only reinforces the case being built by the House Homeland Security that he is in dereliction of his duty as DHS secretary and in violation of his oath of office, and must be removed.

How Biden, Mayorkas Broke Our Immigration System From the Inside Out

From the Tom Homan "How Biden, Mayorkas Broke Our Immigration System From the Inside Out" Heritage Foundation June 2023 article:

With all the focus on the historic immigration crisis brought on by the Biden's mismanagement of our southern border, little attention has been given to immigration enforcement in the interior of our country. Finding, detaining, and removing people who have snuck across the border, evaded Border Patrol, overstayed a visa, ignored a final order of removal, committed additional crimes, or represent active security threats are all the critical functions of interior enforcement.

Yet, this administration, particularly Department of Homeland Security (DHS) Secretary Mayorkas, continues to dismantle the federal government's ability to enforce immigration law. More specifically, Mayorkas has almost completely decimated the country's premier cross-border law enforcement agency: U.S. Immigration and Customs Enforcement (ICE).

I would know, after spending almost my entire career working for ICE or its predecessor agency the Immigration and Naturalization Service, I served as the agency's first director. Today, I hardly recognize the institution. For starters, Mayorkas issued a shocking priorities memorandum in September 2021 that severely limited who ICE was allowed to arrest.

And when I say criminal illegal aliens, I don't simply mean people that crossed the border illegally—though that certainly is a crime in and of itself. See Title 8, USC 1325. No, I am referring to people who have entered the country illegally and have been convicted of a crime or are subject to pending charges.

That's because for Biden and his officials, it isn't enough that these people have entered the country illegally—or in some cases reentered after being formally deported. In many cases, the Democrats don't even care if these same people go on to commit serious crimes in the United States. No, only after they have been convicted of the worst crimes—when it is already too late to act—can these criminals be targeted by ICE. But it doesn't have to be this way. Many of these crimes could easily be prevented if ICE was simply allowed to do its job and enforce the immigration law as written.

Secretary Mayorkas doesn't see it this way. As he recently put it: "Being in the country illegally, on its own, [is] not enough reason for ICE to arrest them." In other words, the unelected and unaccountable Secretary of the Department of Homeland Security made a unilateral decision to overrule the laws written and enacted by the people's representatives in Congress and signed by their president. Today, this truly lawless move has led to immigration officers simply not enforcing our laws.

I testified against Mayorkas's move to undermine ICE last year as an expert witness for the State of Texas. Over the course of a few hours, I explained to District Court Judge Drew B. Tipton how this new instruction did not allow ICE agents to do their job, and fortunately, we won that case. Since then, however, the administration has appealed the decision to a higher court. This won't change the ruling, of course—the U.S. code is clear on who should be arrested and detained, and Mayorkas wrongfully instructed ICE officers to ignore the law—but it has bought the Biden administration more time.

This is bad news for the American people. Since the Mayorkas memorandum came into force, ICE has reported the lowest numbers of arrests and deportations in the history of the agency. It shouldn't come as a surprise, but in that same time period, America has witnessed historic illegal immigration on the southern border.

This alone demonstrates that ICE is essential, and yet Biden dropped the Trump administration's suit against sanctuary jurisdictions shortly after he came into office. Even though Mayorkas has said that arresting serious criminals is a national public safety priority, he and Biden have stood silent while hundreds of jurisdictions across the country have become sanctuary states, counties, and cities, where laws and policies have been put in place that prevent ICE officers from bringing criminals to justice. Many of these jurisdictions will not even give ICE officers access to taxpayer funded jails that harbor known illegal aliens within their facilities. Instead, corrupt Soros-funded prosecutors simply release these criminals back on to the streets to reoffend.

How Alejandro Mayorkas is Shielding Almost a Million Deportable Immigrants From Removal

As per the Nolan Rappaport "How Alejandro Mayorkas is Shielding Almost a Million Deportable Immigrants From Removal" *The Hill* July 2023 story: House Homeland Security Chairman Mark Green (R-Tenn.) recently issued a fact sheet on what he claims to be Department of Homeland Security Secretary Alejandro Mayorkas's "shell game" attempt to hide a startling crisis at the southwest border.

Migrants without visas or other entry documents can install the CBP One app on their mobile phones and use it to schedule an appointment to present themselves at specified southwest border ports of entry. A recent media report shows that 99 percent of the migrants who had these appointments were exempted from Title 42 expulsion and released into the U.S. interior.

CBP has increased the number of CBP One admissions to 1,450 a day.

This shifts the release of undocumented migrants to ports of entry to make it appear that "illegal" crossings are decreasing. "It's clear the Biden administration's approach to 'border management' is to identify more expeditious ways to process illegal aliens and release them into the interior of the United States," said Green.

Illegal entries aren't the only problem. Mayorkas has prohibited enforcement measures against migrants who use non-immigrant visitor's visas to enter the United States lawfully and don't leave when the period authorized for their visit has expired.

According to DHS's Fiscal Year 2022 Entry/Exit Overstay Report, 23,243,127 non-immigrant visitors who entered the United States lawfully at air or seaports of entry were expected to depart in fiscal 2022, and all but 3.674 percent left as required by their visitor's visas.

That seems like a small percentage, but 3.674 percent of 23,243,127 is 853,955 people. This means that the overstays increased the population of undocumented immigrants in the U.S. by almost a million in a single fiscal year.

And there were more than 853,955 overstays in fiscal 2022. The overstay report does not include overstays who entered the United States at a land port of entry. The actual increase in the population of undocumented immigrants may therefore be much larger than a million.

Mayorkas's Guidelines for the Enforcement of Civil Immigration Law shields deportable overstays from being subjected to enforcement proceedings.

According to Mayorkas, most of the deportable immigrants in the U.S. have been contributing members of their communities for years. "The fact an individual is a removable noncitizen therefore should not alone be the basis of an enforcement action against them."

Who were the 853,955 overstays who entered the U.S. at air or sea ports of entry in fiscal 2022?

These include five groups. The first comprises the 97,632 non-immigrant visitor overstays for business or pleasure from Visa Waiver Program (VWP) countries. Then there are 504,636 non-immigrant visitor overstays. Third are 55,023 non-immigrant overstays among student and exchange visitors. Next come the 45,417 non-immigrant overstays (excluding those from Canada and Mexico). Finally, there are 151,247 non-immigrant overstays from Canada and Mexico.

The fact that non-immigrant visitors are not being put in removal proceedings has only become a magnet for more illegal immigration.

According to border security expert Todd Bensman, migrants hear about the Biden administration's lax enforcement policies "from friends, relatives, neighbors, and acquaintances who communicate their good fortune by cellphone calls, texts, chat room discussions, and selfies."

Lastly, the recent Supreme Court decision on standing to challenge the Mayorkas enforcement guidelines makes it unrealistic to expect federal court intervention. Realistically, if Congress doesn't make Mayorkas follow the statutory border security and removal provisions in the Immigration and Nationality Act, then no one will.

Impeaching Mayorkas is a Must, He Violated His Oath and Committed "High Crimes and Misdemeanors"

Per the Hans A. von Spakovsky "Impeaching Mayorkas Is a Must, He Violated His Oath and Committed 'High Crimes and Misdemeanors'" Heritage Foundation February 2023 article:

There is no doubt that impeachment, as renowned Supreme Court Justice Joseph Story said, should be a measure of last resort. But as the Judiciary Committee of the House of Representatives said in 2019, "when faced with credible evidence of extraordinary wrongdoing … the House must investigate and determine whether impeachment is warranted."

The "extraordinary wrongdoing" of Secretary of Homeland Security Alejandro Mayorkas in causing an unprecedented border, national security and illegal immigration catastrophe warrants such an investigation.

We don't take that position lightly. Federal officials should not be impeached for political reasons or because the members disagree with the policy priorities of the administration that controls the executive branch.

But that is not the situation with Mayorkas, who is usurping the powers of Congress on a wide scale.

He has violated his oath of office by repeatedly violating the laws he swore faithfully to enforce. He has abused the powers of his office through reckless conduct that threatens the sovereignty of the U.S. and risks the safety and security of the American people and the law enforcement personnel of the Department of Homeland Security. And he has betrayed the public trust by repeatedly making false statements to Congress and misleading the public about the nature and effects of his misconduct.

No cabinet official has the constitutional authority to ignore the law that he has taken an oath to enforce, and certainly not to violate the law or to instruct executive branch employees to do so. No cabinet official has the right to make misleading statements or to lie to Congress and the public.

Yet that is exactly what Secretary Mayorkas has done since his first day in office.

His impeachable conduct includes throwing open the border and orchestrating the mass release and paroling of millions of illegal aliens in direct contravention of federal immigration law and ignoring the law's mandatory detention and deportation provisions. His new program of preregistering illegal aliens for mass entry and release in the U.S. institutionalizes his flagrant violations of the law.

His classification of almost all illegal aliens as refugees and asylum seekers is an outrageous abuse of his powers, an action that encourages fraud. He is deliberately inducing aliens to put their lives in the hands of ruthless cartel members and human traffickers, whose power and profits Mayorkas is directly benefiting by ensuring the success of their criminal operations.

And his open-border policies have caused a humanitarian disaster and put the American public in danger from unknown quantities of fentanyl and other deadly drugs being smuggled in, along with terrorists and dangerous, violent criminals.

All of these misdeeds fit well within the definition of "High Crimes and Misdemeanors" that the Constitution says merit impeachment, as well as the application by Congress of that clause in the 20 impeachments that have occurred in our history.

There is no question that Mayorkas has acted "in a manner contrary to his trust" as the head of Homeland Security. His defiance of the requirements of federal immigration law and the false testimony he has submitted to Congress are "subversive of constitutional government" and the role of Congress in establishing the laws the executive branch is obligated to enforce.

We agree that impeachment is not appropriate for mere disagreements over an exercise of policy discretion. But when the officer entrusted with the nation's immigration laws and border security deliberately, intentionally and systematically refuses to recognize and uphold the requirements of those laws and assumes instead an unlimited power to suspend and violate the law, that is conduct far beyond simple policy disagreement.

It is extraordinary misconduct that threatens our constitutional form of government and warrants impeachment.

The Case for Impeaching Homeland Security Secretary Alejandro Mayorkas

As noted in the Mark Morgan and Tom Homan "The Case for Impeaching Homeland Security Secretary Alejandro Mayorkas" Heritage Foundation March 2023 update: Impeachment was not designed to settle political scores or policy differences. It is reserved for holding public officials accountable when they violate the law, abuse the power of their office or are dishonest with the American people or Congress.

Our colleagues at the Heritage Foundation recently laid out a clear and compelling legal case for Mayorkas's impeachment along these lines.

First, he has deliberately defied many of the laws he is supposed to execute.

For example, Mayorkas has violated numerous provisions of the Immigration and Nationality Act (INA), which governs much of U.S. immigration law. He has instructed Department of Homeland Security (DHS) officials to mass-parole illegal immigrants into the country, in violation of the statute that dictates parole is to be granted "temporarily" and "only on a case-by-case basis for urgent humanitarian reasons or significant public benefit."

The Fifth Circuit Court of Appeals has even stated that DHS cannot mass parole immigrants into the country, but Mayorkas has expanded the practice.

DHS's newest parole program alone will admit as many as 360,000 Haitians, Cubans, Nicaraguans and Venezuelans per year, clearly violating the statute. The most significant effect of these parole policies has been the mass release of individuals into the country who would otherwise have no legitimate claim to enter.

This has encouraged widespread abuse of the asylum system, which has been a driving force behind the crisis, incentivizing millions of individuals to make the journey in hopes of filing a claim and gaining release into the U.S. All this despite data showing that around 90 percent of those claiming asylum do not get relief.

Mayorkas has further defied duly passed laws by restricting Immigration and Customs Enforcement from deporting individuals in the U.S. illegally. His own guidance even dictates that an individual's presence in the country illegally "should not alone be the basis of an enforcement action against them."

Second, Mayorkas has abused the power of his office. Through his unlawful policies, he has encouraged millions of individuals to cross the border illegally, most of whom place themselves in the vicious hands of the drug cartels to do so.

He has made clear that anyone who makes a "credible fear" asylum claim, legitimate or not, will be released into the U.S., knowingly encouraging and facilitating widespread asylum fraud. Mayorkas is a veteran DHS official who knows the data on these claims and yet continues to look the other way, allowing the system to be exploited.

And he has authorized the use of taxpayer funds to transport illegal immigrants throughout the country, often under the cover of darkness, effectively completing the cartels' work by ferrying individuals from the border to their final destination.

Third, he has repeatedly lied about his policies and their consequences. In March 2021, he told Fox News, "The border is secure, the border is closed." In July 2022, he told the Aspen Security Forum, "Look, the border is secure." On Nov. 15, 2022, he told the House Homeland Security Committee the same thing.

He has even told Congress that DHS maintains "operational control of the border."

Customs and Border Protection (CBP) has recorded more than 5.5 million encounters since Joe Biden took office. Another 1.2 million "got-aways" have evaded Border Patrol altogether and are now at large in the U.S. Among them are violent criminals, including murders, pedophiles, gang members and drug dealers. Fentanyl is now the leading cause of death for Americans 18-45.

As Border Patrol agents are pulled off the line to process the historic flows of illegal immigrants, large areas of our nation's borders are increasingly vulnerable for the cartels to exploit. CBP has recovered more than 1,500 dead migrants on U.S. soil on Biden's watch, another ghastly record.

No objective person would continue to claim the border is secure. DHS does not have operational control. Mayorkas knows this. Finally, he has knowingly misled the public about the conduct of his own agents who were falsely accused of "whipping" Haitian migrants in Del Rio, Texas. Mayorkas's actions have directly contributed to a historic border crisis, the consequences of which continue to affect every city and state in the country.

His "high crimes and misdemeanors" are "acts committed by public officials, using their power or privileges, that inflicted grave harm on our political order." That's the definition from the House Judiciary Committee's 2019 impeachment of former President Trump. That standard certainly applies today.

The case is compelling. The Constitution provides the means. Our public conscience demands accountability.

8 – Trump's Prudent Immigration Policies, Successes & Border Enforcement Champion

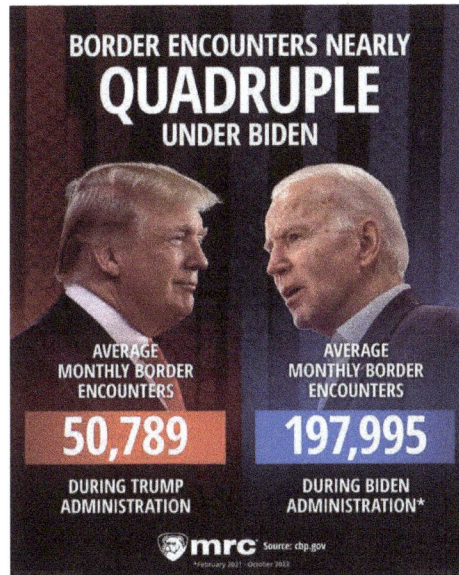

From the Caroline Downey "Trump: Border Crisis Could Have Been Averted If Biden Did 'Nothing'" *National Review* June 2021 article:

The border security that President Trump built, President Biden has quickly torn down. Trump put Americans first with immigration policies that secured the border, enforced our laws, and brought integrity back to our immigration system. President Biden has quickly dismantled those effective policies, opened the border, stopped immigration enforcement, and brought chaos to our immigration system, prioritizing illegal aliens over Americans.

At a joint press conference in June 2021 with Texas governor Greg Abbott at the U.S. border with Mexico, former president Donald Trump suggested that the border crisis could have been averted if Biden simply did nothing. "All Biden had to do was go to the beach," he commented. "If he would have just done nothing, we would have had the strongest border we ever had."

President Ronald Reagan is reported to have once said, "A nation that cannot control its borders is not a nation." During the past three decades, the U.S. has faced a mounting immigration problem as an increasingly larger number of aliens have come into the country illegally— straining government resources, imposing huge costs on taxpayers and state and local governments, and endangering national security, public safety, and the rule of law.

Per the Heritage Foundation team of Charles D. Stimson, Hans A. von Spakovsky, and Lora Ries "Assessing the Trump Administration's Immigration Policies" June 2020 article:

A sovereign country with sound immigration policy controls who is allowed to come into the country, both temporarily and permanently, and selects future citizens, expecting them to become part of the cultural, intellectual, economic, and political body of the republic.

Candidate Donald Trump ran for the presidency in 2016 promising to enforce existing immigration laws and secure the border. That was a radical departure from the Obama administration, which, as we chronicle, abused the authority given to the President—and arguably broke the law and violated the Constitution by issuing executive edicts to satisfy its policy preferences.

Once he became the President, Donald Trump began to enforce immigration law as written, rolling back the extra-constitutional policies put in place by the Obama Administration, and reframed the debate by announcing a tectonic shift in how new immigrants would be chosen.

The Trump Administration's immigration policies have been consistently challenged in the courts, including in the U.S. Supreme Court. The Administration has won many of those challenges, in large part because it was following the law and exercising its discretion accordingly, as we demonstrate.

While the Trump administration implemented numerous immigration policies that protected American workers and deterred illegal immigration, there were still many loopholes in existing policy that encouraged additional illegal immigration and protected the interests of large corporations over small business and American workers. As such, the illegal alien population grew considerably, as did the backlog of cases currently before an immigration judge.

Measuring the Trump Administration's Top Immigration Issues by the Numbers

As shown in the Spencer Raley, Madison McQueen and Jason Pena "Measuring the Trump Administration's Top Immigration Issues by the Numbers" FAIR June 2021 report:

There are literally thousands of immigration-related statistics that can be used to assess the success or failure of a country's immigration policy. This can make the prospect of analyzing the results of policy changes overwhelming. Because of that, the Federation for American Immigration Reform (FAIR) has compiled and organized the most important and commonly requested immigration-related statistics from throughout the Trump administration.

These figures demonstrate several things:

- Policies such as the Migrant Protection Protocols (MPP) were tremendously helpful in deterring illegal immigration and reducing asylum fraud.

- The administration largely removed the handcuffs from federal law enforcement agencies, as evidenced by the steady increase in apprehensions and deportations from U.S. Customs and Border Protection (CBP) and Immigration and Customs Enforcement (ICE).

While the Trump administration implemented numerous immigration policies that protected American workers and deterred illegal immigration, there were still many loopholes in existing policy that encouraged additional illegal immigration and protected the interests of large corporations over small business and American workers. As such, the illegal alien population grew considerably, as did the backlog of cases currently before an immigration judge.

The COVID-19 pandemic led to abnormally low immigration-related figures for FY 2020. While some of this improvement can indeed be attributed to positive policy change, such as placing a temporary pause on many guestworker visa categories, most are due to a weakened economy and international travel restrictions. Because of this, totals for this year should be considered with a grain of salt.

The statistics and figures in this report can serve as an important basis of comparison between the Trump and Biden administrations.

President Biden immediately scaled back or eliminated almost every policy implementation from the Trump administration. Conventional wisdom would suggest that with the reversal of these policies, the positive statistical developments will likely reverse as well. This is already evident with the development of an ongoing crisis at the southern border that developed soon after President Biden's election.

In general, the Trump administration made it much easier for immigration law enforcement officers to do their job and remove immigration lawbreakers from the United States. This is reflected in the preceding data ranging over his four years as president.

However, there were still numerous holes in our nation's immigration policies that allowed the illegal alien population to increase during his tenure. Furthermore, large corporations continued to largely get away with prioritizing foreign labor over unemployed American citizens.

The Border Wall: How Much Was Built?

Per the extensive Claire Hansen "How Much of Trump's Border Wall Was Built?" *U.S. News & World Report* February 2022 article:

Trump's signature promise to build a barrier along the southwest border of the U.S. propelled him to victory in 2016, and his administration during his term appropriated some $15 billion for its construction – a big chunk of which was taken from the Defense Department's budget after Congress refused to meet the administration's funding demands, prompting a lengthy government shutdown.

The wall was a constant source of controversy, prompting fierce criticism from environmentalists and Democrats. Its construction and funding was also the target of a number of lawsuits.

Before Biden stopped new construction on the wall, the Trump administration had built 458 miles of what it dubbed "border wall system," according to final figures compiled by U.S. Customs and Border Protection and provided to *U.S. News*.

The wall consists mostly of 18- to 30-foot steel bollards anchored in concrete. The barriers also feature sensors, lights, cameras and parallel roads in some places.

The vast majority of the 458 miles were constructed in places where some kind of barrier already existed, but most of the preexisting structures were far less imposing than the new wall and included fencing and rudimentary technical barriers. The total figure also includes what the agency calls "secondary border wall" or sections of wall built behind preexisting barriers that ultimately remained in place.

Some 226 miles, or nearly half of the total number of miles built, run along the border in Arizona, including more than 100 miles in both the Border Patrol sector near Yuma and in the sector near Tucson.

About 100 miles were constructed in New Mexico, largely in a stretch along the eastern part of the state's border that bumps into Texas near El Paso. A total of 55 miles were built in the Lone Star State along the Rio Grande by El Paso and in lengths by Laredo and in the Rio Grande Valley.

California saw the completion of construction of 77 miles of wall in areas along the border near San Diego and El Centro.

Stretches of the wall system are not necessarily contiguous. The wall often runs into existing fencing or simply has gaps.

One of the most controversial aspects of the wall was its cost. During his 2016 campaign, Trump pledged that Mexico would foot the bill – a promise that went unfulfilled, leaving taxpayers to fund construction. In some places, Trump's barrier carried a price tag of up to $46 million per mile, according to the Biden administration.

Since taking office and largely stopping wall construction, Biden has canceled border wall projects paid for by Pentagon funds. In June 2021, the administration announced it was returning $2.2 billion in Defense Department funds diverted for the wall in order to use the money for 66 previously deferred defense projects, including a missile field expansion in Alaska and a school for U.S. military children in Germany.

The Biden administration most recently said it would use border security funding allocated by Congress to close small gaps in border barriers and to pay for environmental fixes and the clean-up of border wall construction sites. Work will include projects like the installation of drainage to prevent flooding, addition of missing gates and construction of erosion control measures, Homeland Security Secretary Alejandro Mayorkas said in a December statement.

The administration is also urging Congress to cancel the remaining funding allocated to the wall and instead siphon money toward other border security initiatives.

CBP Apprehension and Inadmissible Totals (Southern Border)

CBP is one of the federal law enforcement agencies under the Department of Homeland Security (DHS). It is charged with enforcing U.S. regulations on customs, immigration and trade. The agency's most extensive duties include protecting and patrolling all U.S. borders.

Apprehensions refer to the temporary detainment of an individual suspected to be illegally present in the U.S. and typically results in an arrest. Apprehensions make up roughly 80 percent of all official CBP encounters at the Southern Border. The Trump administration saw a record number of apprehensions occur during FY 2019.

This was due in large part to the booming economy in the United States, along with numerous mass-migration advocacy groups helping illegal aliens file bogus asylum claims. These apprehensions dropped significantly with the implementation of MPP, which required asylum applicants remain in Mexico while their cases were processed instead of being released into the country. Since the vast majority of asylum applications are found to have no merit, this discouraged individuals from making the long and dangerous trek to the United States.

Inadmissible aliens are those migrants encountered at ports of entry who are seeking lawful admission into the U.S. but are determined to be inadmissible. This encompasses a number of potential situations, including those who withdraw an application for admission and return to their countries of origin, and those who present inaccurate or insufficient documentation.

The total number of inadmissible aliens encountered remained relatively static throughout the Trump administration, increasing by less than 15 percent between FY 2017 and FY 2019, before decreasing drastically in FY 2020. Again, as for many immigration-related statistics, the drop in FY 2020 was due to a drastic decrease in crossings at the southern border.

Inadmissible encounters were especially impacted since many who fall into this category are typically those who are attempting to enter the country on a short-term basis for reasons other than work. Since these kinds of admissions were largely paused during the COVID-19 pandemic, it makes sense that fewer individuals would attempt to enter the country for this purpose.

CBP Total Enforcement Actions (Southern and Northern Border)

Total enforcement actions include both northern and southern border data, as well as actions by the Office of Field Operations (OFO) and the United States Border Patrol (USBP). Total enforcement actions for FY 2020 include Title 42 expulsions and Title 8 apprehensions.

Beginning in March 2020, the Trump administration ordered the expulsion of individuals who pose a potential health risk due to COVID-19, either by previously announced travel restrictions or because they unlawfully entered the country to bypass health screening measures. As a result, in accordance with Title 42 of U.S. Code Section 265, qualifying individuals would not be held in congregate areas for processing but rather be immediately expelled to the country of last transit.

The number of total enforcement actions by Customs and Border Patrol (CBP) dropped in FY 2020 due to the coronavirus pandemic slowing activity at the southern border. However, encounters of unlawfully present or inadmissible migrants were rising in an alarming fashion prior to the COVID-19 era. This increase was primarily due to a growing number of migrants claiming asylum at the southern border. Between 2012 and 2020, the rate of denied asylum applications rose drastically from approximately 45 percent to more than 70 percent.

This is due in part to the fact that, prior to the Trump administration's implementation of Migrant Protection Protocols (MPP) in late FY 2019 (often referred to as the "Remain in Mexico" program), most asylum applicants were released into the country pending their court dates. A large number of these applicants never showed up for their proceedings, opting instead to disappear into the country.

Since MPP eliminated most incentives for filing a bogus asylum claim by requiring applicants remain in a safe third-party country until their court proceedings take place, this contributed to the decrease in the number of claims made in the final year of the Trump administration.

DHS Apprehension Totals

DHS combines data from both CBP and ICE. The DHS apprehension data is larger than the combined totals of ICE and CBP apprehensions. This is likely due to data corrections made by the DHS, arrests made by 287g affiliates, or apprehensions by other agencies which are then turned over to DHS.

The 287g program allows for certain local and state law enforcement officers to partner with DHS in the apprehension and processing of those who are residing in the country illegally. This program is important because it helps relieve some of the currently overwhelming workload shouldered by ICE officials, especially with the ongoing crisis at the southern border.

Unfortunately, the Biden administration is curtailing the use of this program, and it's very existence is in danger. Ending the 287g program puts American communities at risk because it forces local jurisdictions to release potentially dangerous foreign-born lawbreakers back into their communities versus turning them over to ICE for removal.

DHS Returns

Returns are the confirmed movement of an inadmissible or deportable alien out of the United States not based on an order of removal. Often, illegal crossers from Mexico that are apprehended by Border Patrol are given the option to voluntarily return to Mexico. This allows authorities to return illegal aliens back to their home country without going through the deportation proceedings that take more time to complete. Others are individuals who were residing in the United States illegally, but DHS has credible information that the individual left the country and had not returned by the time these annual statistics were curated.

Returns increased throughout the Trump administration (2020 figures were unavailable at the time this report was published). This is likely due to two reasons:

- The Trump administration increased border security personnel and equipment which led to additional apprehensions and an increase in voluntary returns.

- The removal of Obama-era ICE deportation "priorities" that targeted primarily just those with substantial criminal records resulted in more migrants opting to leave the country of their own accord versus being apprehended and removed by ICE.

With the de-prioritization of apprehensions and deportations under the Biden administration, it can be expected that returns will decrease, as illegal aliens feel less pressure to leave the country for fear of apprehension and expulsion.

ICE Apprehension Totals

One of the largest areas of responsibility for ICE is the apprehension, processing, and removal of individuals who are illegally present in the interior of the country.

ICE apprehensions, otherwise known as administrative arrests, occur within the interior of the United States. Under the Trump administration, ICE arrests rose by 30% to 143,470 in FY 2017 compared to 110,104 in FY 2016.

Throughout the Obama administration, ICE was handcuffed by an apprehension "priority" system implemented in a series of policies that built on the infamous "Morton Memos." The policies targeted primarily illegal aliens who committed crimes in addition to unlawful entry (which is considered a civil offense).

As a result, ICE apprehensions and removals dropped significantly during the Obama administration, especially near the end of his time in office. One of the first things President Trump did after taking office was to dismantle this system and allow federal law enforcement to apprehend, process, and remove all immigration lawbreakers.

This new approach was hampered by states and local jurisdictions who chose to release any illegal aliens they arrested back into the public instead of turning them over to ICE as federal law requires. These so-called "sanctuary" jurisdictions make it harder on ICE officers to carry out their federally-mandated duties, and forced them to spend additional time locating often dangerous criminal aliens throughout the country instead of simply picking up the individual at a state/local facility.

In their annual report, ICE identified several factors which contributed to a decrease in interior arrests for FY 2019, noting the growing enforcement needs at the southern border and the lack of cooperation from increasing jurisdictions nationwide.

ICE Removals

ICE removals are simply the deportation of individuals who were apprehended in the interior of the country. These deportations rose every year during the Trump administration except for FY 2020, when COVID-19 precautions hindered apprehension and removal efforts.

As noted in the previous section, the Obama-era apprehension and deportation "priorities" prevented ICE from fully completing their duties. These rules were eliminated during the Trump administration, which lead to an increase in apprehensions, and subsequently, deportations. Unfortunately, the Biden administration has restored these damaging Obama-era deportation priorities. Because of this, it can be reasonably expected that ICE removals will once again decrease.

Moreover, the Biden administration has re-instated Obama-era "catch and release" policies that require CBP release individuals into the country. When this is combined with the new deportation "priorities," it can be expected that the illegal alien population will increase drastically since CBP must release immigration lawbreakers into the country and ICE is not allowed to remove them.

Throughout his presidency, Donald Trump prioritized the apprehension and deportation of illegal aliens. This commitment is reflected in the totals presented here, especially in regard to ICE removals, which increased every year until the pandemic-dampened year of 2020.

Illegal Alien Population (in Millions)

The illegal alien population grew considerably during the Trump administration. This can be attributed to a number of reasons, including a strong economy throughout most of his presidency. However, it can also be attributed to a failure to enforce some existing laws or implement important policies that would deter migrants from coming to the United States illegally, such as mandatory E-Verify or the prosecution of businesses that hire those who are not authorized to work in the United States.

When former President Trump took office, the illegal alien population stood at approximately 12.5 million. When he left, it had bloomed to 14.5 million. The bulk of this increase took place in 2018 and 2019 (before the border wall construction and refurbishment had commenced). The impacts of COVID-19 led to only marginal growth in the illegal alien population during 2020.

As the Federation for American Immigration Reform (FAIR) has noted elsewhere, the illegal alien population is set to surge under the Biden administration. If he implements all of his preferred policies, the population could exceed 20 million.

Of course, the Biden administration has also promised to grant amnesty to essentially all illegal aliens. While this would immediately lower the number of those residing in the United States without authorization, the negative impacts on taxpayers would only increase, as this population would also immediately become eligible for federal welfare programs. Previous reports by FAIR have revealed that illegal aliens earn far less on average than American citizens or lawfully present immigrants.

Backlog of Pending Immigration Cases

One additional element that hinders ICE from deporting more immigration violators is the growing backlog of immigration court cases. In FY 2017, there were 629,051 pending immigration cases. The following fiscal years saw increases in pending cases, subsequently causing the backlog to worsen. The lack of adequate immigration judges and staff to handle these cases has contributed to the backlog as well.

Under the Trump administration, more immigration judges were hired to alleviate the burden. However, the border crisis of FY 2019, which included American-based organizations helping migrants exploit loopholes and abuse the asylum system, led to an extreme uptick in asylum applications. The vast majority of these applications are found to be fraudulent, and more than half of all applicants never even show up for their hearings. Because of this, the immigration caseload has risen to unprecedented numbers.

If not for the implementation of MPP, which required migrants wait in a safe third-party country while their asylum claims are processed, these figures would be far higher. Since President Biden rescinded the program, apprehensions and subsequent notices- to-appear have skyrocketed.

Refugee Arrivals

Under the Trump administration, the number of refugee arrivals to the United States significantly declined. This is largely due to difficulty in vetting individuals from terrorism-prone countries. Additionally, new screening measures were introduced to ensure that all refugee applicants could be properly vetted, and no potentially dangerous individuals were permitted to enter the country.

While totals are not yet available for FY 2020, the administration set the refugee cap at just 15,000 in order to protect American workers and limit the possibility of national security threats entering the country via the refugee program.

The Biden administration initially announced that they intended to keep the refugee cap at 15,000 in order to protect American workers but reversed course after pressure from open borders proponents. Now, for FY 2021, the Biden administration drastically increased the refugee cap to 62,500. That number is higher than it was at any point during the Trump administration.

Asylum

Grants for asylum increased under the Trump administration. Fiscal Year 2017 had 26,199 grants for asylum of foreign nationals. In FY 2018, the number of asylum grants that were issued totaled 37,567. The latest data on asylum admissions revealed 46,508 grants for asylum were issued in FY 2019.

These statistics counter the false assertion that former President Trump "dismantled" the American asylum system, as current President Joe Biden claims. FY 2019 saw the most Asylum claims approved in the 21st Century. And, the administration did this while greatly reducing asylum fraud by implementing MPP which, as previously mentioned, limited the ability of applicants to disappear into the country and never show up for their court dates.

These asylum agreements with Mexico and the Central American countries of El Salvador, Honduras, and Guatemala were immediately revoked by the incoming Biden administration, despite their tremendous success. As a result, a record number of individuals are once again flooding the southern border, hoping to take advantage of a once-again flawed asylum system.

While data for FY 2020 is not yet available, approximately 92,800 affirmative asylum applications and 151,800 defensive asylum applications were filed in the year. Based on prevailing approval rates (which are extremely low), the number of accepted asylum applications most likely decreased in FY 2020. As for almost all other statistics included in this report, the reason for the decrease can largely be attributed to the impacts of COVID-19.

VISA Overstays

Visa overstays occur when a foreign national remains in the United States past their designated date to return home. These overstays account for approximately 60 percent of the illegal immigrant population. The bulk of visa overstays comes from those who overstay tourist visas. While most of these overstayers leave within a year, hundreds of thousands of these individuals remain indefinitely, and resettle into the country.

In FY 2017, there were 701,900 visa overstays. The number of visa overstays decreased to 666,582 the following year before rising slightly in FY 2019. While data remains unavailable for FY 2020, it can safely be assumed that this figure dropped significantly as far fewer visas were issued due to the COVID-19 pandemic, and very few tourists were allowed into the United States.

As the United States continues to restrict entry by tourists, it can be expected that figures near the beginning of the Biden administration may remain low. However, again, with the de-prioritization of apprehensions and deportations as directed by the president, we can expect more and more individuals to overstay their visas once international travel returns to pre-pandemic levels. When there is little risk of removal from the country, many illegal aliens will simply opt to enter the country as a tourist, and then remain in the country beyond their designated date to return home.

H-1B, H-2A, H-2B, F1, J1, Total Non-immigrant Visas Issued

Non-immigrant work and study visas are for foreign nationals who have gained authorization to enter the United States on a temporary basis for purposes other than tourism. Under the Trump administration, the issuance of non-immigrant visas gradually declined. In FY 2017, the total number of work visas issued was 9,681,913. The visa categories that accumulated large numbers of foreign nationals were the H-1B, H-2A, H-2B, F-1, and J-1.

The latest cumulative data available prior to the COVID pandemic shows the grand total of visas issued at 8,742,068. While the total number of work visas given under the Trump administration has declined, other visa categories have experienced higher entries of foreign workers. The H-2A visa category, for example, increased its cap under the administration. In fact, there were more H-2A visas given during the pandemic-stricken year of 2020, when millions of Americans were without work, than in any other year of Trump's presidency.

Still, in FY 2020, the total number of visas issued decreased by 4,728,858, or 54 percent. These measures ensured millions of jobs which would normally go to foreign laborers were given to U.S. citizens instead. This is another move that the Biden administration has reversed despite the unemployment rate in the United States remaining much higher than its pre-pandemic levels.

Approximate Active DACA Recipients

The Deferred Action for Childhood Arrivals (DACA) program is an initiative created by the Obama administration in 2012 that granted a "soft amnesty" to illegal aliens that entered the United States before the age of 16. Under DACA, recipients receive identity documents, work permits, and temporary relief from deportation. Former President Donald Trump attempted to end DACA throughout his administration, but all attempts were blocked by activist judges. These injunctions were highly questionable, as the program was almost certainly illegal to begin with.

Under the Trump administration, the number of illegal aliens enrolled in DACA slowly decreased each fiscal year. In FY 2017, there were approximately 689,800 active DACA recipients. By the end of FY 2020, the number of active recipients decreased to 643,560. The Trump administration attempted to end DACA in June of 2020, but the Supreme Court blocked any efforts to dismantle the program until the case could be decided in its entirety. Subsequently, the Trump administration refused to accept any more applications for DACA.

Since taking office, President Biden has not only began approving new applications for DACA but has promised amnesty to all DACA-eligible individuals, whether they apply for the program or not.

Trump Administration Immigration Accomplishments

As shown in the "Trump Administration Immigration Accomplishments" FAIR December 2023 report:

Throughout his presidency, Donald J. Trump has worked hard to restore the rule of law and make immigration work for America. President Trump's efforts to fulfill his immigration-related campaign promises faced constant obstruction – mainly from the Democrats, but also some Republicans, and activist judges – but the president remained undeterred. Many important pro-American policies consistent with FAIR's vision were implemented.

Below is a timeline of the Trump Administration's immigration accomplishments from the latest to the earliest:

2021:

- 452 Miles of Border Wall Completed (new and refurbished)

2020:

- Trump Extends COVID-19-Related Immigration Restrictions To Protect American Workers
- Refugee Ceiling Reduced To Lowest Level In History
- Criminals Barred From Asylum
- Trump Bars Federal Contractors from Displacing American Workers with Foreign Guestworkers
- Protecting American Workers, Halting Foreign Guest Worker Admissions
- Trump Imposes Anti-Coronavirus Travel Ban on Europe

- Trumps Signs Coronavirus Relief Package Excluding Illegal Aliens
- More Travel Restrictions on Iran
- Trump Administration Takes Action Against Sanctuary Jurisdictions
- Legal Immigration Reduced
- Trump Blocks Travel to China To Stem COVID-19
- Trump Administration Cracks Down on Birth Tourism
- Southwest Border Apprehensions Decline for 8 Consecutive Months
- Travel Ban Expanded to Six More Countries

2019:

- Bar Asylum-Seekers From Receiving Work Authorization While Their Application is Pending
- Trump Administration Signs Asylum Agreement with El Salvador
- Supreme Court Permits Administration to Enforce "Safe Third Country" Rule
- Apprehensions at the Southern Border Continue to Decline
- Trump Administration Paves the Way for the Termination of the Flores Agreement
- U.S. Signs Asylum Agreement with Guatemala
- Arrests at the Southern Border Crossings Down
- ICE to Begin Removing Millions of Illegal Aliens
- President Signs Memo Enforcing the Legal Responsibilities of Immigrant Sponsors
- Trump Signs Memo to End Asylum Abuse
- Attorney General Barr Cracks Down on Catch-and-Release
- President Trump Declares National Emergency
- DHS Announces Final Rule for a More Merit-Based, Effective, and Efficient H-1B Visa Program

2018:

- DHS Announces Major Change to U.S. Asylum Policy
- President Trump Signs Proclamation to Address Deficiencies in the Asylum Process
- President Deploys 5,200 Troops to the U.S.-Mexico Border
- Administration Releases New Rule on Public Charge Exclusions
- Trump Administration Lowers FY 2019 Refugee Cap to 30,000
- Justice Department Touts New Immigration Judges, Quicker Hiring
- President Trump Deports WWII Nazi Collaborator
- Supreme Court Rules in Favor of Trump Administration on Travel Ban
- Trump Administration Terminates TPS for Honduras
- Justice Department Announces "Zero Tolerance Policy" for Illegal Entry
- President Trump Deploys National Guard Troops to Southern Border
- Justice Department Imposes Quotas on Immigration Judges
- Trump Administration Announces Citizenship Question on 2020 Census
- Justice Department Sues California Over Sanctuary Policies

2017:

- Trump Administration Ends TPS for El Salvador
- Trump Administration Terminates Temporary Protected Status for Haiti
- President Trump Fulfills Campaign Promise to End DACA
- President Trump Sets FY 2018 Refugee Cap to Responsible 45,000
- Trump Administration Withdraws DAPA Amnesty
- President Trump Signs Executive Order Establishing the Commission on Election Integrity
- President Trump Signs Buy American and Hire American Executive Order
- President Trump Signs Executive Order Ensuring Proper Vetting of Foreign Nationals Before They Enter the United States
- President Trump Withdraws the United States from the Trans Pacific Partnership (TPP)
- President Trump Signs Executive Order Authorizing Construction of Border Wall on the Southern Border
- President Trump Signs Executive Order Withholding Funds From Sanctuary Jurisdictions
- President Trump Signs Executive Order Protecting the Nation from Foreign Terrorist Entry into the United States

9 – The Shocking Costs to Americans Due to Democrats' Pro Illegal Immigration Policies

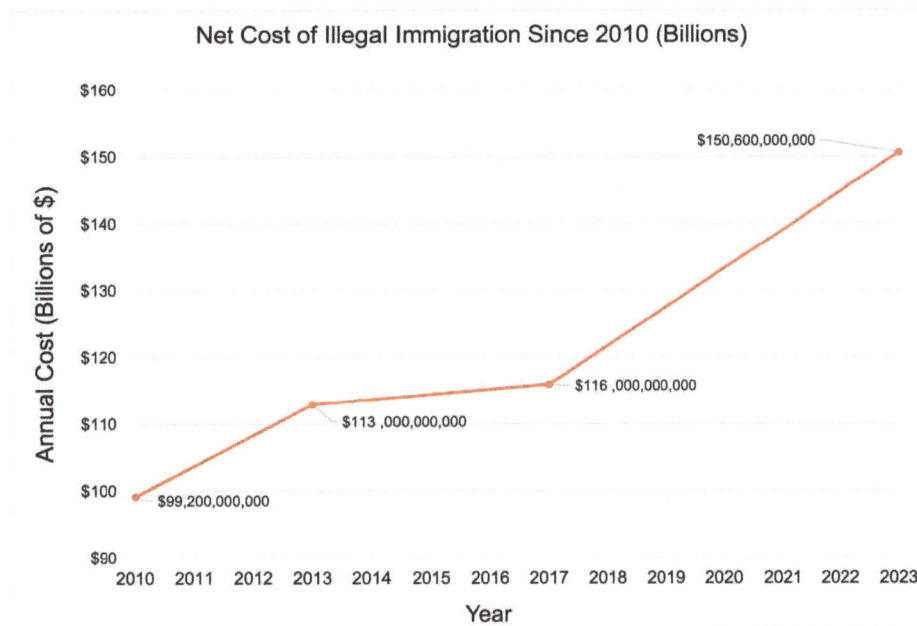

Net Cost of Illegal Immigration Since 2010 (Billions)

- $150,600,000,000
- $116,000,000,000
- $113,000,000,000
- $99,200,000,000

Credit: FAIR.

The costs of building a border wall/fence – usually estimated at $20-25 billion – are dwarfed by the burden of illegal immigration, which currently costs the American taxpayer $151 billion annually, and which may rise to $200 billion by 2025 if current illegal immigration trends continue.

From the Mark Morgan "Cash to Illegal Immigrants Is the New Low in Biden's Open-Borders Push" *National Review* November 2021 article:

It goes without saying: No one should get paid hundreds of thousands of dollars for entering our country illegally. But in September 2021, the *Wall Street Journal* reported that the Biden administration was considering payments of up to $450,000 each to illegal aliens who were caught illegally entering our country in 2018. A family of four could receive almost $2 million. There's since been a confused back-and-forth.

When Biden was initially asked about paying illegal aliens, he gave a refreshingly honest answer: He called the reports "garbage" and waved the topic off. The rare moment of honesty with the American people did not last long.

White House deputy press secretary Karine Jean-Pierre later said the Biden administration might be open to it. Then, in November 2021, Biden said such illegal immigrants "deserve some kind of compensation." Events like this show how beholden Biden is to the far-left open-borders lobby and his own staff. It's not a common thing in American politics for a president to contradict himself so plainly and openly.

The American Civil Liberties Union (ACLU) on Behalf of Illegal-Alien Families

This all stems from a lawsuit brought by the American Civil Liberties Union (ACLU) on behalf of illegal-alien families. They claim that their constitutional rights were violated in 2018 when they were detained, in accordance with U.S. immigration laws, without their children.

Usually, frivolous lawsuits seeking sky-high payouts would be contested and promptly tossed out of court. But these are not usual times. Instead, the Biden administration is acting more like an ACLU co-counsel and looking to give illegal aliens a big payday at American taxpayers' expense.

Unfortunately, this gambit is nothing new. It follows in the footsteps of the Obama era's "Sue and Settle" strategy. It worked like this: The administration would invite lawsuits from politically connected groups, usually over regulations, and then settle, acquiescing to the demands and setting new standards that circumvented the regulatory process. This often involved big payouts to the political allies posing as legal adversaries.

The ACLU suit dovetails nicely with the mission of the president's Interagency Task Force on the Reunification of Families. Created just two weeks after President Biden took office, the task force has a two-fold mission: to get money to illegal aliens via legal settlements and to find illegal aliens deported during the Trump administration and bring them back into the United States.

According to its September 21 interim report, the task force is engaged in multiple settlement negotiations. That means the ACLU lawsuit may be only the tip of the iceberg. And that is why Congress should act now to expressly prohibit any and all payments.

Congress could do a few things. First, it could expressly prohibit any settlement money going to illegal aliens. Full stop. It's really that simple.

Next, it could disband the task force and demand a full accounting of all its activities and meetings. The American people deserve to know which government officials lined up with open-borders advocates to raid the Treasury.

Finally, Congress could put some commonsense limits on the ability of the executive branch to enter into these types of settlements. Requiring congressional approval for settlements above a certain amount would be a good start.

The Biden administration already has the worst record on immigration and border security in American history. But contemplating $450,000 payments to illegal aliens marks a new low. As Senator Tom Cotton (R., Ark.) has noted, the families of American soldiers who lose their lives fighting for our country get only $100,000. The amount an illegal-alien family receives could even far exceed the awards given to some 9/11 victims' families, who were permanently separated from the loved ones when terrorists attacked our country.

The families of Border Patrol agents who die in the line of duty receive nowhere near as much as this. And the Angel Families who have lost loved ones in crimes committed by illegal aliens receive nothing.

Congress must step in to stop this madness. The Biden administration certainly won't stop itself.

The Costs of Biden's Border Crisis: The First Two Years

As per the in-depth Erin Dwinell and Hannah Davis "The Costs of Biden's Border Crisis: The First Two Years" Heritage Foundation March 2023 report:

In President Biden's first two years, the Administration requested and received significant funding to further its open borders agenda. The Biden Administration is using hundreds of billions of federal dollars to shift federal agencies and personnel further away from enforcing the nation's immigration laws and toward processing and accommodating millions more illegal aliens. This policy agenda defies federal law and abuses American taxpayer dollars, and Congress should act to halt it.

Federal Dollars for Illegal Aliens

The Biden Administration has shifted from deterrence, detention, and deportation of illegal aliens toward accommodating an ever-rising wave of illegal immigrants into the United States in parole status. As a result, its demand for federal dollars have increased significantly. As the Administration, through non-governmental organizations (NGOs), disperses millions of illegal aliens into the interior of the country, it expects American taxpayers to pay for their long-term and widespread support, including travel, food, housing, and health care. Under the Biden Administration, government-run or contracted transportation, food, and medical care for illegal aliens have cost taxpayers billions of dollars so far, with no end in sight.

Federal, state, and local government entities all bear the brunt of the federal government's policy decisions. This Backgrounder provides an analysis of costs and priorities at the federal level, as well as an assessment of the strategy and agenda of the Biden Administration.

Biden's Agenda Abuses Taxpayers

President Joe Biden has often said, "Don't tell me what you value. Show me your budget, and I'll tell you what you value."

Taking President Biden at his word, we can evaluate the Budget of the U.S. Government for Fiscal Year 2023 to understand the Biden Administration's values regarding border security and illegal immigration.

This analysis indicates that the Biden Administration values neither securing America's borders nor enforcing the nation's immigration laws. Rather, a high value is placed on allowing as many illegal aliens into the United States as possible and making the American taxpayers provide their transportation, shelter, food, medical care, education, and more during the lengthy, indefinite period needed to determine final immigration status in each case. Very few resources are allocated toward deporting the millions who fail to qualify for asylum or other immigration benefits.

Compared to the Budget of the U.S. Government immediately prior to President Biden taking office, proposed by then-President Donald Trump for fiscal year (FY) 2021, the Biden Administration would increase spending by $98.6 billion over the FY 2022–FY 2030 period on budgetary accounts and programs that facilitate—rather than control—the border crisis.

In contrast, U.S. Customs and Border Protection (CBP) and U.S. Immigration and Customs Enforcement (ICE), the federal agencies tasked with enforcing America's border security and immigration laws, would spend $33 billion less on their important mission-focused accounts over the same FY 2022–FY 2030 period as compared to the previous budget proposal.

Spending Reductions for Border Security and Immigration Enforcement

During his first year in office, President Biden took 296 executive actions relating to the border and immigration. Of these, 89 dissolved the previous Administration's border policies.

Among other things, these orders ended enhanced vetting and processing for those attempting to enter the United States from specific regions; fortified protections for the Deferred Action for Childhood Arrivals program; terminated southern border wall construction; counted illegal aliens in the same way as U.S. citizens in the U.S. Census; and limited ICE's ability to remove illegal aliens who posed national security threats, had previous criminal convictions, or who had recently entered the United States illegally.

The Administration fought hard to terminate the Migrant Protection Protocols, the policy allowing the Department of Homeland Security (DHS) to require non-Mexican aliens arriving from Mexico to return and remain there while waiting for their asylum claims to be heard.

Since April 2021, the Administration has attempted to end the use of Title 42, a law allowing Border Patrol agents to quickly expel aliens for public health reasons. Lawsuits and resulting court orders have prevented them from doing so, but in any case, the Administration has elected to use the authority on fewer than half of those attempting to enter the United States illegally.

The Biden Administration has adamantly refused to enforce interior immigration laws. From FY 2020 to FY 2021, the number of aliens removed by ICE dropped from 185,88411 to 59,011,12 even as monthly encounters at the border soared to record levels.

By doing away with both deterrence at the border and enforcement of immigration law in the interior, in its overall immigration strategy, the Administration continually signals that the southern border is open and puts the lives of millions of citizens and migrants in harm's way.

CBP Procurement, Construction, and Improvements: The Biden Administration would reduce spending for the U.S. Customs and Border Patrol Procurement, Construction, and Improvements account by $14.7 billion over the FY 2022–FY 2030 period.

This account provides vital funding for physical and technological barriers at the border, including the construction of the border wall system as well as aircraft, marine vessels, and tactical infrastructure to protect the nation's borders.

ICE Operations and Support: The Biden Administration would reduce spending for the U.S. Immigration and Customs Enforcements Operations and Support account by $21.7 billion over the FY 2022–FY 2030 period.

This account funds mission support, immigration enforcement and removal operations, the Office of the Principal Legal Advisor, and Homeland Security Investigations operations of ICE so that it can enforce the nation's immigration laws.

Spending Increases to Perpetuate the Border Crisis: The Biden Administration's re-direction of funding includes carving out billions of dollars in massive U.S. aid bills to fund refugee resettlement programs and re-allocating taxpayer-funded government resources to process aliens illegally crossing the border into the United States more quickly. Policy changes include countless memos changing operations across federal agencies to assist in this endeavor.

President Biden set in place new regulations for the "public charge" rule, which would make it easier for illegal aliens to receive governmental benefits such as cash assistance, medical care, food stamps, education, and housing.

HHS Refugee and Entrant Assistance: The Biden Administration would increase spending for the Department of Health and Human Services (HHS) Refugee and Entrant Assistance account by $53.1 billion over the FY 2022–FY 2030 period.

This account provides taxpayer-funded grants to NGOs and states to provide cash, medical assistance, and social services to aliens. It funds the Office of Refugee Resettlement, which transports and settles aliens around the United States.

Department of State Migration and Refugee Assistance: The Biden Administration would increase spending for the Department of State Migration and Refugee Assistance account by $35.1 billion over the FY 2022–FY 2030 period.

This account provides taxpayer-funded grants to NGOs for processing, transporting, and resettling refugees and immigrants to the United States as well as aid to refugees and migrants overseas.

USCIS Operations and Support: The Biden Administration would increase spending for the U.S. Citizenship and Immigration Services Operations and Support account by $7.1 billion over the FY 2022–FY 2030 period.

Historically, this budgetary account has primarily been used to fund the E-Verify program, which acts as a deterrent to illegal immigration. However, the Biden Administration would transform this account, adding billions of dollars in new spending to pay for the immigration application processing fees of aliens. Illegal aliens claiming asylum are not charged fees, even when their claims are fraudulent or frivolous.

Compared to the previous Administration's 2021 refugee admissions cap of 15,000, President Biden's 2022 and 2023 caps of 125,000 admissions each year is excessive, unachievable, and unmanageable.

The CBP is so overwhelmed that it has drastically increased reliance on NGOs as a means of collecting, transporting, harboring, and, ultimately, integrating illegal aliens throughout the United States.

By relying on NGOs to provide "a more orderly, reliable process for the federal government authorities and the border communities receiving them," the Administration, according to Secretary of Homeland Security Alejandro Mayorkas, is "bolstering the capacity of NGOs," which are facilitating what amounts to human smuggling.

In its FY 2023 budget, the Biden Administration requested and received billions of dollars toward embedding illegal aliens in the United States as described below despite the likelihood of high percentages being ruled ineligible to remain after due process.

Customs and Border Protection: The Biden Administration added 300 Border Patrol agents at a cost of $65 million. Rather than being tasked with patrol, their assigned functions now often center around processing and caring for illegal immigrants at the border.

The Administration will also hire 300 Border Patrol processing coordinators at a cost of $23 million. A new Joint Processing Center—including space for migrant processing, housing, food, and medical care, largely provided by contractors and NGOs—will cost $140 million.

It is important to note that of the CBP "Operations and Support" omnibus funding, the $1,563,143,000 for border management requirements is specifically prohibited from being used "to acquire, maintain, or extend border security technology and capabilities, except for technology and capabilities to improve Border Patrol processing."

Rather than fund enforcement of the nation's laws, the Biden Administration's FY 2023 budget allotted $527 million in funding for Alternatives to Detention, an increase of $87 million. However, not only has DHS proven itself unable to keep adequate track of the program's participants, but the program itself is ineffective at replacing detention. (DHS reports that if aliens are never or only briefly detained, they will not be removed 97 percent of the time.

Emergency or temporary beds meant for processing prior to release are funded at $25 million for the year, while the Administration eliminates traditional family detention beds and reduces traditional adult detention beds by 5,000.

As smuggling and trafficking at the southern border increases, Homeland Security Investigations funding is a planned $2.3 billion, a $162 million increase. DHS's Center for Countering Human Trafficking obtains $15 million and the Victim Assistance Program receives $11 million. So much money would not be needed if the Biden Administration prevented illegal immigration in the first place. Instead, it throws good money after bad policy.

Office of Health Security: The newly established Office of Health Security will duplicate HHS functions within DHS—namely, to tend to the health needs of aliens in DHS custody.

This new allocation of resources provides $34.3 million to be used for the new office, including functions never before within the agency's scope. As discussed below, if ICE agents were instead permitted to apprehend, detain, and deport illegal immigrants, the resources required to care for them would be dramatically less.

Federal Emergency Management Agency: As aliens cross the southern border, the Biden Administration requested an increase of $24 million for FEMA in FY 2023 budget34 to provide "food, shelter, transportation, COVID-19 testing, and care" for them through the Emergency Food and Shelter Program—Humanitarian Relief. Now, the 2023 omnibus makes up to $785 million available for this program.

U.S. Citizenship and Immigration Services: At U.S. Citizenship and Immigration Services (USCIS), the Biden Administration prides itself on increasing "humanitarian" functions.

In the FY 2023 budget, $375 million and 1,151 new full-time employees are allocated for asylum adjudications following the Administration's move in 2022 to allow USCIS asylum officers—rather than immigration judges—to adjudicate asylum claims at the border. That decision of dubious legality will expedite erroneous approvals, encourage fraud, and put more vulnerable aliens at risk.

Meanwhile, asylum fraud is rampant at the border, and there are approximately 8.7 million total pending applications (over 571,000 of which are asylum applications) waiting to be adjudicated by USCIS.

Furthermore, Congress more than doubled the President's budget request of $10 million for Citizenship and Integration Grants and provided $25 million. Many of these grants can be traced to NGOs such as Catholic Charities that facilitate support for aliens crossing the border illegally. These grants fuel more actors' capacity for corruption and ability to embed illegal immigrants into communities in violation of the law.

Lame Duck Omnibus Spending Bill Funds Biden's Border Crisis: Compared to the FY 2021 appropriations bills enacted in December 2020 just prior to Biden taking office, the FY 2023 bill significantly increased funding for accounts and activities that advance Biden's irresponsible immigration policies. HHS Refugee and Entrant Assistance receives $8.2 billion, almost $1.9 billion more than President Biden requested. Department of State Migration and Refugee Assistance receives $2.9 billion, about the same as the FY 2021 enacted level. USCIS Operations and Support receive $243 million, the majority of which is for application process subsidies.

In contrast, the omnibus shortchanged appropriations accounts that support border security. CBP Procurement, Construction, and Improvements receives $582 million, only $9 million above the FY 2021 enacted level despite worsening conditions at the border. ICE Operations and Support receives $8.4 billion, a less than $200 million increase from the FY 2021 enacted level. Congress has appropriated these insufficient funding levels when border security and enforcement of immigration laws is sorely needed.

Recommendations

Congress should introduce robust flagship legislation to take control of the nation's borders, stop the uncontrolled flow of illegal immigration, and prevent the Biden Administration from continuing the border crisis. Some solutions include:

Creating a non-public-health authority to immediately expel illegal aliens across the border in a crisis: The current border crisis has shown that, during a crisis, Border Patrol agents should be able to exercise lawful authority to return inadmissible aliens across the border, regardless of country of origin, whether health related or not.

Funding thorough immigration enforcement: Mandating and appropriating resources for completion of the border wall system, increasing ICE resources for deportation officers and detention beds so they are commensurate with the mandatory detention and removal requirements in the law, clarifying deportation officers' authority to make custodial arrests, and detaining aliens would encourage adherence to the nation's laws and disincentivize illegal immigration.

Ending abuse of humanitarian programs: Reining in the rampant abuse of parole authority, the disparate treatment of unaccompanied alien children under the Trafficking Victims Protection Reauthorization Act, terminating the Flores settlement agreement that limits detention of family units to 20 days, and raising the "credible fear" asylum standard would restore integrity to the immigration system as well as safety for citizens and aliens alike.

Additionally, no later than the FY 2024 appropriations bill, Congress should:

Prohibit all dangerous Biden Administration rules and executive orders and reprogram their funding to truly secure the border: Congress should hold the Administration accountable for the border crisis by refusing to fund its open border and immigration-related executive orders, rules, and operations and instead reprogram the funds to successful programs that truly secure the border, including completing wall system construction and fully implementing the Migrant Protection Protocols. Congress should also prohibit implementation of the Administration's open border rules and related memos and guidance documents.

Defund the Biden Administration's open border operations through ubiquitous NGOs: The Administration should be held accountable for its increased reliance on NGOs and efforts to skirt federal law and responsibilities. In addition to defunding detrimental government programs, NGOs facilitating the border crisis should be defunded.

Defund the Office of Health Security: This newly created office unnecessarily takes DHS funding that could be used to secure the homeland, enforce the nation's laws, and uses it to duplicate functions such as alien health care that are the responsibility of HHS.

Utilize the Holman rule to hold executive branch officials accountable: The Holman rule in the House of Representatives permits provisions in appropriations bills to reduce salaries for specific executive branch officials or to eliminate positions entirely. This power should be used to hold Biden Administration officials accountable and to eliminate offices that are using taxpayer funds to weaken border security and enforcement of immigration laws.

Impeach Secretary of Homeland Security Alejandro Nicholas Mayorkas: Secretary Mayorkas has violated his oath of office, purposely neglected his duty to secure the homeland, and instigated and overseen the greatest border crisis is the nation's history.

For the sake of the nation, he deserves to be impeached and removed from office.

Conclusion

More than 5.7 million illegal aliens crossed the U.S. border in the first 24 months of the Biden presidency (between encounters and aliens evading encounter or apprehension). As historic numbers of illegal aliens continue to cross the border and disperse throughout the country, every state has effectively become a border state. The nation is subject to significant preventable expenses and countless crimes committed by illegal aliens. As taxpayers demand change from Congress, elected officials should hold the Biden Administration accountable and put an end to disastrous federal funding priorities and policies that endanger America's lawful society and national security.

The Cost of Illegal Immigration to American Taxpayers 2023

From the updated "The Fiscal Burden of Illegal Immigration on United States Taxpayers: 2023 Cost Study" FAIR March 2023 report:

The following is a summary of the Federation for American Immigration Reform (FAIR) cost study findings. To access our full report, including state-specific information and summary of methodology, follow the link in the Appendix.

Key Highlights

- At the start of 2023, the net cost of illegal immigration for the United States – at the federal, state, and local levels – was at least $150.7 billion.

- FAIR arrived at this number by subtracting the tax revenue paid by illegal aliens – just under $32 billion – from the gross negative economic impact of illegal immigration, $182 billion.

- In 2017, the estimated net cost of illegal migration was approximately $116 billion. In just 5 years, the cost to Americans has increased by nearly $35 billion.

- Illegal immigration costs each American taxpayer $1,156 per year ($957 after factoring in taxes paid by illegal aliens).

- Each illegal alien or U.S.-born child of illegal aliens costs the U.S. $8,776 annually. Evidence shows that tax payments by illegal aliens cover only around a sixth of the costs they create at all levels in this country.

- A large percentage of illegal aliens who work in the underground economy frequently avoid paying any income tax at all.

- Many illegal aliens actually receive a net cash profit through refundable tax credit programs.

Introduction

This cost study report is currently the only comprehensive examination of the financial impact of illegal immigration in the United States. Every day, hundreds of millions of dollars in American taxpayer money are spent on costs directly associated with illegal immigration.

Only a small fraction of these costs is ever recouped from taxes paid by illegal aliens, with the rest falling on the shoulders of American citizens and legal immigrants.

Our aim in this report is to show the American people the fiscal burden of illegal immigration at every level and across nearly all aspects of life. These costs range from emergency medical care to in-state tuition; from incarcerating illegal aliens in local jails to federal budgets that pay out billions in welfare every year.

Because there are so many different ways that money is spent on illegal aliens at both the state and local levels, the information in our report is otherwise hard to find (or even intentionally hidden). This report supersedes FAIR's 2017 cost study and highlights massive increases in spending related to illegal immigration that were implemented while American citizens deal with an uncertain economy.

The Number of Illegal Immigrants in the US

Estimating the fiscal burden of illegal immigration on the U.S. taxpayer depends on the size and characteristics of the illegal alien population. Federation for American Immigration Reform (FAIR) defines "illegal alien" as anyone who entered the United States without authorization or anyone who unlawfully remains once his/her authorization has expired. Unfortunately, the U.S. government has no central database containing information on the citizenship status of everyone lawfully present in the United States.

The overall problem of estimating the illegal alien population is further complicated by the fact that the majority of available sources on immigration status rely on self-reported data. Given that illegal aliens have a motive to lie about their immigration status in order to avoid discovery, the accuracy of these statistics is dubious at best. All of the foregoing issues make it very difficult to assess the current illegal alien population of the United States.

However, now estimates that there were at least 15.5 million illegal alien residents as of the beginning of 2022. This estimate takes into account drastic, ongoing increases in illegal immigration under the Biden administration. This estimate also includes some categories of individuals without legal status, like DACA recipients and parolees, who are illegal aliens under law but misleadingly excluded from many estimates. For more information on how we reached this figure, refer to the FAIR study "How Many Illegal Aliens Live in the United States?"

The Cost of Illegal Immigration to the United States

At the federal, state, and local levels, taxpayers shell out approximately $182 billion to cover the costs incurred from the presence of more than 15.5 million illegal aliens, and about 5.4 million citizen children of illegal aliens. That amounts to a cost burden of approximately $8,776 per illegal alien/citizen child. The burden of illegal immigration on U.S. taxpayers is both staggering and crippling, with the gross cost per taxpayer at $1,156 every year.

Illegal aliens only contribute roughly $32 billion in taxes at the state, local, and federal levels. This means that the net fiscal cost of illegal immigration to taxpayers totals approximately $150.7 billion.

In 2017, FAIR estimated the net cost of illegal immigration at approximately $116 billion. This means that in just 5 years, the cost of illegal immigration has increased by nearly $35 billion. This rapid increase is a consequence of the ongoing border crisis and a lack of effective immigration enforcement. The sections below further break down and explain these numbers at the federal, state, and local levels.

- **Total Governmental Expenditures on Illegal Aliens—$182,057,865**
- **Total Tax Contributions by Illegal Aliens—($31,391,635)**
- **Total Economic Impact of Illegal Immigration—$150,666,230**

Federal Spending

The approximately $66.4 billion in federal expenditures attributable to illegal aliens is staggering, and constitutes an increase of 45 percent since 2017. This amounts to roughly $3,187 per illegal alien, per year.

FAIR believes that every concerned American citizen should be asking our government why, in a time of increasing costs and shrinking resources, it is spending such large amounts of money on individuals who are not authorized to be in the United States. This is an especially important question in view of the fact that the taxes paid by illegal aliens offset very little of the enormous costs stemming from their presence in the country.

- **Federal Education—$6.6 Billion**
- **Total Federal Medical Expenditures—$23.1 Billion**
- **Total Federal Justice Enforcement Expenditures—$25.1 Billion**
- **Total Federal Welfare Programs—$11.6 Billion**
- **Total Overall Federal Expenditures—$66.5 Billion**

Federal Taxes

Taxes collected from illegal aliens help offset fiscal outlays and therefore must be included in any examination of the cost of illegal immigration. However, illegal alien advocates frequently cite the alleged large tax payments made by illegal aliens as a justification for their unlawful presence and as a reason itself to grant them amnesty. That argument is nothing more than a red herring. Such claims rarely look at the costs associated with illegal immigration, and instead only focus on the amounts contributed to the economy and paid in taxes.

Most studies grossly overestimate both the taxes actually collected from illegal aliens and, more importantly, the net amount of taxes actually paid by them (i.e., the amount of money collected from illegal aliens and ultimately kept by the federal government). A predominant reason for this is that in recent years, the United States has focused on apprehending and removing almost solely criminal aliens (and since President Biden took office, many criminal aliens are now protected from deportation as well). Because of this, the majority of illegal aliens seeking employment in the United States now live in an environment where they have little fear of deportation even if discovered.

- **Federal Tax Receipts from Illegal Aliens—$24.6 Billion**
- **Net Federal Impact of Illegal Aliens—$50.2 Billion**

The total fiscal burden of illegal immigration on state taxpayers has now reached a staggering $115.6 billion, which is 30 percent more than it was in 2017. The primary reasons for this, aside from a rapid increase in the illegal alien population, are that a number of states have opted to expand access to state welfare, education, and medical programs to illegal aliens. These expansions have led to taxpayers paying tens of billions in additional funding to cover these costs.

Concerningly, as will be seen in the following section, the taxes paid by illegal aliens to state and local governments fall far short of making up for the numerous additional state-funded benefits they are receiving. Moreover, with many states set to begin offering even more benefits to illegal aliens, as mentioned previously, these costs are only expected to increase even further.

- **State Educational Expenditures—$73.3 Billion**
- **State Medical Expenditures—$18.6 Billion**
- **State Administration of Justice Expenditures—$21.8 Billion**
- **State Welfare Expenditures—$2 Billion**
- **State and Local Expenditures—$115.6 Billion**

State and Local Taxes Collected

As with federal costs, state and local costs are offset—to some degree—by the taxes illegal aliens pay. As noted in the Federal taxes portion of this section, proponents of illegal immigration argue that the taxes paid by illegal aliens result in a net boon to state and local coffers. However, this is a spurious argument. Evidence shows that the tax payments made by illegal aliens fall far short of covering the costs of the services they consume.

It is also important to note that calling illegal alien tax payments a net receipt is a mischaracterization. The overall wage depression inflicted on local labor markets by the presence of large numbers of illegal aliens willing to work for less than market rates has far-reaching fiscal implications that are often not quantified on average balance sheets. Low-wage workers generally access more government benefits than higher-paid employees.

Furthermore, illegal aliens also tend to remit large portions of their earnings back to their home countries, and thus less money is incorporated back into local economies and less is paid in local sales and excise taxes. However, because this study looks at the fiscal impacts of illegal immigration, and tax collections are a fiscal offset, we do our best to estimate how much of the fiscal costs borne by taxpayers are reduced by taxes paid by illegal aliens.

Illegal aliens are not typical taxpayers. First, the large percentage of illegal aliens who work in the underground economy avoid paying any income tax at all. Those that do work in the formal economy often receive back more than they pay to the federal government through refundable tax credit programs. Finally, the average earnings of illegal alien households are considerably lower than earnings of legal aliens and native-born workers, thus they typically fall into the lowest tax brackets.

- **State Taxes Collected—$15.2 Billion**
- **Net State Impact—$100.4 Billion**

The state tax payments made by illegal aliens fall far short of the costs incurred by their presence, as detailed below. These figures negate the argument that illegal aliens represent a net economic benefit to the United States.

- **Federal and State Fiscal Outlays—$182 Billion**
- **Federal and State Tax Contributions—$31.4 Billion**
- **Net Cost of Illegal Immigration—$150.7 Billion**

A Note on the Lack of Transparency in Government Data Reporting

Information transparency is essential to good governance. It encourages a well-informed citizenry to hold their elected officials responsible and motivates those officials to implement policies that benefit their constituents instead of special interest groups.

Furthermore, citizens have the right to know pertinent information, presented in a clear and comprehensible manner, on issues that impact them. Unfortunately, there is a concerning lack of transparency and openness when it comes to the issue of illegal immigration.

So, why are Americans being kept in the dark? Primarily because the political and ideological influence of the open-borders lobby, both within and outside the federal government, holds significant sway over the Biden administration and many state governments. This "hear nothing, see nothing, say nothing" attitude is rooted in the hope that if the American public doesn't have easy access to valid information regarding the impacts of illegal immigration, they will accept the lie that no problem exists.

In carrying out this study, FAIR is advancing the belief that the American people have a right to transparent and accurate information so that they are fully informed of what is occurring in their country and how much it costs them.

How Feds Use Charities to Hide the True Cost of the U.S. Border Crisis

As revealed in the Mark Morgan and Mike Howell "How Feds Use Charities To Hide the True Cost of the U.S. Border Crisis" Heritage Foundation January 2023 story:

Border Patrol simply does not have the capacity to hold the massive number of illegal immigrants crossing the border every day who would normally be transferred to Immigration and Customs Enforcement (ICE). The shocking images we saw last year at the beginning of the Biden border crisis—overcrowded holding facilities with men, women and children on top of one another—drove this point home beyond a doubt.

Credit: Heritage Foundation – USA map of illegal alien NGO assistance groups .

And under the Biden administration, DHS has reinstated catch-and-release, which forces Border Patrol to release these illegal immigrants into our communities, rather than transfer them to ICE.

Enter the non-government organizations (NGOs), which shelter and feed the migrants, as well as purchasing plane and bus tickets and other resources. The NGOs are partly funded by private donations, but a good chunk of their money comes from American taxpayers—thus hiding the true cost of the border crisis behind "charities."

DHS hasn't been shy about it. In April, Secretary of Homeland Security Alejandro Mayorkas told Congress that the department was asking for more funding for this very purpose. Now, they're back at the trough, asking for nearly $1 billion for various NGO programs.

Ultimately, these NGOs operate as the final link in a vast, transnational human-smuggling operation. At one end, the cartels promise that those who pay them to get to the border will be able to go wherever they want in the US. At the other end, the NGOs make it a reality. Naturally, this just enables and encourages more illegal immigration.

That's where the investigation we launched at the Heritage Foundation's Oversight Project comes in. We've long known anecdotally that these NGOs are providing these services. Now we have proof that it's happening at a national, previously unreported scale.

What we did was simple. We purchased commercially available, bulk cellphone data from mobile devices that pinged at more than 30 NGO facilities in border states in the month of January 2022. We then tracked where those cellphones ended up. Altogether, we collected data from around 30,000 unique and anonymized devices in multiple phases.

In one phase, we traced 22,000 devices that pinged at 20 border-state NGOs—they ended up scattered across the country, in 431 out of 435 congressional districts.

Then we captured 3,400 unique device pings on the premises of Catholic Charities' facility in San Juan, Texas. Catholic Charities is a massive NGO, with operations around the country and the world.

Despite such a limited sample over just 30 days, the phones from this one location later pinged from all but two congressional districts.

The Biden border crisis has turned every town and state in this country into a border town and state. This investigation is the proof.

This was just a sample of 30,000 phones in one month. Imagine the data on the more than 5.5 million individuals who have illegally entered or been improperly admitted to our country since Biden and Mayorkas took office.

10 – Mexifornia: California's Largest Ethnic Group is Falling Behind the Others: Why?

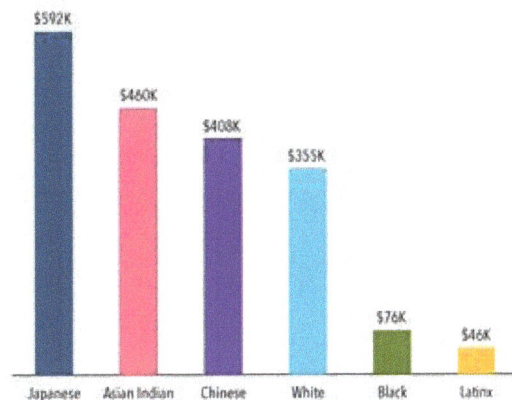

In the Los Angeles Area, Black and Latinx Californians Have Significantly Less Wealth Than Do Other Groups

Household Median Net Worth by Race and Ethnicity, 2014

Per the Raquel Rosenbloom and Jeanne Batalova "Mexican Immigrants in the United States" Migration Policy Institute (MPI) October 2022 analysis:

Mexicans account for the largest group of unauthorized immigrants: 48 percent of the total 11 million people in 2019, according to estimates from the Migration Policy Institute (MPI). Although the number of unauthorized immigrants from Mexico has been on the decline, this trend may have shifted due in part to effects of the pandemic.

As inflation increases in Mexico, climbing to a 21-year high in August 2022, more Mexicans have headed to the U.S. border. In FY 2020, for the first time in five years, Mexicans accounted for more than half of all encounters recorded by U.S. Customs and Border Protection (CBP), and the number of encounters of Mexicans at the border in FY 2022 reached its highest point since FY 2007.

The United States is overwhelmingly the most popular destination for Mexicans living abroad, accounting for 97 percent of all Mexican emigrants. In fact, 8 percent of all people born in Mexico lived in the United States as of 2020. Canada is home to the next largest population of Mexicans (87,000), followed by Spain (61,000), Germany (20,000), and Guatemala (19,000), according to mid-2020 United Nations Population Division estimates.

Within the United States, almost 60 percent of Mexican immigrants live in California or Texas. Most Mexican immigrants are not U.S. citizens, and those who gained permanent resident status in FY 2021 mainly did so via family sponsorship. Compared to both the overall foreign- and U.S.-born populations, Mexican immigrants have lower levels of educational attainment and lower household incomes. They also tend to have lived in the United States for longer than all immigrants and are more likely to be in the labor force than U.S.-born adults.

Mexican Immigrants in the US: Statistics

Per Migration Policy Institute (MPI) data, most immigrants from Mexico lived in California (36 percent) Texas (22 percent), Illinois (6 percent), and Arizona (5 percent) as of the 2015-19 period, which represents the most recent pooled data file available from the U.S. Census Bureau at this writing. (MPI uses the five-year file for more precise estimates for smaller geographies and populations.)

The next six most populous states—Florida, Washington, Georgia, North Carolina, Colorado, and Nevada—were home to an additional 13 percent of the Mexican-born population. The four counties with the most Mexican immigrants were Los Angeles County in California, Harris County in Texas, Cook County in Illinois, and Dallas County in Texas. Together, these counties accounted for 22 percent of the Mexican immigrant population.

English Proficiency

Mexican immigrants are less likely to be proficient in English than the overall foreign-born population. In 2021, about 65 percent of Mexicans ages 5 and over reported limited English proficiency, compared to about 46 percent of all immigrants. Approximately 6 percent of Mexican immigrants spoke only English at home, versus 17 percent of all immigrants.

Note: Limited English Proficient (LEP) status refers to those who indicated on the ACS questionnaire that they spoke English less than "very well."

Age, Education, and Employment

Mexican adults have much lower rates of educational attainment than both the native- and overall foreign-born populations. In 2021, approximately 52 percent of Mexican immigrants ages 25 and older lacked a high school diploma or equivalent, compared to 26 percent of foreign-born adults and 7 percent of U.S.-born adults. About 9 percent of Mexican immigrants reported having a bachelor's degree or higher, compared to 35 percent of U.S.-born and 34 percent of immigrant adults. However, the college-educated share of Mexicans who arrived within the past five years was much higher: 19 percent as of 2019.

Income and Poverty

On average, Mexicans have lower incomes than the overall foreign- and native-born populations. In 2021, households headed by a Mexican immigrant had a median annual income of $56,000, compared to $70,000 for all immigrant- and native-led households.

In 2021, Mexican immigrants were more likely to be in poverty (17 percent) than immigrants overall (14 percent) or the U.S. born (13 percent).

Immigration Pathways and Naturalization

Mexicans are much less likely to be naturalized U.S. citizens than immigrants overall. In 2021, 35 percent of Mexican immigrants were U.S. citizens, compared to 53 percent of the total foreign-born population.

Unauthorized Immigrant Population

MPI estimates that as of 2019, approximately 5.3 million (48 percent) of the estimated 11 million unauthorized immigrants in the United States were from Mexico.

Mexican immigrants are the largest group participating in the Deferred Action for Childhood Arrivals (DACA) program, which provides temporary deportation relief and work authorization to unauthorized migrants who arrived as children and meet the program's education and other eligibility criteria. As of mid-2022, 480,200 Mexicans were active DACA participants, accounting for the vast majority of all 594,100 DACA recipients, according to U.S. Citizenship and Immigration Services (USCIS) data.

Health Coverage

Mexicans have low health insurance coverage rates compared to all immigrants and the U.S. born. In 2021, 37 percent of immigrants from Mexico were uninsured, compared to 19 percent of the entire foreign-born population and 7 percent of the U.S. born.

Diaspora

The Mexican diaspora is comprised of approximately 38.7 million U.S. residents who were either born in Mexico or reported Mexican ancestry or origin, according to MPI tabulation of data from the U.S. Census Bureau's 2019 ACS. The Mexican diaspora is the second largest in the country, after the German-origin diaspora.

Remittances

More than $54.1 billion in remittances was sent to Mexico via formal channels in 2021, according to the World Bank, the vast majority undoubtedly from the United States. Remittances have steadily risen following a dip around the time of the Great Recession in 2008-09 and grew at an even faster rate during the COVID-19 pandemic despite an initial prediction that they would decline. Global remittances represented about 4 percent of Mexico's gross domestic product (GDP) in 2021.

Mexifornia: Why the California's Largest Ethnic Group is Falling Behind the Others. Why?

Per Victor Davis Hanson, renowned author of *Mexifornia: A State of Becoming (third 2021 edition)*:

As I write in mid-March 2021, the southern border of the United States is porous. Traffic across it is fluid and unchecked to a degree not seen in the recent forty-year history of massive illegal immigration.

Tens of thousands of immigrants, most from Central America and Mexico, many of them unaccompanied minors, some of them members or cartels or gangs are crossing illegally every day. They arrive in the country unvetted and unimpeded. Panicked Biden administration officials suddenly assert that the visibly permeable border is "closed."

Millions of would-be immigrants boast of renewed hopes of entering the United States without legal permission. They express relief at the end of the restrictionist Trump administration. They have been incentivized through the celebration of Trump's departure by many of the loudest and most influential people in the U.S. government, popular culture, and academia. Messaging that the new Biden administration is mostly against whatever Trump was for has provided encouragement to make the trek northward, as many border crossers unapologetically admit.

More specifically, illegal immigrants claim they were emboldened by Joe Biden's widely reported executive orders stopping further bordar wall construction. They were heartened by news of an imminent relaxing of border enforcement, a return to "catch and release" policies in the detaining of illegal aliens, promises to allow would-be refugees to have their claims adjudicated inside the United States, and Washington's backing off from agreements in which Mexico was to patrol its borders to prevent Central Americans in transit from entering the U.S. illegally. Many had heard rumors of serial multimillion-person amnesties that would soon make the facts of illegal entry and unlawful residency irrelevant. Optimistic phone texts from friends and relatives who had successfully crossed the border inspired thousands more to try.

Officials in the new Biden administration seem shocked at the public unease with their open-border agenda. They had assumed that the public was more evenly divided over immigration enforcement, given the controversies of the restrictionist Trump years. But polls in March already showed that over 57 percent of Americans were opposed to President Biden's nonenforcement policies.

Apparently the idea of allowing unvetted foreign nationals to enter the United States-and without any testing for Covid-19 when American citizens are still locked down, restricted in their travel, and not yet fully vaccinated--does not win majority support. Yet the Democratic Party's progressive base has persisted in pushing radical changes in immigration policy, despite their increasing unpopularity.

Mexifornia: A State of Becoming

The following issues affecting primarily the Mexican and Central American illegal alien component, are not unique to these ethnic groups, but they are at their worst by degree and shear volume with these ethnic groups. For these reasons, an open U.S. border appears to be losing favor even among Mexicans and Central Americans.

Perhaps they have learned that illegal immigration is ultimately as harmful to their own societies as to America. It breaks families apart. Breadwinners vanish and are unlikely to return permanently. Thousands become ill or fall victim to predation on their way north. Emboldened cartels and criminals profit from the migrations. Some expatriates in the United States grow hostile to their homeland, as the remittances they send back out of their hard-won earnings remind them just how inept and callous are the social services there.

After years of acrimonious negotiations with the Trump administration, Latin American leaders had finally hammered out agreements to keep their own citizens from crossing borders unlawfully. They did so in part to avoid consequences such as trade penalties and U.S. taxes on some $100 billion in remittances sent annually to Central America and Mexico, an astronomical figure four to five times higher than when I first wrote Mexifornia (in 2003).

A few Latin American governments have even shown surprise that the Americans now seem to have broken their Trump-era agreements. They wonder at the logic of encouraging mass migrations at precisely the time they were dramatically waning.

The president of Mexico, Andres Manuel Lopez Obrador frustrated at the thousands crossing through his country from Central America, the manipulation of these masses of humanity by Mexican cartels and smugglers, and the end of carefully negotiated protocols with the Trump administration- seemed to dismiss President Biden as "the Migrant President," a transparently backhanded compliment.

As the numbers of illegal aliens climbed, as American entry -level wages stagnated, and as crime increased in many places, immigration became more politicized and weaponized. The official government response would shift, but there was a fixed theme to America's attitude toward open borders: both poll-driven parties voiced increased concern that immigration laws were "broken."

Securing America's Southern Border With Mexico

Back in the 1990s, the astute, pragmatic, but also cynical President Bill Clinton had been keenly aware of growing political unease with the huge numbers of people crossing the border from the south. In his 1995 State of the Union address with an eye to his reelection bid Clinton spoke of illegal immigration in terms that today would be condemned by his party as nativist and indeed racist:

All Americans, not only in the States most heavily affected but in every place in this country, are rightly disturbed by the large numbers of illegal aliens entering our country. The jobs they hold might otherwise be held by citizens or legal immigrants. The public service they use impose burdens on our tax payers.

That's why our administration has moved aggressively to secure our borders more by hiring a record number of new border guards, by deporting twice as many criminal aliens as ever before, by cracking down on illegal hiring, by barring welfare benefits to illegal aliens. ... We are a nation of immigrants. But we are also a nation of laws so it is wrong and ultimately self-defeating for a nation of immigrants to permit the kind of abuse of our immigration laws, and we must do more to stop it!

Later, President George W. Bush signed into law the bipartisan "Secure Fence Act of 2006," which promised a 700-mile fence from California through parts of Texas. But the barrier was never fully completed. It was also porous and unimpressive in size. Studies showed that it had almost no effect in reducing unlawful entry. Open-borders advocates disingenuously cited the failure of that poorly constructed fence as proof that border walls are futile.

The numbers of people residing illegally in the United States and of those entering unlawfully grew year by year. So did the pool of American citizens born to illegal aliens on U.S. soil. After decades of immigration nonenforcement, first-generation voters and supporters of undocumented aliens were becoming a potent electoral force in the American Southwest, especially as progressives after 2008 began to recalibrate the Democratic Party leftward.

By 2014, not surprisingly, the Obama administration was offering "amnesty" to nearly five million illegal aliens. A series of executive actions encouraged more illegal immigration by sharply reducing the ability of immigration authorities to control the border. In response to a perceived lack of deterrence, so-called "caravans" of illegal immigrants began to swarm the border, creating a human melodrama as thousands of unaccompanied minors-often prompted by their parents crossed without hindrance.

If Latino's Upward Mobility Doesn't Improve—California Will Suffer

This Winter 2012 *City Journal* article "California's Demographic Revolution: If the upward mobility of the impending Hispanic majority doesn't improve, the state's economic future is in peril" is by Heather Mac Donald:

Unless Hispanics' upward mobility improves, the state risks becoming more polarized economically and more reliant on a large government safety net. And as California goes, so goes the nation, whose own Hispanic population shift is just a generation or two behind.

The scale and speed of the Golden State's ethnic transformation are unprecedented. In the 1960s, Los Angeles was the most Anglo-Saxon of the nation's ten largest cities; today, Latinos make up nearly half of the county's residents and one-third of its voting-age population.

A full 55 percent of Los Angeles County's child population has immigrant parents. California's schools have the nation's largest concentration of "English learners," students from homes where a language other than English is regularly spoken. From 2000 to 2010, the state's Hispanic population grew 28 percent, to reach 37.6 percent of all residents, almost equal to the shrinking white population's 40 percent.

Nearly half of all California births today are Hispanic. The signs of the change are everywhere—from the commercial strips throughout the state catering to Spanish-speaking customers, to the flea markets and illegal vendors in such areas as MacArthur Park in Los Angeles, to the growing reach of the Spanish-language media.

The poor Mexican immigrants who have fueled the transformation—84 percent of the state's Hispanics have Mexican origins—bring an admirable work ethic and a respect for authority too often lacking in America's native-born population. Many of their children and grandchildren have started thriving businesses and assumed positions of civic and economic leadership.

California's English Learner students are a diverse group. Of the more than 60 languages spoken, Spanish is by far the most common: 83 percent of ELs in California schools speak it at home. The next most common languages are Vietnamese and Mandarin, spoken by 2 percent and 1.6 percent of EL students, respectively. Arabic, Filipino, and Cantonese each make up about 1 percent of languages spoken.

But a sizable portion of Mexican, as well as Central American, immigrants, however hardworking, lack the social capital to inoculate their children reliably against America's contagious underclass culture.

Furthermore, the *New York Times*, in 2006, wrote an editorial called "Young Latinas and a Cry for Help": "About one-quarter of Latina teens drop out, a figure surpassed only by Hispanic young men, one-third of whom do not complete high school. Latinas, especially those in recently arrived families, often live in poverty and without health insurance.

"Another piece of the puzzle is how to address the complication of very early, usually unmarried motherhood. Religious beliefs in Hispanic families often limit sex education and rule out abortion. Federal statistics show that about 24 percent of Latinas are mothers by the age of 20—three times the rate of non-Hispanic white teens. ... One in four women in the United States will be Hispanic by the middle of the century. The time to help is now."

City Journal's Heather Mac Donald quotes Anita Berry, a case manager who works at Casa Teresa, a California program for homeless single mothers. Berry says: "There's nothing shameful about having multiple children that you can't care for, and to be pregnant again, because then you can blame the system. ... The problems are deeper and wider. Now you're getting the second generation of foster care and group home residents. The dysfunction is multigenerational."

Whether this can be turned around remains to be seen. But it certainly casts doubt on the *Times'* blissful assertion that "a young Latino workforce (will help) the economy."

The Resulting Dysfunction is Holding Latinos Back and California as Well

The complicated reality of Hispanic family life in California—often straddling the legitimate and the criminal worlds, displaying both a dogged determination to work and poor decision making that interferes with upward mobility—helps explain why the state's Hispanic population has made only modest progress up the educational ladder.

Most parents want their children to flourish, yet they may not grasp the study habits necessary for academic success or may view an eighth-grade education as sufficient for finding work. Julian Rodriguez, a Santa Ana gang detective, recalls a case several years ago in which two parents had taken their 14-year-old daughter out of school to care for their new baby—a classic display of "Old World values," he says.

Many of California's Hispanic students who have been schooled in the U.S. for all their lives and are orally fluent in English remain classified as English learners in high school because they have made so little academic progress. In the Long Beach Unified School District, for example, nearly nine-tenths of English learners entering high school have been in a U.S. school at least since first grade.

The lack of progress isn't due to bilingual education: Long Beach got rid of its last bilingual program in 1998, and the current ninth-grade English learners have been in English-only classrooms all their lives. Some come from families that immigrated to the U.S. two or three generations ago.

True, Hispanics' cognitive skills have been improving over the last decade; the percentage of Hispanic eighth-graders deemed proficient in math and reading on the California Standards Tests doubled from 2004 to 2010.

But the gap between Hispanics' performance and that of whites and Asians narrowed only modestly, since white and Asian scores rose as well. Latino students' rate of B.A. completion from the University of California and California State University is the lowest of all student groups, reports the Institute for Higher Education Leadership and Policy at California State University, Sacramento.

The state spends vast sums each year trying to get more Hispanics into college and to keep them there—$100 million in 2009, for instance, on the education of full-time community-college students who dropped out after their first year, according to the American Institutes for Research. (Facilitating transfers from community college is a favored strategy for increasing Hispanic enrollment in four-year colleges.)

Latino Student Underperformance Contributes to California's Dismal Educational Statistics

More from their 2012 "California's Demographic Revolution: If the upward mobility of the impending Hispanic majority doesn't improve, the state's economic future is in peril" is by Heather Mac Donald:

Only Mississippi had as large a percentage of its eighth-grade students reading at the "below basic" level on the 2011 National Assessment of Educational Progress (NAEP); in eighth-grade math, California came in third, after Alabama and Mississippi, in the percentage of students scoring "below basic." Only 56 percent of ninth-graders graduate in four years in Los Angeles; statewide, only two-thirds do.

Since the 1980s, California's economic growth has been powered by skilled labor. Silicon Valley, for example, added jobs at a rate of 3.2 percent for the year beginning in November 2010, despite the continuing economic slump. If current labor-market trends continue, 41 percent of California's workers will need a B.A. by 2025, according to the Public Policy Institute of California (PPIC).

Because it can't produce all the skilled workers that it needs, it imports them: in 2006, for example, 33 percent of all college-educated California workers had been born in other states and 31 percent had been born abroad, PPIC says. Moreover, since 2000, more college graduates have been exiting California than entering. California will need to attract almost 160,000 college-educated workers annually for 20 years in a row to meet the projected demand, PPIC estimates—three times the number who have been arriving from elsewhere since 2000.

Unfortunately, though Hispanics will make up 40 percent of the state's working-age population by 2020, just 12 percent of them are projected to have bachelor's degrees by then, up from 10 percent in 2006.

Moreover, their fields of academic concentration are not where the most economically fertile growth will probably occur. At California State University in 2008, just 1.7 percent of master's degree students in computer science were Mexican-American, as were just 3.6 percent of students in engineering master's programs. The largest percentage of Mexican-American enrollment in M.A. programs was in education—40 percent—despite (or perhaps because of) Mexican-Americans' low test scores.

The future mismatch between labor supply and demand is likely to raise wages for college-educated workers, while a glut of workers with a high school diploma or less will depress wages on the low end and contribute to an increased demand for government services, especially among the less educated Hispanic population.

U.S.-born Hispanic households in California already use welfare programs (such as cash welfare, food stamps, and housing assistance) at twice the rate of U.S.-born non-Hispanic households, according to an analysis of the March 2011 Current Population Survey by the Center for Immigration Studies. Welfare use by immigrants is higher still. In 2008–09, the fraction of households using some form of welfare was 82 percent for households headed by an illegal immigrant and 61 percent for households headed by a legal immigrant.

Higher rates of Hispanic poverty drive this disparity in welfare consumption. Hispanics made up nearly 60 percent of California's poor in 2010, despite being less than 38 percent of the population. Nearly one-quarter of all Hispanics in California are poor, compared with a little over one-tenth of non-Hispanics.

Nationally, the poverty rate of Hispanic adults drops from 25.5 percent in the first generation—the immigrant generation, that is—to 17 percent in the second but rises to 19 percent in the third, according to a Center for Immigration Studies analysis. (The poverty rate for white adults is 9 percent.) That frustrating third-generation economic stall repeats the pattern in high school graduation and college completion rates as well.

How Unskilled Immigrants Hurt Our Economy

Per the *City Journal* Summer 2006 "How Unskilled Immigrants Hurt Our Economy: A handful of industries get low-cost labor, and the taxpayers foot the bill" report from Steven Malanga:

Since the mid-1960s, America has welcomed nearly 30 million legal immigrants and received perhaps another 15 million illegals, numbers unprecedented in our history. These immigrants have picked our fruit, cleaned our homes, cut our grass, worked in our factories, and washed our cars. But they have also crowded into our hospital emergency rooms, schools, and government-subsidized aid programs, sparking a fierce debate about their contributions to our society and the costs they impose on it.

Advocates of open borders immigration argue that welcoming illegal immigrants, versus skilled based immigrants, is essential for our American economy because our businesses need them due to a shortage of people willing to do low-wage work. Moreover, the free movement of labor in a global economy pays off for the United States because immigrants bring skills and capital that expand our economy and offset immigration's costs. Like tax cuts, supporters argue, immigration pays for itself.

As many sapient Americans sense and so much research has demonstrated—America does not have a vast labor shortage that requires waves of low-wage immigrants to alleviate; in fact, unemployment among unskilled workers is high—about 30 percent. Moreover, many of the unskilled, uneducated workers now journeying here labor, in shrinking industries, where they force out native workers, and many others work in industries where the availability of cheap workers has led businesses to suspend investment in new technologies that would make them less labor-intensive.

Yet while these workers add little to our economy, they come at great cost, because they are not economic abstractions but human beings, with their own culture and ideas—often at odds with our own. Increasing numbers of them arrive with little education and none of the skills necessary to succeed in a modern economy. Many may wind up stuck on our lowest economic rungs, where they will rely on something that immigrants of other generations didn't have: a vast U.S. welfare and social-services apparatus that has enormously amplified the cost of immigration.

California Sets a Bad Example With the Largest Share of America's Illegal Immigrants

Just as welfare reform and other policies are helping to shrink America's underclass by weaning people off such social programs, we are importing a new, foreign-born underclass. As famed free-market economist Milton Friedman puts it: "It's just obvious that you can't have free immigration and a welfare state."

The flood of immigrants, both legal and illegal, from countries with poor, ill-educated populations, has yielded a mismatch between today's immigrants and the American economy and has left many workers poorly positioned to succeed for the long term.

Unlike the immigrants of 100 years ago, whose skills reflected or surpassed those of the native workforce at the time, many of today's arrivals, particularly the more than half who now come from Central and South America, are farmworkers in their home countries who come here with little education or even basic training in blue-collar occupations like carpentry or machinery. (A century ago, farmworkers made up 35 percent of the U.S. labor force, compared with the under 2 percent who produce a surplus of food today.)

Nearly two-thirds of Mexican immigrants, for instance, are high school dropouts, and most wind up doing either unskilled factory work or small-scale construction projects, or they work in service industries, where they compete for entry-level jobs against one another, against the adult children of other immigrants, and against native-born high school dropouts.

Of the 15 industries employing the greatest percentage of foreign-born workers, half are low-wage service industries, including gardening, domestic household work, car washes, shoe repair, and janitorial work. To take one stark example: whereas 100 years ago, immigrants were half as likely as native-born workers to be employed in household service, today immigrants account for 27 percent of all domestic workers in the United States.

Although open-borders advocates say that these workers are simply taking jobs Americans don't want, studies show that the immigrants drive down wages of native-born workers and squeeze them out of certain industries.

Harvard economists George Borjas and Lawrence Katz, for instance, estimate that low-wage immigration cuts the wages for the average native-born high school dropout by some 8 percent, or more than $1,200 a year. Other economists find that the new workers also push down wages significantly for immigrants already here and native-born Hispanics.

Consequently, as the waves of immigration continue, the sheer number of those competing for low-skilled service jobs makes economic progress difficult.

If the Benefits of the Current Generation of Migrants Are Small, the Costs Are Large

If the benefits of the current generation of migrants are small, the costs are large and growing because of America's vast range of social programs and the wide advocacy network that strives to hook low-earning legal and illegal immigrants into these programs. A 1998 National Academy of Sciences study found that more than 30 percent of California's foreign-born were on Medicaid—including 37 percent of all Hispanic households—compared with 14 percent of native-born households.

The foreign-born were more than twice as likely as the native-born to be on welfare, and their children were nearly five times as likely to be in means-tested government lunch programs. Native-born households pay for much of this, the study found, because they earn more and pay higher taxes—and are more likely to comply with tax laws. Recent immigrants, by contrast, have much lower levels of income and tax compliance (another study estimated that only 56 percent of illegals in California have taxes deducted from their earnings, for instance). The study's conclusion: immigrant families cost each native-born household in California an additional $1,200 a year in taxes.

Immigration's bottom line has shifted so sharply that in a high-immigration state like California, native-born residents are paying up to ten times more in state and local taxes than immigrants generate in economic benefits. Moreover, the cost is only likely to grow as the foreign-born population—which has already mushroomed from about 9 percent of the U.S. population when the NAS studies were done in the late 1990s to about 12 percent today—keeps growing. And citizens in more and more places will feel the bite, as immigrants move beyond their traditional settling places.

Almost certainly, immigrants' participation in our social welfare programs will increase over time, because so many are destined to struggle in our workforce. Despite our cherished view of immigrants as rapidly climbing the economic ladder, more and more of the new arrivals and their children face a lifetime of economic disadvantage, because they arrive here with low levels of education and with few work skills—shortcomings not easily overcome.

Mexican Immigrants Are Six Times More Likely to be High School Dropouts Than Native-Born Americans

Mexican immigrants, who are up to six times more likely to be high school dropouts than native-born Americans, not only earn substantially less than the native-born median, but the wage gap persists for decades after they've arrived.

A study of the 2000 census data, for instance, shows that the cohort of Mexican immigrants between 25 and 34 who entered the United States in the late 1970s were earning 40 to 50 percent less than similarly aged native-born Americans in 1980, but 20 years later they had fallen even further behind their native-born counterparts.

Today's Mexican immigrants between 25 and 34 have an even larger wage gap relative to the native-born population. Adjusting for other socioeconomic factors, Harvard's Borjas and Katz estimate that virtually this entire wage gap is attributable to low levels of education.

Meanwhile, because their parents start off so far behind, the American-born children of Mexican immigrants also make slow progress.

First-generation adult Americans of Mexican descent studied in the 2000 census, for instance, earned 14 percent less than native-born Americans. By contrast, first-generation Portuguese Americans earned slightly more than the average native-born worker—a reminder of how quickly immigrants once succeeded in America and how some still do.

One reason some ethnic groups make up so little ground concerns the transmission of what economists call "ethnic capital," or what we might call the influence of culture. More than previous generations, immigrants today tend to live concentrated in ethnic enclaves, and their children find their role models among their own group.

Thus the children of today's Mexican immigrants are likely to live in a neighborhood where about 60 percent of men dropped out of high school and now do low-wage work, and where less than half of the population speak English fluently, which might explain why high school dropout rates among Americans of Mexican ancestry are two and a half times higher than dropout rates for all other native-born Americans, and why first-generation Mexican Americans do not move up the economic ladder nearly as quickly as the children of other immigrant groups.

11 – GOP, States & Courts Take Action on Illegal Immigration, Laws, Enforcement & Solutions

BID=N'S BORDER CRISIS

GOVERNOR DESANTIS SIGNED SB 1718
THE STRONGEST ANTI-ILLEGAL IMMIGRATION BILL IN THE NATION TO COMBAT THE BIDEN BORDER CRISIS

Requires employers to use E-Verify to check the employment eligibility of employees, and fines employers who fail to use E-Verify $1,000 per day.

E-Verify

Suspends licenses of any employer who knowingly employs illegal aliens, and makes using a fake ID to gain employment a felony.

CLOSED

Enhances penalties for human smuggling, including making knowingly transporting five or more illegal aliens or a single illegal alien minor a second-degree felony subject to a $10,000 fine and up to 15 years in prison.

Provides $12 million to continue the Unauthorized Alien Transport Program to relocate illegal immigrants to sanctuary jurisdictions.

Bans local governments and NGOs from issuing identification documents to illegal aliens and invalidates all out-of-state driver licenses issued exclusively to illegal aliens.

Requires hospitals to collect and report healthcare costs for illegal aliens.

Credit: Office of Governor Ron DiSantis.

From the Hans von Spakovsky and Charles Stimson "Enforcing Immigration Law: What States Can Do To Assist the Federal Government and Fight the Illegal Immigration Problem" Heritage Foundation October 2019 report: States play, and should continue to play, an important role in enforcing federal immigration law—but more can be done by the states.

The problem is many state politicians are not aware of all that they can do at the state level to fight illegal immigration. This research paper should act as their guide in that effort. True, the federal government has the primary role in establishing immigration rules for the country, including the employment rules governing noncitizens. But the states do have a supporting role.

It is "well settled," says the U.S. Supreme Court, that it is the federal government, not state governments, that "has broad, undoubted power over the subject of immigration and the status of aliens." But the "pervasiveness of federal regulation does not diminish the importance of immigration policy to the States," which bear the many "consequences of unlawful immigration."

States can legislate and act in this space to a limited—but crucial—extent as long as their actions are not preempted by federal law. For example, states can pass licensing and similar laws directed at those who employ, recruit, or refer for a fee illegal aliens. There is no doubt, given the enormity of the problem and the limited resources of the federal government, that the assistance and support of the states is essential to comprehensive and effective enforcement of our immigration laws.

How Great Is the Problem?

The federal government, despite its vast financial resources and expansive workforce, simply does not have the manpower to enforce every federal immigration law. That is where the states come in, as they are force multipliers in confronting the problem—and no one can rationally deny that we have an illegal alien problem in this country. According to the U.S. government, there were 12 million illegal aliens residing in the U.S. in 2015.[3] Another study says the number in 2016 may have ranged from almost 17 million to as high as 22 million.

Illegal aliens have a fiscal impact on local governments due to costs incurred for public education, health care, law enforcement,[5] and other government services.[6] States primarily fund those local essential government services, and, as a result, bear the burden of those costs. States, and the citizens who live there, feel the impact of illegal immigration much more than federal bureaucrats squirreled away in Washington, DC.

States and, in some instances, counties within states, can—and indeed should—play a crucial role in the enforcement of federal immigration law. For too long, opponents of commonsense, step-by-step immigration reform have repeated the myth that only the federal government can enforce immigration law or pass immigration laws. That is simply not true.

H.R.2 - Secure the Border Act of 2023 Proposal to the End Border Crisis & Reduce Illegal Immigration

As reported in the "Heritage Hails Well-Timed Passage of Historic Proposal to End Border Crisis, Reduce Illegal Immigration" Heritage Foundation May 2023 article:

House Republicans today passed May 11, 2023 the strongest border security and enforcement legislation put forward to date, addressing nearly every policy recommendation provided by a coalition led in part by the Heritage Foundation. Meanwhile, Title 42 is set to expire at 11:59 p.m. the same day.

The Secure the Border Act (H.R. 2)—which was opposed by every House Democrat—seeks to end the abuse of U.S. immigration laws by illegal aliens and the Biden administration alike.

Tom Homan, Heritage visiting fellow and former acting Immigration and Customs Enforcement (ICE) director, released the following statement in response to the passage of H.R. 2:

"Last fall, I noted that the time for excuses was coming to an end, and that Congress must take actual steps to hold the Biden administration accountable for the chaos and carnage they have unleashed on our southern border. Thankfully, that is exactly what House Republicans did today.

"Passage of the Secure the Border Act fulfills promises to the American people on delivering solutions to a self-inflicted crisis that harms not just cities and states along the border, but every city and state around the country. The bill's intentions and contents are clear: It would end the crisis and restore sanity, safety, and security at our borders. It is vital that the Senate takes note of what the House did and swiftly brings this bill to the floor."

Mark Morgan, Heritage visiting fellow and former acting Customs and Border Patrol (CBP) commissioner, released the following statement in response to the end of Title 42, a contrasting backdrop to what happened in Washington today:

"Rather than replacing Title 42 with a strong and proven deterrence-and-consequence strategy—giving the Border Patrol a fighting chance to regain operational control of our borders from the cartels—Secretary Mayorkas has chosen to re-write the law, abuse authority, and continue to transform the statutory mission of Department of Homeland Security law enforcement agencies away from their national security responsibilities.

Make no mistake: As Title 42 goes away, more dangerous narcotics, criminals, and potential national security threats will pour across our borders, as agents are preoccupied fulfilling their new mission as a 'processing enterprise.'"

Background: H.R. 2 would close loopholes used for asylum fraud, fortify border security by ending "catch-and-release," end the illegal use of mass parole, expand penalties for visa overstays, reduce incentives for illegal immigration by mandating nationwide E-Verify, and close longstanding loopholes in the processing of both accompanied and unaccompanied alien children.

The bill also resumes construction of the border wall, provides essential support for CBP, and prohibits the Biden administration's reliance on non-governmental organizations to process and transport illegal aliens into American communities.

This firm display of leadership from House Republicans stands in stark contrast to the Biden administration and its policies that seek to worsen, not address the worst border crisis in American history.

This bill addresses issues regarding immigration and border security, including by imposing limits to asylum eligibility. For example, the bill:

- Requires the Department of Homeland Security (DHS) to resume activities to construct a wall along the U.S.-Mexico border;

- Provides statutory authorization for Operation Stonegarden, which provides grants to law enforcement agencies for certain border security operations;

- Prohibits DHS from processing the entry of non-U.S. nationals (*aliens* under federal law) arriving between ports of entry;

- Limits asylum eligibility to non-U.S. nationals who arrive in the United States at a port of entry;

- Authorizes the removal of a non-U.S. national to a country other than that individual's country of nationality or last lawful habitual residence, whereas currently this type of removal may only be to a country that has an agreement with the United States for such removal;

- Expands the types of crimes that may make an individual ineligible for asylum, such as a conviction for driving while intoxicated causing another person's serious bodily injury or death;

- Authorizes DHS to suspend the introduction of certain non-U.S. nationals at an international border if DHS determines that the suspension is necessary to achieve operational control of that border;

- Prohibits states from imposing licensing requirements on immigration detention facilities used to detain minors;

- Authorizes immigration officers to permit an unaccompanied alien child to withdraw their application for admission into the United States even if the child is unable to make an independent decision to withdraw the application;

- Imposes additional penalties for overstaying a visa; and

- Requires DHS to create an electronic employment eligibility confirmation system modeled after the E-Verify system and requires all employers to use the system.

On Immigration, Republicans Are Starting to Think Creatively and Constructively

From the Fred Bauer "On Immigration, Republicans Are Starting to Think Creatively and Constructively" *National Review* September 2023 story:

In the *Washington Post*, Ramesh Ponnuru praises the "Higher Wages for American Workers Act," which would couple a minimum-wage increase with universal E-Verify. He writes that this bill, which is sponsored by a range of Republican senators, "is a sign that Republicans might be recovering their ability to engage in creative and constructive policymaking."

I might add that the internal logic of this bill is a reversal of the thinking behind many immigration proposals during the George W. Bush and Barack Obama years. Back then, the general architecture of "comprehensive immigration reform" was about expanding legal migration pathways in order to compensate for the promise of enforcement that—theoretically, at least—would curtail future illegal immigration. Thus guest-worker proposals as well as expansive amnesty provisions characterized the failed "grand bargains" on immigration of 2006, 2007, and 2013.

This fusion of promised enforcement, amnesty, and expanded legal immigration (and guest-worker programs) ultimately proved dissatisfying to many people. The first iteration of that paradigm (the 1986 amnesty paired with 1990's expansion of legal immigration) was followed by an explosion of illegal immigration in the 1990s and 2000s. No version of "comprehensive immigration reform" ever passed, and grassroots frustration with immigration issues helped power Donald Trump's 2016 campaign.

The Higher Wages for American Workers Act reverses that dynamic. Rather than trying to prioritize high rates of migration, it instead focuses on tightening the labor market. Its two prongs work in tandem: Implementing universal E-Verify helps ensure that a federal minimum wage is actually a floor (employers can't evade it by recruiting illegal labor). Moreover, E-Verify also helps tighten the labor market up the chain by restricting employment only to those with legal authorization. Universal E-Verify might be a tool for managing illegal immigration and controlling the border, but it also has economic effects. This is immigration policy as labor policy.

Governor Ron DeSantis Signs Strongest Anti-Illegal Immigration Legislation in the Country to Combat Biden's Border Crisis

Per the "Governor Ron DeSantis Signs Strongest Anti-Illegal Immigration Legislation in the Country to Combat Biden's Border Crisis" press release from the Governor Ron DeSantis' Staff in their May 2023 publication:

On May 10, 2023, Governor Ron DeSantis signed Senate Bill 1718 to combat the dangerous effects of illegal immigration caused by the federal government's reckless border policies. This legislation makes using E-Verify mandatory for any employer with 25 or more employees, imposes enforceable penalties for those employing illegal aliens, and enhances penalties for human smuggling. Additionally, this bill prohibits local governments from issuing Identification Cards (ID) to illegal aliens, invalidates ID cards issued to illegal aliens in other states, and requires hospitals to collect and submit data on the costs of providing health care to illegal aliens.

"The Biden Border Crisis has wreaked havoc across the United States and has put Americans in danger," said Governor Ron DeSantis. "In Florida, we will not stand idly by while the federal government abandons its lawful duties to protect our country. The legislation I signed today gives Florida the most ambitious anti-illegal immigration laws in the country, fighting back against reckless federal government policies and ensuring the Florida taxpayers are not footing the bill for illegal immigration."

"Our Southern Border has been dealing with a manmade crisis under the ineptness of President Biden, allowing more than 6.3 million illegal immigrants to flood our border," said Senator Blaise Ingoglia. "Today, under the leadership of Governor Ron DeSantis, Florida made history signing into law the strongest state-led anti-illegal immigration bill ever brought forth. It was an honor to usher this bill through the process, knowing we are safeguarding Floridians and serving as the model for the nation to combat this crisis created by our very own President."

"Today, Florida sent a strong message that as a state we will protect our resources, our communities, and our families," said Representative Kiyan Michael.

This legislation will require private employers with 25 or more employees to use the E-Verify system for new employees, beginning on July 1, 2023. This bill also expands penalties for employers who fail to comply with E-Verify requirements, including the possible suspension and revocation of employer licenses and the imposition of specific penalties on employers that knowingly employ illegal aliens.

Additionally, this legislation creates a third-degree felony for an unauthorized alien to knowingly use a false ID document to gain employment and prohibits a county or municipality from providing funds to any person or organization for the purpose of issuing IDs or other documents to an illegal alien.

Importantly, illegal aliens will no longer be permitted to rely on out-of-state driver licenses.

If another state issued a license to an illegal alien who was unable to prove lawful presence in the U.S. when his or her license was issued, that person is prohibited from operating a motor vehicle in Florida.

Senate Bill 1718 also enhances the crime of human smuggling when smuggling a minor, when smuggling more than five people, and when the defendant has a prior conviction for human smuggling. This bill also adds the crime of human smuggling to the list of crimes allowed for prosecution under the Florida Racketeer Influenced and Corrupt Organization (RICO) Act.

This legislation will additionally require each hospital that accepts Medicaid to include a question on admission or registration forms that asks whether the patient is a U.S. citizen or lawfully present in the U.S. or is not lawfully present in the U.S. Hospitals will be required to provide a quarterly report to the Agency for Health Care Administration detailing the number of patients that visited the emergency department or were admitted to the hospital in each category of the citizen status question on the admission or registration forms.

20 Ways States Can Prevent Illegal Immigration

Utilizing the "20 Ways States Can Prevent Illegal Immigration" Heritage Foundation article:

Illegal immigration has soared to record highs under the Biden Administration's purposeful dismantling of our nation's borders and our immigration enforcement infrastructure. Due to radical open-border policies and the current border crisis, states across the country are bearing the consequences of illegal immigration like never before.

While it is true that the federal government has primary responsibility to enforce our immigration laws, they are failing to do so. States can play a crucial role in upholding our country's laws and fighting illegal immigration, protecting their own citizens. States can help enforce the law by deterring illegal aliens from residing in their states and publicizing the problems caused by uncontrolled, illegal immigration. The list that follows can act as a roadmap and starting point in that effort.

1. **Require E-Verify**
   Requiring licensed businesses to use this Web-based verification system can quickly and accurately reveal the authenticity of the information and credentials offered by new hires so employers hire authorized workers.

2. **Target Business Licenses of Employers Hiring Illegal Aliens**
   Requiring employers to use the federal government's own system and laws for checking immigration status, then suspending or revoking the license of a business if an employer knowingly hires an illegal alien is a right held by states and upheld by the Supreme Court since 2011—it helps fight willful ignorance of immigration status by businesses.

3. **Pass Vehicle Laws Preventing Day Labor**
   Passing vehicle laws—such as those making it illegal to stop and impede traffic to hire someone or pick up a passenger—cuts down on the "day labor" practices of illegal aliens trying to avoid official work verification.

4. **Require State/Local Law Enforcement to Determine/Communicate Immigration Status**
   Requiring law enforcement to attempt to determine the immigration status of anyone (if reasonable suspicion exists that the person is unlawfully present in the United States) they stop, detain, or arrest is reasonable and doable through U.S. Immigration and Customs Enforcement (ICE)'s 24-hour Law Enforcement Support Center and allows agencies to report illegal aliens' status to the federal government.

5. **Prevent Sanctuary Cities and Counties**
   Passing state laws forbidding state, county, or local jurisdictions and officials from operating under "sanctuary policies" (withholding information from federal law enforcement) protects law enforcement, Americans, and migrant communities.

6. **Empower State Residents to Sue Officials Who Obstruct Federal Law Enforcement**
   Allowing legal residents to sue officials who carry out sanctuary policies reinforces opposition to sanctuary policies and prevents political subdivisions within the state from obstructing the state's cooperation with federal law enforcement.

7. **Require the Majority of Law Enforcement Agencies to Participate in the 287(g) Program**
   Requiring state and local law enforcement agencies to participate in this program—authorizing U.S. Immigration and Customs Enforcement (ICE) to enter into agreements with the agencies, train local and state officials, and supervise them—expands immigration enforcement.

8. **Require Small, Rural Jurisdictions to Enroll in the Warrant Service Officer Program**
   Enrolling law enforcement officials from rural or low-budget jurisdictions in the 1-day training for the Warrant Service Officer (WSO) program, rather than the full, 4-week

287(g) program training, allows warrant service officers in these smaller jurisdictions to at least serve administrative warrants and execute arrests on behalf of ICE.

9. **Enact Laws Making It a Crime to Transport/Conceal/Induce an Illegal Alien**
Passing laws making it a crime to knowingly transport and further the illegal presence of an alien in the U.S., harbor an alien from detection in any place or building in the state, or encourage an alien to come into the state, discourages residents from aiding illegal aliens.

10. **Prohibit Illegal Aliens from Receiving Driver's Licenses/License Plates/Business, Commercial, Professional Licenses**
Prohibiting driver's licenses prevents illegal aliens from obtaining downstream benefits, such as voter registration, government benefits, bank accounts, and credit cards. Prohibiting license plates makes it difficult to drive undetected and unlicensed.

11. **Collect Data and Publish Crimes Committed by Illegal Aliens**
Collecting data on immigration status of arrested and incarcerated criminals in state and local prisons and jails provides states with valuable information to address the problem. Publishing this data and these stories fights the open borders narrative that Americans are unharmed by high illegal immigration and sanctuary policies.

12. **Prevent or Tax Remittances Sent Abroad**
Requiring banks to verify immigration status or imposing taxes on remittances sent abroad disincentivizes illegal aliens from sending wages back to their home country.

13. **Prohibit State and Local Taxes from Funding Attorneys for Removeable Aliens**
Pass laws stating that taxpayer funds shall not go to attorneys or NGOs to pay for aliens' legal representation in immigration proceedings, including appeals, as they seek relief from removal.

14. **Revise Definition of State Residence**
Ensuring that "state residents" are clearly defined as legal citizens and lawful aliens helps to prevent illegal aliens from obtaining state benefits, voter registration, identification, etc.

15. **Prohibit Business Licenses/ Contracts/Grants for NGOs Transporting/Smuggling**
Prohibiting licenses/contracts/grants for NGOs transporting or assisting in the transport of aliens discourages organizations from funding, operating, or aiding smuggling operations.

16. **Prevent Biggest State Costs for Illegal Aliens**
Requiring agencies and social service providers to verify immigration status and benefit eligibility by using SAVE (a U.S. Citizenship and Immigration Services online tool to quickly verify a benefit applicant's immigration status) prevents aliens from illegally obtaining public funds for education, health, social services, etc.

17. Require Voter ID and Clean Voter Rolls Regularly

Requiring Voter ID would prevent aliens from voting illegally. Cleaning up voter rolls regularly ensures that aliens who have purposely or inadvertently been registered to vote are removed.

18. Sue the Federal Government

As seen in Biden vs. Texas, suing federal government officials for reckless or illegal changes made to immigration policies—as well as disregard for states' interests—can better force accountability for the federal government when it comes to the enforcement of proper immigration law and policy.

19. Pass Laws Prohibiting State Colleges/Universities from Giving In-State Tuition to Aliens

Passing state laws preventing colleges and universities from offering in-state tuition to illegal aliens upholds and reinforces existing federal immigration law and makes it harder for future governors to ignore.

20. Provide a Private Right of Action for Citizens of the State to Sue State Colleges/Universities That Offer In-State Tuition to Aliens

Setting up treble damages for each violation or setting a high fine (e.g., $1 million per violation) within the statute empowers taxpayers who have been forced to subsidize the education of illegal aliens to hold the state accountable to the law.

Texas Passes Bill Allowing State Police to Arrest, Deport Illegal Immigrants

As per the David Zimmermann "Texas Passes Bill Allowing State Police to Arrest, Deport Illegal Immigrants" *National Review* November 2023 article:

The Texas House passed legislation making it a state crime to illegally cross the southern border, empowering state and local police to arrest and in some cases deport illegal immigrants, in what the bill's supporters claim is a response to federal inaction.

Senate Bill 4 gives local and state government the authority to arrest illegal immigrants who enter Texas from Mexico between official ports of entry. Under SB 4, those who unlawfully cross the border can be charged with a state misdemeanor and face up to one year in prison. A felony charge, carrying a maximum sentence of 20 years, can be leveled if illegal immigrants are charged with additional crimes or don't comply with a judge's orders.

The bill also authorizes state judges to deport illegal aliens to Mexico rather than pursue prosecution under federal law. After getting approval from the Texas senate last week, the latest version of SB 4 now heads to Republican governor Greg Abbott's desk, where he is expected to sign it into law.

Critics argue that the bill runs afoul of a decade-old Supreme Court ruling, *Arizona v. United States*, which forbids states from implementing their own immigration laws. That responsibility is left entirely to the federal government, but Texas Republicans believe the ongoing border crisis necessitates state action.

Republican state representative David Spiller, a sponsor of the landmark bill, said SB 4 intends to "stop the flow of illegal immigration" and that is not designed to prevent legal migrants from lawfully seeking asylum in the U.S. The state lawmaker also claimed SB 4 is constitutional because it's "not in conflict" with *Arizona v. United States,* despite Democratic claims to the contrary.

"SB 4 intends to challenge the decade-long holding of Arizona versus United States, given the new makeup of the United States Supreme Court, which we have seen has already overturned [the] 50-year long precedent of *Roe v. Wade*," Democratic state representative Victoria Neave Criado said. Spiller argued he is not attempting to overturn the Supreme Court decision.

The ACLU of Texas expressed opposition to SB4, saying it "overrides federal immigration law, fuels racial profiling and harassment, and gives state officials the unconstitutional ability to deport people without due process, regardless of whether they are eligible to seek asylum or other humanitarian protections."

The state House also approved $1.5 billion in border barriers as part of a separate bill.

Abbott personally thanked Spiller and Republican state representative Jacey Jetton for pushing both bills in the Texas House. "I look forward to working with both chambers to get these priorities across the finish line," the governor posted on X. "Texas won't wait on Biden to secure the border."

Nearly 189,000 illegal migrants crossed the southern border in October, according to a U.S. Customs and Border Protection report released. That figure decreased 14 percent from the month prior.

Migrant Busing Turned Out to Be a Political Coup for Republicans

From the Noah Rothman "Migrant Busing Turned Out to Be a Political Coup for Republicans" *National Review* May 2023 article:

Who would have thought that, for the low, low price of a bus ticket, you could compel your political opponents to make the very arguments against unchecked illegal immigration that you've been making for years? Apparently, the Republican governors of Texas and Florida, among others—though even they probably couldn't have imagined what a spectacular political success their respective migrant-relocation programs would be.

We have "reached our limit," said a spokesman for New York City mayor Eric Adams. The city has been compelled to engage in emergency measures including requisitioning gyms to house the number of migrants seeking asylum in the Big Apple. But with over 61,000 migrants descending on the city in the last year, New York is out of contingency plans. The mayor's office revealed last night that it would suspend its policy of guaranteeing the "right to shelter" to migrants crossing America's southern border.

Officially, the rationale justifying New York City's reluctant decision to temporarily abandon its sanctuary policies is the expiration of the pandemic-era border restrictions contained within Title 42. But as the *New York Times* confessed, the relatively modest volume of migrants relocated to the city via programs pursued by red-state governors such as Ron DeSantis and Greg Abbott have focused the minds of the city's policy-makers. And it's not just New York City that's feeling the heat.

Outgoing Chicago mayor Lori Lightfoot declared a state of emergency amid the influx of thousands of migrants that has overwhelmed the city's social services. "We've reached a breaking point in our response to this humanitarian crisis," Lightfoot said. Immigrants are reportedly forced to sleep on the floors of police stations and have limited access to showers and sanitation facilities. Chicago, too, has been compelled to rethink its sanctuary policies in response to the sunsetting of Title 42, but Lightfoot herself confessed that the city's "breaking point" was accelerated by the migrant-busing program.

Washington, D.C. has already spent the $10 million set aside to help its migrant population, and the hotel space Mayor Muriel Bowser's administration blocked out to house immigrants is full. The city is now seeking reimbursement from FEMA to maintain its support for migrants. Last year, in response to the pressure the border states had imposed on the nation's capital, the city pared back its sanctuary policies in a move the *Georgetown Voice* called "anti-immigrant."

Both Lightfoot and Adams lashed out at the governors representing border states. "Not only is this behavior morally bankrupt and devoid of any concern for the well-being of asylum seekers," Adams said in a statement, "but it is also impossible to ignore the fact that Abbott is now targeting five cities run by Black mayors."

Lightfoot struck a similarly accusatory note. "We're not just warehousing people," she insisted. "We're not gonna treat them in the same way that we've seen Governor Abbott do, without any regard for their humanity." But the busing programs have contributed only modestly to the increase in both cities' migrant populations. And if that increase is enough to break these "sanctuary cities," imagine what border communities are facing.

This isn't the first time these mayors have articulated essentially the same arguments that Republican border hawks have been making.

"This is not a new challenge at the border," Lightfoot confessed in September 2022 after a collection of red-state governors set out to disprove Vice President Kamala Harris's absurd contention that "the border is secure." It is, however, "a new challenge for us," Lightfoot added. Illinois governor J. B. Pritzker called out the National Guard to meet the modest pressure that had sent his state "unnecessarily scrambling." As a stopgap measure, Lightfoot shuttled nearly 150 migrants onto buses and sent them packing from her "sanctuary" city into the confines of the suburbs.

The story is much the same in D.C., where one city councilmember complained that Republican governors had "turned us into a border town." Eric Adams was equally distressed. "The city's prior practices, which never contemplated the busing of thousands of people into New York City, must be reassessed," he confessed last year. These Democratic city officials did their best to tee up the reliable effect of negative partisanship by accusing Republicans of being heartless and opportunistic, but it didn't work.

Within short order, Governors Abbott and DeSantis were joined by Colorado's Democratic governor, Jared Polis.

"We refuse to keep people against their will if they desire to travel elsewhere," Polis said in a statement. Though his state's relocation program has since ended, his decision to implement it complicated a nascent Democratic effort to polarize the issue.

The underlying conditions fueling this interstate dispute—the crisis at the border—are only getting worse. Border Patrol agents reported encounters with over 10,000 migrants, the third day in a row on which encounters had passed that mark. And with the conditions worsening, the migrant-busing programs are set to intensify.

"Until Biden secures the border to stop the inflow of mass migration, Texas will continue this necessary program," Texas governor Abbott wrote at the beginning of May. Earlier this year, the Florida legislature passed, and Governor DeSantis signed, a bill funding and expanding the state's migrant-relocation program. Florida's Division of Emergency Management confirmed this week that the state has "selected multiple vendors based on their capabilities to carry out the program."

The hardships experienced by the migrants who flood across America's borders and the municipalities tasked with keeping them sheltered, fed, and safe are not evenly endured. The busing program has rendered America's border crisis a far more visible nightmare by exposing the nation's political and media professionals to it. In objecting to their treatment by the border states, Democratic lawmakers in America's most permissive municipalities are inadvertently popularizing the case against lax immigration policies. If that becomes a catalyst for political change, it will have done more for the security of America's borders and the migrants already inside them than any "sanctuary city" policy ever could.

The Bipartisan Border Solutions Act: Rewarding President Biden for His Border Crisis

As per the Lora Ries and Mike Howell "The Bipartisan Border Solutions Act: Rewarding President Biden for His Border Crisis" Heritage Foundation April 2021 article:

Far from offering solutions, the proposed Bipartisan Border Solutions Act is a bipartisan failure. Caused willfully by President Biden's undoing of the Trump Administration's border security and immigration measures, the artificially created humanitarian and security disaster can only be alleviated by reinstituting the Trump-era policies and closing legal loopholes.

Passing this utterly misguided act would simply increase the U.S. capacity for processing illegal aliens in order to release them into the interior of the country, acting as a direct incentive for yet more illegal immigration.

The Issue

The proposed Bipartisan Border Solutions Act, introduced by Senators John Cornyn (R–TX) and Krysten Sinema (D–AZ) and Representatives Henry Cuellar (D–TX) and Tony Gonzales (R–

TX), is a poorly informed policy that would simply increase the U.S. capacity for processing illegal aliens in order to release them into the interior of the country, acting as a direct incentive for yet more illegal immigration.

The Biden Administration knowingly caused the current border crisis by undoing Trump-era border security and immigration measures for political purposes. Ending this artificially created humanitarian and security disaster requires restarting the Trump-era policies and closing legal loopholes. This bill does neither. Instead, it:

Establishes "Reception Centers" for Quick, Mass Processing. Establishing at least four "regional processing centers" on the border will provide legal guidance and medical attention to illegal aliens as they go through immediate document issuance and other checks. These reception centers will bring in relevant personnel from Immigration and Customs Enforcement (ICE), Customs and Border Protection (CBP), the Federal Emergency Management Agency, Citizenship and Immigration Services, and the Department of Health and Human Services (HHS). Illegal aliens will be processed and released within 72 hours.

Establishing giant one-stop-shop "reception" centers will be a boon for human traffickers, allowing them to drop off future waves of illegal aliens. Refugees from other countries should apply for protection in their regions at existing centers run by the United Nations Refugee Agency.

Moves Illegal Aliens into U.S. Communities. At taxpayer expense, the bill orders the Secretary of Homeland Security to "expand and improve the capability of the Department to conduct ground transportation of migrants." In this expanded system, state, local, or tribal governments to which the illegal alien is being transferred are only afforded at least four hours advance notice. The governments are not allowed to refuse the illegal aliens.

Plays Woke Word Games to Blur the Line Between Legal Immigrants and Illegal Border Crossers. In line with the Biden Administration's objective of changing immigration terminology, the bill creates new language to reframe mass illegal immigration. The bill introduces the following two terms:

(4) IRREGULAR MIGRATION INFLUX EVENT —The term "irregular migration influx event" means a period during which there is a significant increase in, or a sustained large number of, Department of Homeland Security encounters with aliens who—(A) do not use the formal immigration system of the United States or the countries they are traveling through; and (B) intend to enter the United States. (Emphases added.)

An "irregular migration influx event" is a border crisis. Not using "formal immigration systems" means breaking U.S. law to cross the border illegally. We do not need new terms to obscure the consequences of these actions.

Meaningless Asylum Improvement Pilot Program

The problems with U.S. asylum laws and the rampant abuse of them are well known. The Biden Administration must return to the Migrant Protection Protocols and Asylum Cooperation Agreements so that far fewer people show up at the southern U.S. border to claim asylum fraudulently.

Furthermore, Congress must remove the many benefits it provided to unaccompanied children in past legislation, as these resulted in more children making the dangerous journey north in the hands of human traffickers to obtain those benefits. In a nod to border security, the bill authorizes a pilot program to develop strategies to prevent abuse of U.S. asylum laws, though the program exempts unaccompanied children, pregnant women, and sick or disabled individuals. In doing so, the program fails to acknowledge that such categorical exceptions simply amount to incentives for those within those categories to make the dangerous journey to the U.S.

Increased Access to U.S. Immigration System for Open-Border NGOs and Attorneys

The bill contains several provisions aimed at increasing the role of, and access for, attorneys and non-governmental organizations (NGOs) to the immigration system. Current law already states that aliens may have representation, but at no expense to the government. This is a sound fiscal and equitable policy that must be maintained. U.S. taxpayers should not pay for aliens' legal orientation or counsel. It would be a bottomless fiscal pit. It is also important to note that U.S. citizens do not receive public attorneys in civil proceedings. Attorneys and NGOs often benefit from mass illegal immigration and play a strong advocacy and organizing role in pushing illegal aliens into the United States.

The bill allows the U.S. government to solicit donations from NGOs and the private sector for toys, clothes, and other supplies for border crossers. These entities will have access to the processing facilities, now called reception centers. Instead of supporting this increased access, policymakers should work to dramatically reduce illegal immigration in the first place, thereby reducing the need for these open-borders organizations and lawyers and extinguishing their advocacy role for policies that support illegal immigration.

Dangerous Sponsor Placement of Unaccompanied Children

While the bill would mandate criminal background checks for the U.S. sponsors of unaccompanied minors, it would still allow these children to be placed with illegal-alien and criminal sponsors. Only certain convictions and current trials would bar a person from sponsorship.

By placing unaccompanied children with illegal aliens, the U.S. government is directly complicit in the final act of the human trafficking scheme. The bill also kneecaps law enforcement by prohibiting the HHS from sharing sponsor fingerprints or DNA with the Department of Homeland Security.

More Personnel

The bill increases the CBP's Border Patrol by 600 officers, adds 300 personnel to ICE, adds 150 new immigration judges, adds 300 asylum officers, and adds other relevant support staff. While more personnel is needed, until the legal loopholes are closed, additional resources will merely accelerate the processing of illegal aliens into the U.S. instead of preventing the waves of illegal immigration in the first place.

12 – Biden's Immigration Policy Proposals vs. "Blue"

Sanctuary States, Cities & Orgs Hypocrisy

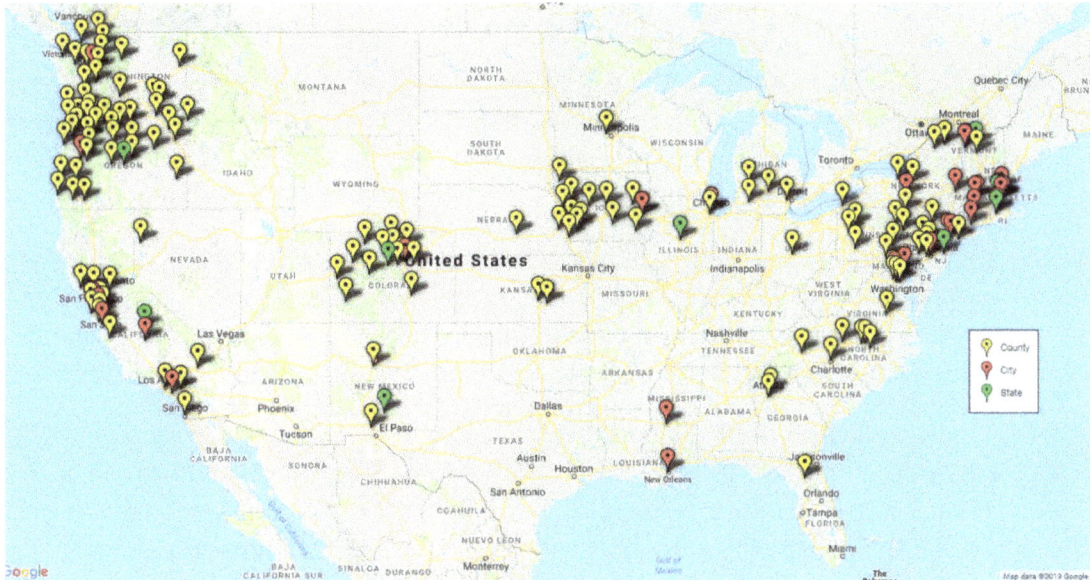

Credit: Pacific Standard – Sanctuary County, City and State Map (as of May 3, 2019).

Sanctuary policies are those followed by towns, cities, counties, states, and other jurisdictions that restrict most forms of cooperation with federal immigration authorities. There are 564 lawless "sanctuary" jurisdictions throughout the United States as of May 2018. The number rose sharply under Presidents Obama (from 40 in 2009 to 338 in 2016) and Trump.

From the "Sanctuary Policies" section of the FAIR website: Sanctuary jurisdictions frequently release dangerous convicted illegal alien felons – including rapists, murderers, and pedophiles – into the general population. The Supreme Court has declared immigration an exclusively federal domain in *Arizona v. United States* (567 U.S. 387) in 2012. This makes sanctuary policies illegal and unconstitutional.

Because they undermine federal law and give aid and comfort to illegal alien criminals, the U.S. government is well within its right to defund sanctuary jurisdictions and demand that they change these harmful policies.

The Truth About "Sanctuary" Policies

Sanctuary policies are those followed by towns, cities, counties, states, and other jurisdictions that restrict most forms of cooperation with federal immigration authorities.

They are explicitly forbidden under federal law (8 USC § 1373) and violate the supremacy clause of the United States Constitution (Article VI, Clause 2) and the 10th Amendment. They also undermine the rule of law by violating federal immigration policies. By refusing to hand over criminal aliens to federal authorities for deportation and releasing them, noncompliant jurisdictions are irresponsibly exposing their residents to potential harm.

In fact, American citizens (and sometimes illegal aliens themselves) have been killed or otherwise victimized by criminal illegal aliens who benefited from sanctuary policies. Sanctuary jurisdictions serve as an attractive magnet for illegal aliens, criminals among them in particular.

Although sanctuary policies have been around since the late 1970s, they were relatively rare until quite recently. Only eleven had been adopted before 2000 (including New York City and San Francisco, as well as the country's first sanctuary state, Oregon, in 1987).

Only 40 had been adopted by the time President Barack Obama was inaugurated in 2009. During the Obama era, the number of sanctuary jurisdictions grew by 650 percent. That exponential growth was spurred on by the Obama administration's efforts to dismantle immigration enforcement and its tacit encouragement of local governments to do the same.

By contrast, during the Trump administration, sanctuary policies have served as a way for left-leaning state and local governments to "virtue signal" by demonstrating their anti-Trump bona fides and emphasizing their opposition to the President's pro-enforcement rhetoric and policies. At the end of the day, however, the main victims of these foolish policies are American citizens, legal immigrants, and even illegal aliens.

The Whole Justification for Sanctuary Cities Is Wrong

Per the Steven A. Camarota and Jessica Vaughan "The Whole Justification for Sanctuary Cities Is Wrong" *National Review* October 2021 article:

Noncitizen Hispanics theoretically should be the most fearful of police because a large share are in the country illegally. In government surveys such as the National Crime Victimization Survey (NCVS), we estimate that roughly two thirds of noncitizen Hispanics are either illegal immigrants or live with one. And yet the NCVS shows that 57 percent of serious crimes against noncitizen Hispanics were reported to police, compared with 53 percent for the U.S.-born.

Immigration advocates have long asserted that local law-enforcement agencies should not cooperate with federal immigration authorities because doing so would cause immigrants to avoid reporting crimes out of fear of deportation. This justification for "sanctuary" jurisdictions has always been dubious, but now we have data that directly refute it as noted above.

Starting in 2017, the Department of Justice (DOJ) added a citizenship question to its annual NCVS, which is the largest and most authoritative survey of crime victims. The 2017–19 NCVS indicates that the whole basis for sanctuary polices is a myth; it turns out that crimes against immigrants are reported to police at rates that match or often exceed those for crimes against the U.S.-born.

With no evidence that immigrants are less likely to report crimes, the primary objection to cooperation between police and ICE appears to be invalid. However, the public-safety benefits of such cooperation are real. When local officers and ICE are able to share information, criminal aliens who are causing problems can be identified and deported instead of returned to the streets. Federal immigration authorities can remove criminal aliens, even when witness intimidation is a problem, as it often is with gang members, because deportation typically does not require witness testimony. None of this can happen if police are not allowed to work with ICE.

How Texas Gov. Greg Abbott Divided Democrats on Immigration With Migrant Busing

For more than a year, Texas Gov. Greg Abbott has regularly sent busloads of migrants to cities that have deemed themselves sanctuaries to immigrants. It's a controversial practice, with officials on the receiving end saying the busing comes without warning or coordination and with an intent of creating chaos. Since April 2022, the Abbott administration has bused some 75,500 migrants from Texas to six cities, according to the governor's office.

Abbott has said it all began from sheer desperation while overseeing small border towns bursting at the seams with migrants. That's something he blames on President Joe Biden's border policies, which he says are lax as reported in the Natasha Korecki "How Texas Gov. Greg Abbott Divided Democrats on Immigration With Migrant Busing" NBC News December 2023 news story:

Along the way, however, a different phenomenon has taken over—Democrats are raising the alarm on immigration, with the leaders of sanctuary cities and blue states thousands of miles from the southern border now warning their situation is dire. Democrats are calling on the White House for more funding and to seize control over the interior operations to ensure migrants are sent to areas that have the capacity to take them in.

It has all added up to a shift in the immigration debate, where Democrats are calling out the president of their own party to do more to contain what they call a crisis. And this winter could make it worse.

Asked if the busing would continue through the winter months in cold-weather places like Chicago and New York, Abbott spokesperson Renae Eze said in a statement to NBC News, "Until President Biden does his job and secures the border, Texas will continue busing migrants to sanctuary cities to provide much-needed relief to our overwhelmed border towns."

From Abbott's standpoint, it's a shift that's long overdue.

"Before we began busing illegal immigrants up to New York, it was just Texas and Arizona that bore the brunt of all of the chaos and all of the problems that come with it," Abbott said in an interview with ABC News' "Nightline" a year ago. "Now the rest of America is understanding exactly what's going on."

Not only are Democrats warring with each other, there are signs that the party is losing the public's faith in whether it can handle the issue better than Republicans.

A September 2023, NBC poll showed that 50% of the registered voters surveyed said that the Republican Party was better at dealing with border security, compared to 20% of voters who chose Democrats. And 18% more registered voters in that survey chose Republicans over Democrats when asked who they thought was better at dealing with immigration overall.

The White House, too, has rebuked Abbott's practices, citing one of Abbott's bus deployments dropped off families outside of Vice President Kamala Harris' residence on Christmas Eve last year.

Abbott's reasoning for the busing, a review of his public comments over the last year show, is that the Biden administration isn't enforcing immigration laws already on the books. With a record number of migrants coming over the border and seeking asylum, systems are overwhelmed in Texas. Abbott has deployed groups of migrants after they're processed by Border Patrol to places where he says there's more room. He's chosen sanctuary cities because they are supposed to be welcoming to immigrants, he says, and insists no newcomer to the country is forced to get on a bus; only those who raise their hands to travel to other cities are sent.

John Wittman, a former communications official who previously served in the Abbott administration, said the governor has helped shift the conversation about immigration in the country with places like New York, Chicago and Boston talking about the border.

"There is no doubt that the busing strategy is having an impact," Wittman said. "All of a sudden, there does seem to be some actual bipartisan support for securing the border, which, before this busing strategy the governor implemented, I don't think anyone saw coming.

"Who would have thought Eric Adams would be calling on the Biden administration to do something about the border?"

Now, Abbott argues that Chicago, New York and other big cities see the emergency for what it is. "This is something that's unsustainable. Those are the words of your mayor," Abbott told a New York City crowd at the Manhattan Institute in September. "Those are the words of the mayors of Chicago and L.A. Those are the words of the governor of Texas."

CNN Host Admits Red State Strategy of Bussing Migrants to Sanctuary Cities 'Has Worked' to Pressure Biden

As disclosed in the Kristine Parks "CNN Host Admits Red State Strategy of Bussing Migrants to Sanctuary Cities 'Has Worked' to Pressure Biden" Fox News December 2023 news story:

CNN panel discusses immigration crisis, argues GOP strategy has been effective as a coalition of Democratic mayors demanded President Biden declare a national emergency on the border.

CNN host Kasie Hunt argued on the network that Republican governors' strategy of sending migrants to blue sanctuary cities "has worked" to highlight the immigration crisis and put pressure on President Biden. Hunt's comments come as Biden faces increased demands from beleaguered Democratic mayors to address the border.

New York City Mayor Eric Adams, Chicago Mayor Brandon Johnson and Denver Mayor Mike Johnston held a virtual press conference asking Biden to declare a national emergency and provide additional funding to their cities, which have been overwhelmed by the surge in migrants.

"Yeah, I mean, that right there is the problem that Joe Biden has, right, in a nutshell," Hunt responded to the mayors' comments.

Democrats had long dismissed Republican concerns about the border as "alarmist," she said, but they are now seeing how the crisis "has gotten worse, not better."

"And, frankly, the strategy that these red state governors have had of sending a lot of these migrants up to blue states has worked from a political perspective. And it is very, very hard for these cities to absorb them. And, you know, the Biden team, I think, knows that, or they wouldn't be willing to make these concessions in these policy negotiations that they're having with Capitol Hill," the anchor argued.

'They Will Hurt': Eric Adams Warns of Painful Budget Cuts to NYC Essential Services Due to Migrant Crisis

Per the Ari Blaff "'They Will Hurt': Eric Adams Warns of Painful Budget Cuts to NYC Essential Services Due to Migrant Crisis" *National Review* September 2023 update:

With the growing financial toll of providing for over 100,000 illegal immigrants, New York City mayor Eric Adams said agencies will need to cut expenses, with some departments facing cuts of up to 15 percent.

"While our compassion is limitless, our resources are not," Mayor Eric Adams said during a recorded address. "We have not received substantial support from the federal or state governments to handle those costs or change the course of this crisis."

"The simple truth is that longtime New Yorkers and asylum seekers will feel these potential cuts and they will hurt," Adams warned.

Amid declining city revenues and a projected $12 billion migrant-related tab the Big Apple has been forced to pay in recent years, Adams is demanding municipal agencies trim as much as 5 percent of their upcoming three budgets, the first of which will be publicized in November.

In recent months, the mayor has become increasingly vocal that New York City's problems have been exacerbated by the failure of the Biden administration and federal agencies to proactively address the migrant crisis. "I want to be clear: these tough decisions are a direct result of inaction in Washington and in Albany," Adams added during his remarks, which were released on YouTube.

"But the die is not yet cast, and we can still avoid these cuts if Washington and Albany do their part by paying their fair share, and coming up with a decompression strategy that reduces the pressure on New York City, so we are not forced to manage this crisis almost entirely on our own. "

"Since the large influx of asylum-seekers to our city began last spring, we have warned New Yorkers that every city service could be impacted by this crisis if we did not get the support we needed."

Although Adams has insisted that such budget cuts will not translate to job losses, one source familiar with the situation told the *New York Post* that such thinking is farcical. "There's no scenario of a 5 percent cut at every agency without layoffs," the individual said. "It will mean dirtier streets and crime could go up."

City councilors weighed in and voiced their frustration.

"Oh, my God! I don't think any agency could take a 5 percent cut," Gale Brewer, a Democratic representing Manhattan, reflected. "It would be detrimental to quality of life—no question."

"We're talking about programs that support essential workers, social workers, housing, health care. I don't know if you could do it without layoffs."

Across the aisle, David Carr, a Republican representative from Staten Island, insisted such budget cuts demonstrate the shortcomings of "carte blanche" asylum-seeking policies the city had long-embraced. "This is going to hurt services and new hires," Carr told the Post. "I hope that everyone who has been in favor of an open-ended commitment to housing migrants as they come are thinking twice about that."

New York City has opened over 200 emergency shelters to accommodate the influx of illegal migrants, the continued strain of which has prompted Adams to request city agencies incorporate cost-saving measures four times already.

"New Yorkers are angry and frustrated, and they are right to be. I am, too," Adams insisted.

New York City Asks Judge to Suspend Right-to-Shelter Mandate Amid Migrant Crisis

From the David Zimmermann "New York City Asks Judge to Suspend Right-to-Shelter Mandate Amid Migrant Crisis" *National Review* October 2023 article: New York City moved toward halting the city's 42-year-old right-to-shelter mandate, asking a state judge to modify or temporarily suspend the law as its unprecedented migrant crisis persists.

New York City's senior counsel Daniel Perez, on behalf of Democratic mayor Eric Adams, submitted a letter to state supreme court justice Erika Edwards, requesting the court reconsider the city's legal obligation to offer temporary housing to anyone who asks. The right-to-shelter consent order was passed in 1981, making New York the only major city in the U.S. to have such a law.

The letter clarified city officials do not intend to "terminate" it, though.

"We seek only the immediate relief that present circumstances demand. New York City has done more than any other city in the last 18 months to meet this national humanitarian crisis," the letter reads. "The Judgment's onerous terms are demonstrably ill-suited to present circumstances and restrain the City at a time when flexibility to deal with the emergency is paramount."

The city continues to struggle to provide housing to over 117,000 migrants who have entered its borders since spring 2022, and that number is only expected to rise. With only 210 shelter sites open, government officials are overwhelmed by the record influx of asylum-seekers as Adams continues pressing for federal and state aid.

The recent letter is part of Adams's ongoing attempt to weaken the city's right-to-shelter mandate, arguing it "has become outmoded and cumbersome in the face of the present migrant crisis." In May, Adams filed a court motion to modify the law. Deputy chief administrative judge Deborah Kaplan agreed to let the case move forward and assigned it to Edwards.

Despite his calling for limitations to be put on the mandate, Adams slammed Staten Island judge Wayne Ozzi's ruling last week for banning the city from using a former Catholic school as a migrant shelter. Ozzi's decision, as Adams's office put it, "threatens to disrupt efforts to manage this national humanitarian crisis" and "jeopardizes our ability to continue providing shelter at that scale."

"We need to counteract those forms of communications that are basically saying, 'You come to the City of New York, you're going to automatically have a job, you're going to be in a five star hotel,'" Adams added.

Still, he called an open southern border "the official position of the city."

Chicago Residents Explode With Anger Over Migrants, Sanctuary Policies: 'They Are Not Listening'

Per the Elizabeth Heckman "Chicago Residents Explode With Anger Over Migrants, Sanctuary Policies: 'They Are Not Listening'" Fox News November 2023 news report: "Do you as a resident of the City of Chicago believe that we should remain a sanctuary city?" asked 41st Ward Alderman Anthony Napolitano at a city council meeting.

The crowd responded by yelling a resounding "no" and erupting with boos and catcalls.

"We're spending a lot of money every single day. We're up to $40 million a month," said 9th Ward Alderman Anthony Beale, according to Fox 32.

A majority of the crowd was African American residents who were angry about how much money is being spent on illegal immigrants.

"The most outrageous thing about it is the local community. I've been contacted by two pastors in the Black community who are up in arms, saying the Black community has been left behind," said Tom Homan.

Homan compared how struggling Chicago residents are supported versus the illegal immigrants, who are receiving free meals and hotel rooms at taxpayers' expense.

"The community is outraged and they should be," he told co-host Lawrence Jones, adding that sanctuary policies make the community less safe.

"The sanctuary is for criminals. ... That means local law enforcement can't work with ICE agents to deport somebody who is a public safety threat. ... For instance, an illegal alien commits a serious crime, gets booked in a jail. ICE isn't even allowed to go into that jail and talk to them to put a detainer on to set them up for removal," he said.

City officials say the Windy City has accepted more than 19,000 migrants since August 2022, but they are not the only ones who will need assistance during the winter. There are over 68,000 Chicagoans experiencing homelessness, according to a recent study, the city says.

In a recent interview with FOX News host Jesse Watters, a Chicago resident expressed her dismay over migrants being housed at O'Hare Airport, police stations and even youth sports fields. The interview with Cata Truss came after an October city council meeting unfolded in similar fashion, as residents raged at new Democratic Mayor Brandon Johnson.

"They are not listening. ... In Chicago, it's unfortunate that our elected officials have always taken us for granted, but we are tired of being taken for granted. We are standing up and we are fighting back," Truss said.

D.C. Mayor Declares Emergency over Migrant Buses: Crisis 'Certainly Not of Our Making'

As reported in the Brittany Bernstein "D.C. Mayor Declares Emergency over Migrant Buses: Crisis 'Certainly Not of Our Making'" *National Review* September 2022 article: Washington, D.C., mayor Muriel Bowser declared a public emergency in September 2022 in response to the arrival of thousands of migrants in the district on buses from Texas and Arizona.

The declaration allocates funding to create an Office of Migrant Services, which will provide migrants with temporary accommodations and transportation, as well as meet their urgent medical needs.

"We're putting in place a framework that would allow us to have a coordinated response with our partners," the mayor said. "This will include a program to meet all buses, and given that most people will move on, our primary focus is to make sure we have a humane, efficient, welcome process that will allow people to move on to their final destination."

"Regardless of the federal response—which I think has been lacking in some respects—that the District of Columbia would continue to work with partners to advance what we need and ensure our systems in D.C. are not broken by a crisis that is certainly not of our making," Bowser added.

The declaration comes after Texas governor Greg Abbott said the Lone Star state is "filling gaps left in Biden's absence at our border," in part by busing illegal immigrants to sanctuary cities.

Abbott noted late last month that Texas has "made over 19,000 arrests, seized over 335.5M lethal fentanyl doses, & sent over 7,400 migrants on buses to DC and over 1,500 to NYC."

Abbott previously said he decided to send busloads of migrants to Washington, D.C., and New York City "because of President Biden's continued refusal to acknowledge the crisis caused by his open border policies," saying that "the State of Texas has had to take unprecedented action to keep our communities safe."

San Diego Declares Humanitarian Crisis as Federal Government Drops Thousands of Migrants on Streets

Per the Caroline Downey "San Diego Declares Humanitarian Crisis as Federal Government Drops Thousands of Migrants on Streets" *National Review* September 2023 article: The San Diego board of supervisors voted unanimously on to declare a humanitarian crisis as thousands of illegal immigrants flooded into the city, courtesy of the federal government.

More than 8,100 migrants have arrived in the area in the last two weeks, the San Diego Union Tribune reported, citing county officials. Many of the migrants have been dropped off on the streets of San Diego by the U.S. government, according to the Wall Street Journal.

Supervisor Jim Desmond and Chair Nora Vargas proposed the declaration, which would authorize the county to petition the federal government for more funding to address the untenable situation. The county's office of immigrant and refugee affairs will now send a letter asking for more federal assistance for the local organizations combatting the crisis.

Many representatives of aid groups spoke at the board of supervisors meeting, calling on the officials to secure a federal response.

"These releases occur with little direction and minimal resources, leaving local communities grappling with an increasingly untenable situation," Desmond said in a statement. "While we are a community that values compassion and empathy, we must also acknowledge the practical limits of our capacity to meet the needs of those who arrive in our region."

Desmond said the county has been diverting resources away from the local homeless population to provide help to the migrants

"If you want us to fund this response, what program would you have us take that money from?" he asked at the board of supervisors' meeting, according to the Journal.

Massachusetts Becomes Latest in String of Blue States to Declare State of Emergency Over Illegal Migrant Surge

From the Ari Blaff "Massachusetts Becomes Latest in String of Blue States to Declare State of Emergency over Illegal Migrant Surge" *National Review* August 2023 article: During an afternoon press conference at the Massachusetts state house, Governor Maura Healey declared a state of emergency following the influx of thousands of illegal migrants that has pushed social services across the state to a breaking point.

"Due to the rapid and unabating increases in the number of families with children and pregnant people," the governor said in a prepared statement, "The need for action is urgent."

"Right now, more than 5,500 families," Healey, the former Massachusetts Attorney General, continued, "They are in danger of going without the most basic of human rights in one of the most prosperous places on earth: the ability to lay their heads down in a safe place every night with a roof over their heads and with access to fundamental human necessities. They have called upon us to help give them shelter and the ability to work."

The Democratic governor alluded to the potential need for a state of emergency during a speech in June. "I am going to do whatever I can to maximize resources and funding and support from the federal government as we continue to work with communities and nonprofits around the state," Healey told reporters at the time.

The move now permits the state to seek federal assistance and the governor to enlist the help of the National Guard to address the ongoing crisis.

States Say ICE Stops Issuing Detainers for Illegal Immigrant Convicts, Revokes Them for Dozens

Shown in the "States Say ICE Stops Issuing Detainers for Illegal Immigrant Convicts, Revokes Them for Dozens" *Judicial Watch* April 2021 report:

Immigration and Customs Enforcement (ICE) has long complained about police in sanctuary cities that fail to honor its detainers, instead releasing serious criminals in the U.S. rather than turn them over to get deported. Now two states are suing the Homeland Security agency for failing to issue detainer requests for convicted felons in the country illegally, forcing local authorities to free them after completing their sentence rather than turning them over to the feds for removal. It seems that the tables have turned under the Biden administration, according to the lawsuit, filed this month by officials in Texas and Louisiana.

The states claim that ICE has reversed a Trump era policy and is not issuing detainer requests for dangerous illegal aliens imprisoned in their jurisdiction. "As a result, many convicted criminal aliens have been released to society after their sentences, contrary to Congress's mandate that they be detained pending their removal from the United States," according to their complaint, filed this month in the United States District Court for the Southern District of Texas Victoria Division.

Besides ICE, the defendants include the Department of Homeland Security (DHS) and its secretary, Alejandro Mayorkas, U.S. Citizenship and Immigration Services (USCIS), U.S. Customs and Border Protection (CBP) and various officials at the DHS agencies. The lawsuit begins by stating that "the Biden Administration is refusing to take custody of criminal aliens despite federal statutes requiring it to do so."

Instead, the document reads, defendants "have issued and implemented unlawful agency memoranda that allow criminal aliens already convicted of felony offenses to roam free in the United States. Such aliens belong in federal custody, as Congress required."

Adding insult to injury, officials in the Lone Star State reveal in the court document that the Biden administration has taken the extra step of revoking ICE detainer requests for a multitude of illegal immigrants convicted of felonies and serving sentences in prisons operated by the Texas Department of Criminal Justice.

Many were found guilty in a U.S. court of serious drug offenses, including possession, manufacturing, and sale. "President Biden's outright refusal to enforce the law is exacerbating an unprecedented border crisis," said Texas Attorney General Ken Paxton in a statement announcing the lawsuit.

"By failing to take custody of criminal aliens and giving no explanation for this reckless policy change, the Biden Administration is demonstrating a blatant disregard for Texans' and Americans' safety. Law and order must be immediately upheld and enforced to ensure the safety of our communities. Dangerous and violent illegal aliens must be removed from our communities as required by federal law."

In 2019 Texas housed nearly 9,000 undocumented criminal aliens at a cost of more than $152 million, according to the lawsuit.

In Louisiana ICE is not removing individuals subject to mandatory deportation, the complaint says, causing convicted felons incarcerated in state facilities to be released in local communities throughout the Bayou State. Louisiana, more than any other state, has greater risk due to the large number of local jails that are used to house detainees prior to removal, according to Attorney General Jeff Landry. "The President's refusal to enforce the law only worsens an already dire border crisis," Landry said.

"Law and order must prevail; dangerous and violent criminal aliens must not be allowed to roam free in our communities." Both states assert that the administration is violating binding agreements with DHS to assist in immigration enforcement and national security missions as well the Constitution, Immigration and Nationality Act and Administrative Procedure Act, which require the government to post proposed substantive rule changes in the Federal Register and allow the public to comment on them before enacting them.

For years ICE has slammed sanctuary cities nationwide for refusing to honor a local-federal partnership known as 287(g) that notifies the agency of jail inmates in the country illegally so that they can be deported after serving time for state crimes.

Before Biden became president, ICE repeatedly issued statements reminding sanctuary cities and states that when law enforcement agencies fail to honor immigration detainers and release serious criminal offenders onto the streets, it undermines its ability protect public safety and carry out its mission. The agency even launched a billboard campaign seeking the public's help in capturing felons released by one state's sanctuary policy.

Honduran Drug Dealers Say They've Flocked to San Francisco Because of Sanctuary Laws

Per the Caroline Downey "Honduran Drug Dealers Say They've Flocked to San Francisco Because of Sanctuary Laws" *National Review* July 2023 article: Honduran drug dealers have made a business hub out of San Francisco due to the progressive city's sanctuary laws for illegal immigration, fueling the nation's fentanyl epidemic and the visible decline of a major American city.

San Francisco's accommodative approach to illegal immigration makes it appealing to sell there, Honduran dealers told the *San Francisco Chronicle* as part of an in-depth investigation into how Honduran nationals have come to play a dominant role in the city's drug crisis.

Under current San Francisco law, last amended in July 2016, city employees are forbidden from using city resources to cooperate with any ICE investigation, detention, or arrest relating to an illegal immigration case. The law also prohibits ICE from placing holds on local prisoners so they can be deported upon their release from jail, the publication noted.

A Honduran dealer told the *Chronicle* that San Francisco is a hot spot for drug work because those illegal immigrants who are caught are less likely to be deported.

"The reason is because, in San Francisco, it's like you're here in Honduras," another dealer said. "The law, because they don't deport, that's the problem. … Many look for San Francisco because it's a sanctuary city. You go to jail and you come out."

13 – Skills Based & Assimilated Immigrants Needed for the 21st Century—Not Chain Migration

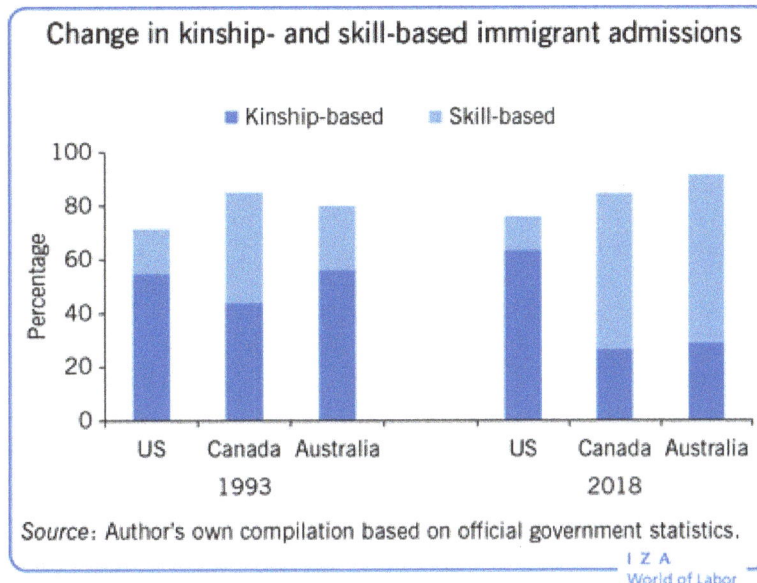

Change in kinship- and skill-based immigrant admissions

Source: Author's own compilation based on official government statistics.

I Z A
World of Labor

Utilizing the Jennifer G. Hickey "Foreign-Born Workers in the United States" FAIR December 2019 update:

According to the latest figures from the Bureau of Labor Statistics (BLS), in 2018, there were 28.2 million foreign-born individuals legally working in the U.S. labor force, which is 17.4 percent of the total workforce. The actual number of foreign-born workers likely is higher as this data does not include either persons illegally employed or illegal immigrants who have been granted temporary protection under the Deferred Action for Childhood Arrivals (DACA) or Temporary Permanent Status (TPS) programs.

The share of the labor force which is foreign-born has continued to increase over the decades. For example, in 2000, foreign nationals made up 13.3 percent of the labor force, compared to 17.4 percent in 2018. With a robust economy, the trend is unlikely to reverse course in coming years.

Types of Work Visas

The U.S. is home to a diversity of industries, so it is no surprise that the types of work visas are varied and numerous. The several options available to foreign nationals to gain employment in the U.S. include green cards (for permanent residency), temporary work visas, seasonal work visas, and exchange worker visas. Several of the most popular visa categories are detailed below.

Permanent Workers

According to U.S. Citizenship and Immigration Services (USCIS), each fiscal year about 140,000 visas are available for aliens (and their spouses and children) to come to the U.S. for the purposes of work. There are five separate employment-based (EB) visa categories offered to those who have particular skills. They are ranked in terms of "preference" and include:

- EB-1: Workers "with extraordinary ability in the sciences, arts, education, business, or athletics; outstanding professors and researchers; or certain multinational managers and executives

- EB-2: Professions requiring advanced degrees or who have exceptional ability

- EB-5: This controversial "immigrant investor visa" is reserved for those who invest $1 million or $500,000 in a commercial enterprise which employs at least 10 full-time U.S. workers

- H-2B Temporary Non-Agricultural Visas: These visas are open to workers in non-agricultural fields, provided there is an insufficient number of domestic laborers to fill the position. These visas are given to those working in jobs like ski resorts, hotels, beach resorts, amusement parks, or other service-related industries. The number of visas is currently capped at 66,000 annually. The maximum period of stay in H-2B classification is 3 years. While someone with H-2B non-immigrant status for a total of 3 years must leave the country, they can seek readmission as long as they remain outside the United States for an uninterrupted period of 3 months.

- H-2A Temporary Agricultural Workers: This visa is available to those seeking work that is of a temporary or seasonal nature, as long as an employer can demonstrate that there are not enough U.S. workers who are able, willing, qualified, and available to do the temporary work. There also must be some evidence provided that hiring H-2A workers will not adversely affect the wages and working conditions of similarly employed U.S. workers. While an H-2A worker's spouse and unmarried children under 21 years of age may seek admission in H-4 non-immigrant classification, those family members are not eligible to work while on H-4 status. Like the H-2B visa, the maximum period of stay is three years.

Optional Practical Training (OPT) Guestworker Program

The Optional Practical Training (OPT) program is operated by the Department of Homeland Security (DHS) that grants work authorization to foreign nationals who are full-time students at American colleges or universities.

Unlike the H-1B program, the OPT program does not require applicants to be sponsored by an employer, and it does not set a cap on the number of people who can participate. They are permitted to work in the U.S. for up to 12 months after graduation, but it can be extended to a maximum of 36 months for those with a degree in a science, technology, engineering or math (STEM) field.

Many of the companies who employ these foreign students also heavily utilize the H-1B program, including Amazon, Google, and Intel.

Other more specific visa categories are granted to internationally recognized athletes (P-1A), persons with extraordinary ability in sciences, arts, education, business, or athletics and motion picture or TV production (O-1), religious workers (R-1), North American Free Trade Agreement (NAFTA) temporary professionals from Mexico and Canada (TN).

Merit-Based Immigration

From the Heritage Foundation team of Charles D. Stimson, Hans A. von Spakovsky, and Lora Ries "Assessing the Trump Administration's Immigration Policies" June 2020 report: Arguably the most far-reaching and boldest aspect of the Trump Administration's immigration-reform platform is the proposal to base the selection of future immigrants on their skills and potential contribution to our economy.

Moving from a family-based immigration system to a merit-based system would upend the status quo and move from a system in which non-citizens and lawful permanent residents select future American citizens based solely on familial ties—to a system in which we choose future American citizens based on the skill sets we need and their ability to contribute to our economy.

This sounds radical, but it is not: Other countries have already implemented merit-based immigration systems. Those countries include Australia, Austria, Canada, the Czech Republic, Denmark, Germany, Hong Kong, Japan, New Zealand, Romania, South Korea, and the United Kingdom.

In October 2017, less than one year into office, President Trump submitted a letter to the House and Senate, laying out his vision of how best to reform the immigration system in the United States. Included in that letter was a section entitled "Merit-Based Immigration System," arguing for the need to transition from a family-based immigration system, which we currently have, to a merit-based system.

The Administration's merit-based concept contained four main parts:

1. Ending family-based chain migration as it currently exists by limiting family-based green cards to immediate family members, and replacing it with a system based on merit, with a special emphasis on "skills and economic contributions" to the U.S. economy;

2. Establishing a point system for green cards;

3. Eliminating the "visa lottery" program, which provides 50,000 immigrant visas annually to random individuals from countries with low rates of immigration to the United States; and

4. Limiting the number of refugees to "prevent the abuse of the generous U.S. Refugee Admissions Program and allow for effective assimilation of admitted refugees into the fabric of our society."

Like with all recent immigration reform proposals, the call to fundamentally reform our immigration system into one that puts America first was aspirational, as there is, as a political reality, very little likelihood that bipartisan immigration legislation can pass both houses of Congress, no matter how commonsense the legislation might be.

The lack of political will in Congress, however, did not stop the Administration from pushing forward with its plans. On January 25, 2018, three months after sending the reform vision letter to Congress, the White House published the framework document on how it would implement its overall goals. In addition to proposing the legalization of all Deferred Action for Childhood Arrivals (DACA) recipients, the Administration proposed to "promote the nuclear family" by limiting family migration to "spouses and minor children only, thus ending chain migration." The changes would be applied prospectively so as not to harm those already in the queue.

The Administration's plan to shift to a predominately merit-based legal immigration system is noteworthy in one other respect: It does not lower, or raise, the number of legal immigrants allowed to come into the United States each year.

Despite media fearmongering to the contrary, the Trump Administration has not lowered the number of legal immigrants admitted to the United States each year (over 1.1 million)—nor would a merit-based system.

Rather, a merit-based system would radically shift the percentage of family-based lawful immigrants from a majority to a minority, while increasing the percentage of merit-based immigrants dramatically for the good of our economy. In sum, the Administration is proposing a rebalancing of the current numbers.

With respect to the visa-lottery program, the Administration proposed to eliminate it because it was "riddled with fraud and abuse and does not serve the national interest." Furthermore, the program selects individuals "at random;" it does not take into consideration "skills, merit or public safety." By eliminating the lottery program, the Administration aimed to reallocate those 50,000 annual visas to reduce the family-based backlog and the high-skilled employment backlog.

The Heritage Foundation also proposed a shift to a merit-based immigration system. In our Special Report entitled "An Agenda for Immigration Reform," we laid out, in detail, the policy reasons why the shift makes sense, both economically and culturally.

The RAISE Act

Per the "RAISE Act" Numbers USA October 2017 update: The RAISE Act was introduced by Senators Tom Cotton (R-Ark.) and David Perdue (R-Ga.) in 2017. The bill would eliminate the family chain migration green card categories and the visa lottery and transform the current employment-based system to a merit-based system, potentially reducing legal immigration by 50% over 10 years. The bill earned the endorsement of Pres. Donald Trump who praised the bill's introduction at a White House event.

"For decades, the United States was operated and has operated a very low-skilled immigration system, issuing record numbers of Green Cards to low-wage immigrants. This policy has placed substantial pressure on American workers, taxpayers and community resources. Among those hit the hardest in recent years have been immigrants and, very importantly, minority workers competing for jobs against brand-new arrivals. And it has not been fair to our people, to our citizens, to our workers.

"The RAISE Act ends chain migration, and replaces our low-skilled system with a new points-based system for receiving a Green Card. This competitive application process will favor applicants who can speak English, financially support themselves and their families, and demonstrate skills that will contribute to our economy."

President Donald Trump, August 2, 2017

The RAISE Act would:

Eliminate Outdated Diversity Visa Lottery: The Lottery is plagued with fraud, it advances no economic or humanitarian interest, and it does not even deliver the diversity of its namesake. The RAISE Act would eliminate the 50,000 visas arbitrarily allocated to this lottery.

Place Responsible Limit on Permanent Residency for Refugees: The RAISE Act would limit refugees offered permanent residency to 50,000 per year, in line with a 13-year average. (This is the same annual refugee cap in Pres. Trump's executive order. It is also the cap recommended in the 1980 Refugee Act, which is current law but which Presidents have routinely exceeded.)

Prioritize Immediate Family Households. The RAISE Act would retain immigration preferences for the spouses and minor children of U.S. citizens and legal permanent residents.

Eliminated would be green card categories for foreign citizens who are:

- Adult parents of U.S. citizens
- Adult brothers and sisters of U.S. citizens
- Unmarried adult sons & daughters of U.S. citizens
- Married adult sons & daughters of U.S. citizens
- Unmarried adult sons & daughters of legal permanent residents

Create Temporary Visa for Parents in Need of Caretaking: For U.S. citizens who wish to bring elderly parents in need of care-taking to the United States, the RAISE Act creates a renewable temporary visa on the condition that the parents are not permitted to work, cannot access public benefits, and must be guaranteed support and health insurance by their sponsoring children.

Opening the Golden Door

As noted in the Daniel Di Martin "Opening the Golden Door" *City Journal* November 2022 article: New polling shows that most Americans recognize the need for more high-skilled immigration.

Americans want to admit more high-skilled legal immigrants like doctors and engineers, according to a new poll by the Manhattan Institute. The poll found that Americans want a system that, above all, admits people who won't be dependent on government welfare and who want to assimilate into the American economy and society.

Americans show their understanding of an important problem in the current system. Though the border crisis and illegal immigration get more attention, the United States faces an invisible immigration tragedy in all the physicians, engineers, entrepreneurs, and innovators who never make it to the U.S. because of our outdated process for legal immigration.

These missing doctors, engineers, and entrepreneurs hold back American innovation. Meantime, China has been making rapid progress in the number of patent filings relative to the United States. Canada and the U.K. are now the preferred destinations for international students seeking to study abroad. And a shortage of doctors exists in areas of the U.S. that are home to 98 million people. These are all symptoms of a breakdown that, if left unaddressed, will cause the U.S. to lose ground relative to China and other countries in the innovation race.

The Manhattan Institute poll, conducted by WPA Intelligence, found that more than 60 percent of Americans want legal immigration to be maintained or increased, while only 33 percent want it to be reduced. Half of Americans want more high-skilled immigrants, while only 13 percent want fewer. Even among those who want to reduce legal immigration, one-third want more high-skilled immigrants.

Majorities of all ethnic groups, and especially Hispanics and Asians, support increasing high-skilled immigration. Regarding low-skilled immigration, 33 percent want more, 23 percent want less, and the rest want no change.

Americans' support for high-skilled immigration may reflect a recognition of the fact that the U.S. currently places severe limits on it. Our current system is the product of the 1965 Immigration Act, which repealed the racial quotas prevalent since the 1920s and replaced them with a system that prioritizes family ties.

The United States has changed a lot since 1965, and so has the world.

We should revamp the system to prioritize immigrants based on their potential to assimilate and thrive economically, recognizing that we have a welfare state that traps generations of families in dependency.

The United States currently admits two categories of permanent newcomers: on the one hand, the immediate relatives of American citizens, who aren't subject to quotas; and, on the other hand, non-immediate family members, workers sponsored by employers, refugees, and those belonging to other small categories—all of whom are subject to quotas.

Immediate relatives include the minor children, spouses, and parents of U.S. citizens who are at least 21 years old. Foreigners are generally eligible for permanent residence (green cards) by virtue of their immediate relationship to an American relative, unless they have violated certain laws. The U.S. admits nearly 500,000 immediate relatives every year.

All other categories are subject to quotas. Congress updated the 1965 quota in 1990 to admit up to 421,000 immigrants to adjust for population growth during that period. Of these 421,000 spots, 226,000 are reserved for non-immediate family members of U.S. citizens and permanent residents, such as siblings and adult children of U.S. citizens.

Some 140,000 green cards are issued to immigrants because of their skills or because their work is in high demand in the U.S. (this includes investors). Finally, the U.S. awards some 55,000 green cards randomly in the annual "diversity" lottery to foreigners with at least a high school degree from countries that don't typically send many immigrants to the United States. Other immigrants are admitted as refugees, so long as they meet the legal definition, in numbers chosen by the president.

The 140,000 green cards issued to high-skilled foreigners represent only about 14 percent of all green cards issued. And only about 70,000 of these go to the high-skilled immigrants themselves since their dependents also get green cards and they count against the overall quota.

What's more, though the 1965 Immigration Act officially repealed racial quotas, in reality, it merely replaced discrimination by ethnicity with discrimination by country of birth. Per-country limits have resulted in decades-long wait times for Indian-born high-skilled immigrants living in the U.S. on temporary visas. And some of the children of these immigrants must self-deport once they turn 21, even though they have lived almost their whole lives in the U.S.

While skills- and employment-based immigrants all must meet stringent requirements—such as college degrees, extensive experience, and high salaries—family-based legal immigrants face no skills requirements or tests, not even for English-language ability. This is a senseless system, and Americans know it.

Our Manhattan Institute poll found that about two-thirds of Americans agree with the proposition that these qualities—willingness to assimilate, ability to fill needed jobs, low likelihood of dependence on government welfare, English proficiency, and family ties—should improve an immigrant's chances of being admitted. When asked to choose which factor is most important, 35 percent chose low likelihood of dependence on government welfare. In second and third place, respectively, are willingness to assimilate (24 percent) and ability to fill needed jobs (20 percent).

The literature on immigrant assimilation and economic outcomes backs up Americans in these views.

Like all Americans, immigrants earn higher incomes if they speak English well and hold a college degree. While a lively academic debate persists about whether recent immigrants are assimilating at the same rate as past ones, we know that the most successful immigrants are those who come to the U.S. when they're young, spend years here, have lined up job offers, have obtained higher education, and speak English.

A better approach to legal immigration would pool all green cards together and award points to applicants based on age (youth), education, employment, and English proficiency. This would result in immigrants who rely on less government assistance, pay more taxes, and perform jobs more likely to contribute to American innovation.

Other English-speaking developed countries learned long ago that prioritizing high-skilled immigration is good policy. Canada and Australia implemented points systems in 1967 and 1973, respectively, and now have the most highly educated immigrant populations of any developed nation. The United Kingdom followed suit after Brexit, and it's on track to admit fewer less-educated Europeans and more highly educated Asians (debunking any potential criticism that such a system would be racist or discriminatory).

Shifting the U.S. system toward allowing more high-skilled immigrants wouldn't require a major legislative overhaul by Congress. One simple but potent change would be to allow unused employment-based green cards from one year to carry over to the next in the same category, instead of going into the family-based system as they do now.

At the same time, all unused family-based green cards in each category could be carried over to the employment-based categories directly rather than into other family-based categories. Making this fix could shift tens of thousands of green cards toward high-skilled immigrants every year. Legislators could also divert the diversity and sibling green-card categories into the employment-based system. Both measures could end the decades-long green-card backlog for high-skilled immigrants from India and increase high-skilled immigration substantially.

An overlooked impact of shifting some family-based green-card categories into the employment-based system is that these high-skilled immigrants would sponsor family members who are likely, on average, more highly educated due to assortative mating. Therefore, expanding employment-based immigration would also raise the average education of the fewer family-based migrants that are admitted.

Most Americans want a system that opens golden doors to immigrants eager and able to contribute to our society. Such a system harmonizes with Ronald Reagan's vision of America as a "shining city upon a hill," one "teeming with people of all kinds living in harmony and peace." That's how Americans see their country, too.

Establish a Merit-Based Immigration System

From the "Solutions/Legal Immigration" section of the Heritage Foundation website dated August 2020:

The expression "a nation of immigrants" reflects the unique benefits that immigration has provided to the U.S. throughout our history. But the current legal immigration system is not designed for the 21st century, and it is failing both to maximize the benefits of legal immigration and to minimize the costs.

Under the current system, the U.S. provides lawful permanent residence—a green card—to around one million foreigners each year. In fiscal year (FY) 2017, for example, the U.S. granted 1.127 million green cards. Green cards are allotted according to decades-old statutes. As a result, the largest category of green card distribution is to family members of U.S. citizens and lawful permanent residents. In 2017, the U.S. granted 748,746 green cards—or about two-thirds—on the basis of a recipient's status as a family member or an immediate relative.

Of this subtotal, over half a million were given to spouses, children, and parents—"immediate relatives" under U.S. law—who are able to receive an unlimited number of green cards each year. By contrast, only 137,855 green cards were awarded based on employment. The Diversity Visa Program lottery issued around 50,000 visas, while refugees, asylees, and other categories totaled approximately 180,000 green cards.

By comparison, Canada granted 56 percent of its green cards in 2017 for economic reasons and Australia gave 62 percent of its permanent visas for economic reasons. Other nations also define "immediate relatives" more narrowly to include only spouses and minor children. These policies make sense because these countries are using immigration to maximize national interests.

By focusing on merit-based immigration, countries can ensure that immigrants contribute to the economy and will not consume government benefits at the expense of existing taxpayers. The U.S. system, however, for the most part, does not consider economic or fiscal considerations, and thus fails to maximize its national interests.

Beyond issues of money and economic growth, immigration is also about assimilating people with certain values and principles. Historically, governments and institutions at all levels have played an active role in the Americanization process. The Founders knew that the new country would attract even more immigrants, so they believed in assimilating and educating them, as well as the native-born, to inculcate the nation's philosophy into a new population, giving American democracy its "demos."

Over the past few decades, however, America has drifted away from assimilating immigrants: Elites in government, culture, and academia have led a push toward multiculturalism, which emphasizes group differences. Instead of E pluribus unum—out of many, one—assimilation is seen as a humiliating demand that the purportedly marginalized conform to the identities of their supposed oppressors. This view must not be allowed to control U.S. policies.

Recommendation: Establish a Merit-Based Immigration System

Congress should modify the family preference system and move to a new merit-based system of visas. A shift from family-based immigration to merit-based immigration would prioritize economically and fiscally beneficial immigration and better serve our national interest. Such a system should be designed in a way that recognizes that the market is the best and most objective way to identify those who will benefit the economy.

This starts with requiring immigrants to have an offer of employment (an objective market signal) or financial means of self-support before entering the country. The government would not be picking winners and losers among industries, job categories, or immigrants.

If there are more requests than available green cards, Congress could consider a limited points system or an auction that again would place emphasis on the market. For example, a company's offered compensation to the immigrant would have significant priority, as compensation provides objective evidence of market demand.

Other heavily weighted factors could include financial resources and assets, educational achievement, professional credentials, job experience, and fluency in English. These factors, while not perfect or completely objective measures, would focus on reasonable measures of economic and fiscal impact, avoiding both government micromanagement and burdening American taxpayers with higher levels of government welfare assistance.

One way to ensure that merit-based green card candidates are indeed working or otherwise providing significant benefit to the U.S. would be to make their legal permanent residence conditional for the first several years. To transition from a conditional lawful permanent resident (LPR) to full LPR status, immigrants should be required to maintain employment for most of the conditional period, although they would be allowed to switch jobs. The total period of time required to hold a green card before becoming a citizen—five years—would remain unchanged, but a requirement that the holder not be a public charge before becoming a U.S. citizen could be added.

Focus on the nuclear family and end chain migration. Congress should allow the number of immediate relatives granted residency to remain uncapped while restricting the definition of immediate relatives to spouses and minor children. Congress should cut all or almost all of the current family preferences for extended family, thus ending chain migration.

U.S. citizens could continue to sponsor their parents, but only for a renewable temporary visa that would not make them eligible for welfare benefits and that would require the citizens to provide proof of health insurance and financial support of their parents. It is also worth noting that extended family members may have other legal avenues for immigrating to the U.S.

End the Diversity Immigrant Visa ("Lottery") Program. Congress should eliminate the Diversity Immigrant Visa (DV) Program, which provides 50,000 immigrant visas annually to random individuals from countries with low rates of immigration to the United States. The United States should evaluate potential citizens individually.

Rather than leave to chance the question of who gets an immigrant visa, Congress should decide based on the qualifications of potential citizens, taking into consideration experience, professional credentials, and education. The Diversity lottery treats people not as individuals, but as the means to artificially create representation from various countries. Congress should end this system because it does not serve the national interest and discriminates based on national origin.

End per-country immigration caps. Under the Immigration and Nationality Act, immigrants are subjected to a per-country ceiling or cap. The arbitrary per-country caps should be eliminated and replaced with a system that serves the national interest. Over the years, numerous proposals have been introduced in Congress to revise or eliminate the per-country ceiling on the number of people granted employment-based lawful permanent residency.

Eliminating this cap could be done in a number of ways. H.R. 392, which was introduced in 2017 by then-Representative Jason Chaffetz (R–UT) and eventually gained over 300 cosponsors, is one example. H.R. 392 would have eliminated the per-country "limits for employment-based green cards, while doubling the limits for family-based immigrants."

End universal birthright citizenship. The granting of birthright citizenship to all children born in the United States regardless of the parents' immigration status is the result of a misinterpretation of the Fourteenth Amendment and is inconsistent with the intent of the amendment's framers. The legislative history of the amendment makes clear that its purpose was to bestow citizenship only on those who owed their permanent, undivided allegiance to the United States and were subject to the fullest extent of its jurisdiction.

In particular, this meant the newly freed slaves, who were lawful and permanent U.S. residents and not subject to any foreign power. Congress should clarify the federal definition of "citizenship" in a manner that conveys its consistency with the original understanding of the Fourteenth Amendment by explicitly stating that only the U.S.-born children of individuals subject to the complete jurisdiction of the United States are citizens by virtue of birth on U.S. soil. This would include the children of lawful permanent resident aliens referred to in *United States v. Wong Kim Ark*, but would exclude the U.S.-born children of illegal or temporarily present aliens.

Promote patriotic assimilation. Policymakers should overhaul policies that do not blend well with immigration. Concepts such as victimhood, oppressor–oppressed, compensatory justice, racial preferences, coercive diversity, etc., are harmful and should not govern policy. Congress must put an end to measures that coerce immigrants and their American children and grandchildren into pan-ethnic identity traps.

We must stop categorizing people as victims with protected status, and we should start mandating that they participate in all aspects of society. Immigrants come to the United States to be American, not to join synthetic nations within the nation. The executive branch should stop dividing society into groups by rescinding the 1977 Office of Management and Budget (OMB) directive, and its 1997 revision, that divides the population into "Hispanics," "Asians," etc., and the courts should finally declare racial preferences in admissions and government contracts to be unconstitutional.

Candidates for citizenship should demonstrate a strong understanding of America's language, history, and civic life. The patriotic rituals surrounding the naturalization ceremony should be augmented to reinforce the transformational character of the event. Once immigrants go through naturalization, they are expected to have no other national loyalty, whether to the lands of their birth or to a "nation within a nation."

The government should return to the guiding principle that once an immigrant is naturalized, he or she should be encouraged, in George Washington's words, to "get assimilated to our customs."

Public schools should reinforce these values and should not use "culturally responsive" teaching methods (used to teach even math), which divide children into different ethnic boxes. Rigorous studies indicate statistically significant positive effects of school choice or private schooling on the teaching of civic values, while the civics education provided by public schools is currently falling short.

Government schools must do a better job of instilling civic values, and policymakers at the state level should provide more charter schools and private school choice options for families.

Assimilation and Americanization is an essential correlate to immigration.

George Washington stated that immigration succeeds when "by an intermixture with our people, they, or their descendants, get assimilated to our customs, manners and laws: in a word, soon become one people."

Abraham Lincoln pointed out that the Founding ideas present in the Declaration of Independence can be grasped by immigrants. He said that they act as "the electric cord in that Declaration that links the hearts of Patriotic and liberty-loving men together."

In a 1919 letter to the American Defense Society, Theodore Roosevelt emphasized the importance of assimilation into American society, saying that "we should insist that if the immigrant who comes here in good faith becomes an American and assimilates himself to us, he shall be treated on an exact equality with everyone else."

14 - How Rampant Illegal Immigration Destroys the American Dream & Social Cohesion

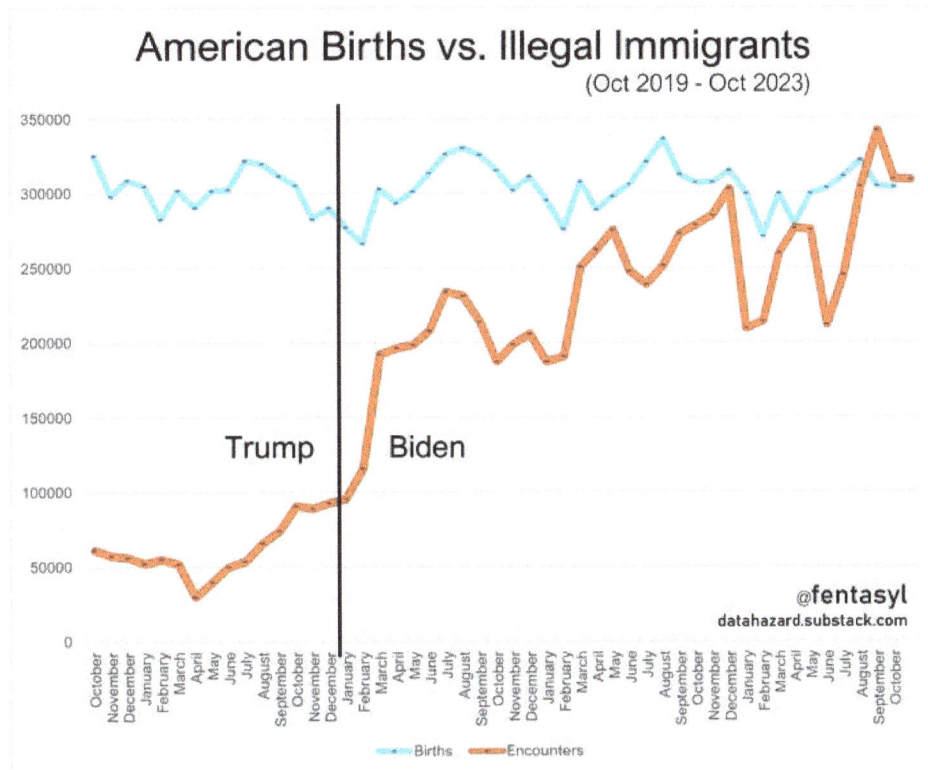

American Births vs. Illegal Immigrants
(Oct 2019 - Oct 2023)

Trump | Biden

@fentasyl
datahazard.substack.com

Births — Encounters

The Biden Administration remains committed to unlimited illegal immigration and is using sleight of hand and administrative abuse to achieve it. Meanwhile, it threatens that "unless Congress comes together in a bipartisan way to address our broken immigration and asylum system," which is code for mass amnesty, this deliberate chaos will continue.

No one should fall for the Biden Administration's misleading numbers or word games. Congress needs to defund these open-border operations, increase U.S. Immigration and Customs Enforcement resources to find and remove the Biden-released masses, and pass H.R. 2 through the Senate to bring true and lasting border security to America.

Since President Joe Biden took office, the number of illegal aliens encountered at the U.S. border has exceeded all historical records. Despite the legal requirement for mandatory detention of those caught entering illegally, the Administration's strategy has been to admit as many as possible on the pretext that they are seeking asylum.

The seemingly lower numbers now being claimed for encounters at the border post–Title 42 are an illusion created by the Department of Homeland Security's (DHS's) deliberate channeling of those seeking to enter the U.S. illegally to ports of entry (POEs) using Custom and Border Protection's CBP One mobile-phone application and through rampant abuse of parole.

Neither Congress nor the American people should be fooled by this charade: Illegal immigration remains at unprecedented, dangerous levels and will never be under control without an end to open borders and a change in policy.

Deceptive Numbers and Word Games Are Hiding Continued Mass Illegal Immigration Post–Title 42

As per the Simon Hankinson and Lora Ries "Deceptive Numbers and Word Games Are Hiding Continued Mass Illegal Immigration Post–Title 42" Heritage Foundation June 2023 update:

The Biden Administration claims that its "historic expansion of lawful pathways" has reduced "unlawful entries between ports of entry…70 percent since May 11, 2023," the day when Title 42 authority ended. When Title 42 expired, the US returned to using the decades-old Title 8.

But there has been no significant reduction of illegal entrants—they have simply been renamed and re-directed. Tens of thousands of illegal aliens whom the Border Patrol would have "encountered"—that is, administratively arrested—are now allowed to enter the country by the CBP Office of Field Operations inspectors at air and land POEs.

The crucial number for tracking the Biden surge in illegal immigration is how many total foreign nationals are allowed into the U.S. nationwide despite having no visa. That number remains exceptionally high, and April 2023 was the fourth-highest month on record. The Biden Administration is attempting to obscure this reality through unlawful action, botched accounting, manipulation of statistics, and taking advantage of a pliant and incurious press corps.

DHS's deceptive spin on numbers.

In a June 6, 2023, press release, the DHS boasted that border encounters were lower as a result of its supposedly tougher "Comprehensive Plan to Manage the Border After Title 42." In fact, the plan is a smokescreen for the underlying strategic objective: to let in as many illegal aliens as possible and punt them into a backlogged asylum and court system, in most cases without tracking their locations or court appearances.

Encounters with the Border Patrol have averaged 3,400 per day since May 11. Another 1,070 inadmissible aliens presented themselves at a POE each day, using Secretary Mayorkas' erroneously named "lawful pathway," and the CBP has expanded daily appointments to 1,250. That is 37,500 inadmissible aliens each month. This number does not include an additional 23,000 supposedly vetted and sponsored Cuban, Haitian, Nicaraguan, and Venezuelan nationals who entered in May through a special parole "pathway" that started in January.

These two mass-parole port programs add up to 60,500 inadmissible aliens per month. If this number were shifted back to the Border Patrol encounter data on the southwest land border, encounters would be back at, or above, the record 200,000 a month.

President Biden's "lawful pathways" are fictional—and illegal.

Since President Biden took office, the number of illegal aliens allowed into the U.S. has exceeded every historical record. In May 2023, the Administration put into effect its new Circumvention of Lawful Pathways rule. The intent of this rule was not to bring illegal immigration under control, much less to a halt. It was to channel as many illegal arrivals as possible toward POEs, away from the open border in between.

President Biden's DHS invented these "lawful pathways" by abusing limited immigration-parole power under current law, which Congress explicitly stated is to be approved "only on a case-by-case basis for urgent humanitarian reasons or significant public benefit." In clear violation of the law, the DHS has granted parole in blanket fashion to entire nations.

The DHS also expanded its mobile-phone application, CBP One, to aid the legal fiction and allow foreigners outside the U.S. to get advanced permission to apply for parole at a land port or interior airport. Successful applicants are allowed to enter the U.S.—without a visa, proven identity, or any evidence of persecution. They then receive parole from the CBP upon arrival.

The "[un]lawful pathways" programs so far include Afghanistan (evacuees), Ukraine, Cuba, Haiti, Nicaragua, and Venezuela, with 30,000 monthly appointments reserved for the latter four countries alone. The DHS is clearly intending to expand this abuse of parole to additional countries. The migrant processing centers that the State Department has just negotiated to build in Guatemala and Colombia are not intended to screen refugees under the long-established U.S. Refugee Admissions Program, but to identify yet more customers for the unconstitutional and unlawful parole programs.

Illegal entries are skyrocketing and removals cratering.

The "stiffer consequences for unlawful entry" that the DHS threatens are simply not credible, given its fiscal years 2023 and 2024 budget targets to deport only 29,389 criminal illegal aliens, and no apparent target for the millions of others in the U.S. illegally, including those with final orders of removal. The Administration is neither using all the detention beds that Congress provided nor adequately using GPS tracking in its alternatives-to-detention program.

The cartels and coyotes are well aware of the Administration's true agenda, and they will continue to make billions from trafficking people to the U.S. Congress must defund these open-border operations, increase U.S. Immigration and Customs Enforcement resources to find and remove the Biden-released masses, and pass H.R. 2 through the Senate to bring true and lasting border security to America.

The Biden Administration Has Finally Conceded We Have a Border Crisis. Now it's Time For Congress to Act

Per the Dan Stein "Stein: The Biden Administration Has Finally Conceded We Have A Border Crisis. Now It's Time For Congress to Act" Daily Caller October 2023 article:

Thirty-two months and nearly 9 million illegal border crossings (including "gotaways") into President Biden's term in office, his administration has finally acknowledged that there is a crisis at our border.

On October 5, 2023, the Department of Homeland Security (DHS) announced that it will waive 26 laws to "install additional physical barriers and roads (including the removal of obstacles to detection of illegal entrants) … to deter illegal crossings in areas of 'high illegal entry' into the United States" [emphasis added]. Mayorkas stated there was an "acute and immediate need to construct physical barriers and roads in the vicinity of the border of the United States."

In plain English, the DHS announcement indicates the administration's intention of resuming construction of the border wall that the president cancelled on his first day in office. It is also a tacit admission on the part of the administration that physical barriers along the border are effective at stemming the flood of illegal migration, and that halting construction of the wall was a mistake. So, too, were other policy decisions, like resuming large-scale catch-and-release of illegal migrants, ending the Remain in Mexico policy and terminating country of first refuge agreements with Central American governments.

The Biden administration, which has brazenly ignored countless requirements to enforce immigration laws, claimed that the decision to construct new wall was solely due to a legal requirement that they could not evade. Whether the move was precipitated by a sudden compulsion to comply with the law, or the realization that Election Day is only 13 months off and the American public is understandably alarmed about the disaster he has created at the border and in communities all across the country, Congress must act now to ensure that the border is secured.

The House of Representatives has already acted to achieve that goal. In May 2023, the House approved H.R. 2, the Secure the Border Act, and has continued to fight to include substantial parts of that bill in its FY 2024 DHS Appropriations bill.

Now that the White House has admitted we have a serious problem at our borders, it is time for the Democratic-controlled Senate to act as well. Republican Sen. Ted Cruz of Texas has introduced H.R. 2 in the Senate, which Majority Leader Chuck Schumer can schedule for a vote as a free-standing bill, or accept as part of a final budget deal that is hammered out between now and November 17. It should not go unnoticed that Sen. Schumer makes his home in New York City, which is reeling under the impact of the migrant influx that Mayor Eric Adams says "will destroy" the Big Apple if it continues.

Resuming border wall construction is a good first step to regaining control of the border, but it will take time.

There is much more that needs to be done that can have an immediate impact on the situation. Enactment of H.R. 2 would provide immediate relief at our borders and for communities all across the country that are being overwhelmed by this crisis.

The legislation now awaiting action by the Senate requires the construction of the border wall along no less than 900 miles of our southern border. Among other provisions, the bill provides funding to increase the ranks of the beleaguered Border Patrol to 22,000 agents and increases detention space, an essential step in ending wholesale catch-and-release of migrants pouring across the border. H.R. 2 also prevents this and subsequent administrations from creating unauthorized back doors to allow otherwise inadmissible aliens to enter the country by asserting virtually unlimited parole authority.

Sen. Cruz and his Republican colleagues have vowed to do all within their power to ensure strong border enforcement measures are included in the final FY 2024 funding bill. The announcement by the administration that it will resume building the border wall should open the door to bipartisan support for the common sense reforms that the bill offers to bring an end to a crisis that is overwhelming red and blue states alike.

It will be hard to undo the damage that has been caused by the Biden administration's systematic dismantlement of border and immigration enforcement. But the Senate, following the lead by the House, now has a green light to prevent the situation from getting even worse.

ESL Students Deserve a Better Education

From the Ohan Krishan "ESL Students Deserve a Better Education" *National Review* July 2022 article: With this century's influx of immigration into the United States, the number of students in American public schools who study English as a second language (ESL) has risen dramatically.

In 2020, the number of students enrolled in ESL classes was estimated at nearly 5 million. That's about 10 percent of all K–12 students in American public schools, and the number is projected to increase in the next decade. According to the Department of Education, from 2009 to 2015, the percentage of ESL students, also known as English learners (EL), "increased in more than half of the states, with increases of over 40 percent in five states." From 2010 to 2019, the percentage of ESL students in public high schools increased by 13 percent, from 9.2 to 10.4 percent.

Although many of the ESL students in American classrooms arrived in the United States as immigrants or refugees, most such students today are American citizens who were born here, commonly to immigrant parents. Though native-born, these students continue to have a poor grasp of English and lag behind their peers, with many remaining in ESL programs throughout their school years.

Graduation rates for ESL students lag behind those for non-ESL learners. To take the example of New York City, in 2017 the graduation rate for ESL students was 27 percent, compared with the average graduation rate for all New York City students of 72.6 percent, and a national graduation rate of 82 percent. ESL students rarely attend college, with a mere 1.4 percent of these students in New York State even taking college-entrance exams like the SAT or ACT.

Given the abysmal academic performance of ESL students in this country, the American education system should adopt policies to improve their academic outcomes. Let's start with the fact that the faculty for most ESL programs in the United States tend to be ill-equipped. The majority of states (31 states and the District of Columbia) have reported a shortage of teachers for ESL students as the population of English learners has grown dramatically.

Consequently, ESL education is often subpar, in that many ESL teachers lack the training or experience to meet the needs of ESL students. Jennifer Samson, an associate professor at the Hunter College School of Education in New York City, stated that "there's been a large increase in students who come from diverse backgrounds that are in schools and unfortunately, in many instances, teachers aren't adequately prepared to address their needs."

For children in immigrant communities, a deficient education results in a less successful integration into society and greater disparities in academic achievement. For instance, in 2018, a California education report showed that the academic performance of ESL students was lower than all other subgroups of students, including students of all races and socioeconomic levels and with disabilities.

Moreover, the results also indicated that the ESL students showed little to no improvement in reading and math scores despite increased funds to districts with more English learners. With lower graduation rates and test scores, ESL students are less likely to move on to higher education and high-skilled jobs.

The Left's Latest Political Scheme: Let Noncitizens Vote

As reported in the John Fund "The Left's Latest Political Scheme: Let Noncitizens Vote *National Review* January 2022 article: Despite misgivings, New York City's new mayor, Eric Adams, has rolled over for the city council and allowed more than 800,000 noncitizen residents to vote in future elections for mayor and all other city officials.

Starting in 2023, the city will have to print separate ballots for city races, since noncitizens will still be barred from voting in statewide and presidential elections. But make no mistake. The new New York law is part of a nationwide push to blur the very meaning of citizenship and promote noncitizen voting everywhere and for all offices.

There are few limits on how far the "woke" Left will go to change the rules of voting. In 2019, a majority of House Democrats voted to lower the federal voting age to 16 years, from 18. This week, Senate Democrats will try to ram through a bill that would nationalize elections by taking away the right of states to determine their own voting systems. Liberals will use any hysterical argument to justify this power grab: Representative Eric Swalwell (D.,

Calif.) even told MSNBC last week that if Republicans win November's midterm elections, "voting in this country as we know it will be gone."

New York City's law was promoted by former councilman Ydanis Rodríguez, who immigrated to the city from the Dominican Republic and is now the commissioner of the New York City Department of Transportation. If noncitizens "pay their taxes as I did when I had a green card," he says, "then they should have a right to elect their local leaders." He notes that the new law will limit the right to vote to legal residents and green-card holders.

But that's only because an earlier version of his legislation from 2013 that would have given the vote to illegal aliens simply generated too much political heat. Many backers of noncitizen voting acknowledge that since many illegal aliens also pay income, payroll, and sales taxes, they too should be allowed to vote. No doubt the advocates of the plan hope that the example of New York will fuel their goal of extending rights to illegal aliens. "As New York City goes, so goes the rest of the world," former New York City councilman David Dromm, an original backer of noncitizen voting, has boasted.

Until now, the movement he's a part of had made only snail-like progress. Six communities in Maryland allow it for local elections. Even in radical San Francisco, only 54 percent of voters in 2016 approved a measure to give voting rights to noncitizens in school-board elections. No significant legal challenges have been mounted against the smattering of cities that have allowed noncitizen voting.

But the new law in the nation's largest city will throw noncitizen voting into a high-stakes legal battle. The constitution of New York State clearly states that all citizens over the age of 18 are entitled to vote. While it is silent on allowing noncitizen voting, judges may require that right to be made explicit through the laborious process of amending the state constitution.

Given that 80 percent of noncitizens lean Democratic, they cite Al Franken 's 312-vote win in the 2008 U.S. Senate race in Minnesota as one likely tipped by noncitizen voting. That election also had profound consequences. As a senator, Franken cast the 60th vote to break the filibuster—a vote that was needed to make Obamacare law.

That kind of impact on national policy has prompted Senator Marco Rubio of Florida, himself the son of Cuban immigrants, to introduce a bill to prohibit federal funding to states and localities that allow foreigners to vote. "It's ridiculous that states are allowing foreign citizens to vote," Rubio says. "However, if states and localities do let those who are not U.S. citizens to vote in elections, they shouldn't get U.S. citizen taxpayer money."

I'm very much in favor of having people legally living in this country establish ties to the community and have a say in their governance. As Howard Husock, a senior fellow at the American Enterprise Institute, says, "the right way to bring noncitizens into the electoral process at the federal, state, and local levels is old-fashioned: encourage them to become citizens." It's not hard to go that route for legal residents—they must have been in the U.S. for five years, pay some fees, and pass a test, given in English, on U.S. institutions.

What is so unfair about the system we have now? The answer is that it doesn't suit the blatantly political imperatives of the woke Left, and that is a key reason the reason noncitizen voting must be rejected.

How Removing Unauthorized Immigrants From Census Statistics Could Affect House Reapportionment

From the Jeffrey S. Passel and D'Vera Cohn "How Removing Unauthorized Immigrants From Census Statistics Could Affect House Reapportionment" Pew Research Center July 2020 report:

Projected change in congressional seats after 2020 census

	Current # of House seats	Gain/loss due to census count based on ...		Projected total based on ...	
		Population change	Minus unauthorized immigrants	Population change alone	Pop. change minus unauthorized immigrants
Texas	36	3	-1	39	38
Florida	27	2	-1	29	28
Arizona	9	1	-	10	10
Colorado	7	1	-	8	8
Montana	1	1	-	2	2
North Carolina	13	1	-	14	14
Oregon	5	1	-	6	6
Alabama	7	-1	1	6	7
Minnesota	8	-1	1	7	8
Ohio	16	-1	1	15	16
Illinois	18	-1	-	17	17
Michigan	14	-1	-	13	13
New York	27	-1	-	26	26
Pennsylvania	18	-1	-	17	17
Rhode Island	2	-1	-	1	1
West Virginia	3	-1	-	2	2
California	53	-1	-1	52	51

Note: Current number of House seats based on 2010 census counts.
Source: Method of equal proportions applied to Pew Research Center projections based on Census Bureau population estimates and Pew Research Center estimates of unauthorized immigrants.

PEW RESEARCH CENTER

Since the first census of the United States in 1790, counts that include both citizens and noncitizens have been used to apportion seats in the House of Representatives, with states gaining or losing based on population change over the previous decade.

If unauthorized immigrants in the U.S. were removed from the 2020 census apportionment count – which the White House seeks to do – three states could each lose a seat they otherwise would have had and three others each could gain one, according to a Pew Research Center analysis based on government records.

If unauthorized immigrants were excluded from the apportionment count, California, Florida and Texas would each end up with one less congressional seat than they would have been awarded based on population change alone. California would lose two seats instead of one, Florida would gain one instead of two, and Texas would gain two instead of three, according to analysis based on projections of Census Bureau 2019 population estimates and the Center's estimates of the unauthorized immigrant population.

Alabama, Minnesota and Ohio would each hold onto a seat that they would have lost if apportionment were based only on total population change. Alabama filed a lawsuit in 2018 seeking to block the Census Bureau from including unauthorized immigrants in its population count.

In addition to these states, 11 more would gain or lose seats based on population change alone, whether unauthorized immigrants are included or excluded. Five states would gain one seat each: Arizona, Colorado, Montana, North Carolina and Oregon. Six states would lose one seat each: Illinois, Michigan, New York, Pennsylvania, Rhode Island and West Virginia.

The apportionment of seats in Congress is required by the U.S. Constitution, which says that the census will be used to divide the House of Representatives "among the several States according to their respective numbers, counting the whole number of persons in each State," except for enslaved people, who, until the late 1800s, were counted as three-fifths of a person, and certain American Indians.

The 14th Amendment eliminated the partial count of enslaved people, and the total American Indian population was added later to congressional reapportionment calculations. The number of seats in the House was fixed at 435 following the 1910 census. Each state gets one seat, and the remainder are assigned according to a complex formula based on relative population size.

The census count includes everyone living in the United States, except for foreign tourists and business travelers in the country temporarily, according to Census Bureau rules. For apportionment purposes since 1990, military and civilian federal employees stationed abroad and their dependents are counted as living in a state if they provided a state address in their employment records. The District of Columbia, Puerto Rico and U.S. Island area populations are excluded from the apportionment total because they have no voting representation in Congress.

Federal law requires the population totals from the decennial census be delivered to the president nine months after Census Day, meaning Dec. 31, 2020. The Census Bureau has requested Congress extend the deadline to April 30, 2021, due to the coronavirus pandemic, although the White House reportedly may push for a "timely census" fueled by $1 billion in additional funding. States would redraw congressional district boundaries to fit the new totals. The results would take effect for the Congress that meets in 2023.

In his memorandum announcing a new policy "to the extent practicable" in how congressional seats are divided up, President Donald Trump asserted that the president has discretion to decide who is considered an inhabitant of the U.S. for apportionment purposes. Some of the same groups that successfully challenged the White House attempt to add a citizenship question to the census last year said they also would sue to block any change in apportionment policy. Democrats announced they would hold an emergency congressional hearing to respond.

The Census Bureau does not regularly publish counts or estimates of unauthorized immigrants, although the Department of Homeland Security has done so. Last year, after the U.S. Supreme Court ruled against including a question about citizenship on the 2020 census, the president ordered the Census Bureau to assemble a separate database, using other government records, on the citizenship status of every U.S. resident. This has also been challenged in court.

The Center's analysis relies on assumptions about populations to be counted in the 2020 census and estimates of unauthorized immigrants. The actual figures used for apportionment will be different from these, and so the actual apportionment could differ regardless of whether unauthorized immigrants are excluded from the apportionment totals.

Our Missing Workers Are Not Missing Immigrants

As revealed in the Steven A. Camarota "Our Missing Workers Are Not Missing Immigrants" *National Review* April 2023 analysis:

The key problem for the U.S. labor market is not a lack of immigrant workers; rather, it's that too many working-age natives are sitting on the sidelines. Excluding inmates, the share of working-age U.S.-born men who hold a job, or are at least looking for one, has declined steadily since the 1960s.

The labor-force-participation rate of U.S.-born women rose until about the year 2000 and has declined since, even as the share of U.S.-born women with children has also declined significantly. The decline in employment is primarily among the U.S.-born non-college-educated, and this holds true whether one studies the 16-to-64, 18-to-64, or 25-to-54 age range.

Recessions tend to accelerate the decline: The labor-force-participation rate recovers somewhat with the economy but never reverts to where it was before the downturn. For example, the labor-force-participation rate for U.S.-born adults aged 18 to 64 without a bachelor's degree was 70.3 percent in the fourth quarter of 2022, compared with 71.4

percent in 2019 (before the pandemic), 74.8 percent in 2006 (before the Great Recession), and 76.4 percent in 2000 (before the dot-com crash).

We probably can never get back to the labor-force-participation rates for men that we observed in the 1960s or even the 1980s. But if U.S.-born men and women of working age had participated in the labor force in the fourth quarter of 2022 at the same rates at which they did in 2000, there would be an additional 6.4 million workers today.

Although rarely discussed in the context of immigration policy, the decline in the labor-force-participation rate of the native-born is hardly a secret. It has been studied extensively, for example, by the Obama White House and the Federal Reserve. One of the best books on the subject is Nicholas Eberstadt's Men without Work.

One reason why all the potential workers on the economic sidelines are often ignored in the public discourse is that many observers are distracted by deceptively low unemployment rates. But these statistics include only those who report that they have sought work in recent months. They do not include the roughly 54 million working-age people who are neither working nor looking for work.

The explanations for the decline in labor-force participation are as varied as the proposed solutions. Some blame the easily accessible welfare and disability systems. Others emphasize the large number of less educated men with criminal records, who have an especially difficult time finding willing employers. Some believe that structural changes in the economy—particularly the declining wages of the non-college-educated—are the real problem. Eberstadt emphasizes changes in the expectations and values related to work, including a decline in institutions that encourage it, particularly the family.

Competition with immigrants has also played a role in reducing the labor-force participation of natives. One large 2016 study by the National Academies of Sciences, Engineering, and Medicine concluded that immigration reduces wages for some U.S.-born workers, mainly the less educated, which reduces the incentive to work. An analysis of Equal Employment Opportunity Commission discrimination cases by my colleague Jason Richwine found that employers tend to favor foreign-born over native-born workers for manual-labor jobs.

More specifically, there is research showing that immigrants displace high-school-age Americans from the labor force.

More than one recent academic paper finds a geographic crowd-out effect: Immigrants tend to move into economically dynamic areas, reducing the incentive for natives to relocate there. Of course, not every job taken by an immigrant is one lost by a native, but allowing in millions of immigrant workers has consequences.

Some may think that immigrants take only the jobs that Americans don't want, but the U.S.-born make up the majority of workers in all but six of the 474 government-defined occupational categories. Even in the 20 occupations with the highest shares of immigrants, there are still 3.5 million U.S.-born workers. The idea that immigrants and natives never compete is simply untrue. It is true that most workers in agriculture are immigrants, but they constitute less than 1 percent of the total workforce, and there is already an unlimited guest-worker program to serve the needs of this tiny sector.

Beyond direct job competition between immigrants and natives, there is perhaps a more profound issue: Bringing in so many immigrant workers year after year allows us to simply ignore all the Americans who are out of the labor force and the social and other pathologies that follow their joblessness. After all, why worry about people on the economic sidelines when we can hire eager immigrants instead?

It may be tempting to throw up our hands and say, "Forget lazy Americans, let's just bring in immigrants who will work." But the higher costs of welfare, disability, law enforcement, and health care associated with low labor-force participation are paid by taxpayers. Moreover, the crime and social dysfunction that are so common among men who do not work affect everyone around them, and as more kids grow up in households where work is not the norm, the problem is likely to get worse.

Perhaps the most important reason we should care about those who remain out of the labor force is that they are our fellow Americans, even if some of them have made bad choices. Most immigrants, even illegal immigrants, are decent people who come to America for the same reasons people have always come: They are simply looking for a better life.

But our fellow Americans, particularly those who are struggling, should have a much greater claim on us than prospective immigrants. Immigration is much more than a way for employers to hire new workers, and the current level has serious implications for everything from schools to the health-care system to physical infrastructure to culture.

To allow more immigration simply as a way to address a labor-force shortage is to turn a blind eye to the destructive impact of idleness among our fellow citizens. Our fellow citizens are entitled to the American Dream—but evidence indicates that upward economic mobility has declined and income inequality has risen in the United States in recent decades.

Sadly, in 2020, a poll found only 54 percent of American adults thought the American Dream was attainable for them, 28 percent believed it was unattainable for them personally, while 9 percent rejected the idea of the American Dream entirely. Younger generations were also less likely to believe in the American Dream than their older counterparts and women are more skeptical of achieving the American Dream than men are.

15 – Common Sense Legislation to Fix America's 'Broken' & 'Abused' Immigration System

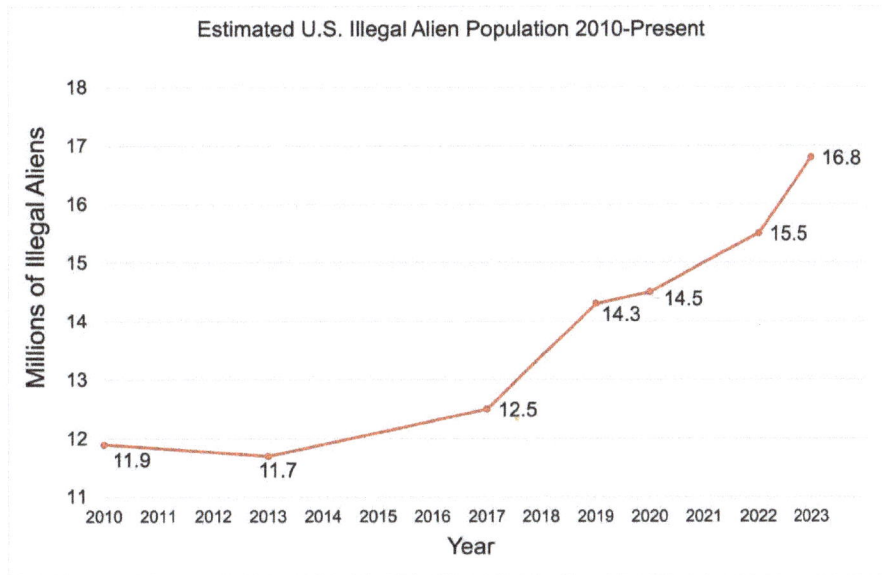

Estimated U.S. Illegal Alien Population 2010-Present

Credit: FAIR.

As our final chapter, it's longer than usual, but extremely important, because it covers many action plans and proposal to fix America's immigration system, and the Heritage Foundation is leading the way in this regard.

From the "What Immigration Reform Should Look Like" Heritage Foundation December 2023 policy paper: For over two centuries, the United States has welcomed millions of people from every corner of the globe. And today, we lawfully admit over one million people every year. That is more than any other country in the world.

The debate is not about whether we should allow immigration – it's about how we do so in a way that protects American sovereignty, respects the rule of law, and is beneficial to all Americans. So what does a thoughtful agenda for American immigration reform look like? Here are four guiding principles:

Number one: We must respect the consent of the governed, that is the will of the people. Individuals who are not citizens do not have a right to American citizenship without the consent of the American people.

That consent is expressed through the immigration laws of the United States. Through those laws, we the people invite individuals from other countries, under certain conditions, to join us as residents and fellow citizens.

Number two: We cannot compromise national security and public safety. Every nation has the right, recognized by both international and domestic law, to secure its borders and ports of entry and control what and who is coming into its country.

A disorganized and chaotic immigration system encourages people to go around the law and is a clear invitation to those who wish to take advantage of our openness to harm the nation. Secure borders, especially in a time of terrorist threat, are crucial to American national security.

Number three: Becoming a citizen means becoming an American. We must preserve patriotic assimilation. The founding principles of this nation imply that an individual of any ethnic heritage or racial background can become an American. That's why we have always welcomed immigrants seeking the promises and opportunities of the American Dream.

Patriotic assimilation is the bond that allows America to be a nation of immigrants. Without it, we cease to be a country with a distinct character, becoming instead a hodgepodge of different groups.

If we are to be a united nation, living up to our motto of e pluribus unum, out of many, one...we all must understand and embrace a common language, history, and civic culture. And that not only benefits America, but also those immigrants and their families who aspire to prosper here.

Number four: Our lawmakers must respect the rule of law and immigration is no exception. Failure to enforce our immigration laws is unfair to those who obey the law and follow the rules to enter the country legally. Those who enter and remain in the country illegally should not be rewarded with legal status or other benefits. When politicians condone such behavior they only encourage further illegal conduct.

Based on these principles, immigration reform should include transitioning to a merit-based system. We should end practices like chain migration, birthright citizenship, the visa lottery, arbitrary per-country immigration caps, and any form of amnesty for those here illegally. We must close loopholes that prevent enforcement of our laws and have overwhelmed immigration courts, allowing illegitimate asylum claimants and other lawbreakers to remain in the U.S. indefinitely.

And we must take on these issues one by one. A comprehensive "deal" subjects the fate of policies with universal appeal to the fate of the most controversial topics. The key is to begin by working on the solutions on which most Americans agree.

We must and can address this issue in a manner that is fair, responsible, humane, and prudent. This is too important an issue to not get right and too important an issue to be driven by partisan agendas. Let's stay focused on what is best for the welfare of all Americans, both those of today and those of the future.

The Biden Border Crisis Has Gone on Long Enough (How Congress Can Help)

Per the Lora Ries "The Biden Border Crisis Has Gone on Long Enough (How Congress Can Help)" Heritage Foundation November 2022 policy proposition:

Earlier this year, the Heritage Foundation, the America First Policy Institute, the Federation for American Immigration Reform (FAIR), the National Border Patrol Council, and other organizations put forward a plan the next Congress should follow. It was endorsed by border security professionals like former acting Customs and Border Protection Commissioner Mark Morgan, former acting Immigration and Customs Enforcement (ICE) Director Tom Homan, and former DHS acting deputy secretary Ken Cuccinelli—and for good reason. The letter dated May 11, 2022 stated:

Dear Congressional Leaders,

When the 118th Congress opens with new majorities in both chambers, it will be in large part because Americans have rejected the Biden Administration's purposeful dismantling of our nation's borders and our immigration enforcement infrastructure. Congress should be emboldened with the mandate to immediately legislate unflinchingly, ensuring that neither this nor any future administration is again able to weaponize loopholes in the immigration system—and defiantly refuse to follow plain law—to purposefully drive mass illegal immigration to the United States. Such weaponization has dramatically reduced the security of the border, allowing cartels to expand their operational control, which seriously jeopardizes our nation's safety, health, and national security. The opportunity to legislate has been missed in several previous Congresses but the stakes are too high for it to be missed again.

As of the writing of this letter, over 2.8 million illegal aliens have been apprehended at our southwest border entering or attempting to enter the United States since Biden took office. The administration has admitted that at least 42 of these aliens were on the terror watchlist. Over 1.6 million illegal aliens, including known gotaways, are now in the interior of the United States—more than the population of states such as Hawaii, Maine, Montana, and New Hampshire. Moreover, these record numbers largely occurred prior to the lifting of Title 42, the last remaining significant measure holding back even higher, crushing numbers. The worst is yet to come.

The results for the United States have been devastating. Criminal transnational cartels have increased their control. According to some reports, they are now making more money in controlling human smuggling than they make from drugs. As the border is overwhelmed, the drugs are flowing in. Fentanyl deaths are now the leading cause of death for Americans ages 18-45.

This purposeful crisis was made possible by glaring loopholes in our immigration system that have been allowed to persist for far too long. This problem is most evident with the asylum system, which Congress intended to protect a narrow category of people persecuted by their governments based on one of several enumerated grounds. In practice, economic migrants without viable claims for protection continue to flood the system by simply claiming "credible fear" and are released into the interior of the country where their likelihood of being removed when their claims are denied is minimal.

To regain our sovereignty, integrity, and security, Congress must close these loopholes and make other changes so that the Biden Administration cannot continue this self- inflicted crisis. It is not enough for the next Congress to simply restart construction of the border wall system or adjust resources at Customs and Border Protection.

While those are important measures required to secure the borders, without closing the loopholes and other changes, the Biden Administration's policies will continue to act as a powerful magnet, attracting millions of illegal aliens into our country.

To retake control of our border and properly address what is sure to be an electoral mandate, we urge you to unite behind flagship introductory legislation for the upcoming Congress. Most importantly, it must include the following components:

- Exclude amnesty of any type;

- Create an authority to immediately expel illegal aliens across the border;

- Substantially reform the asylum system, including clarifying that an alien is ineligible for asylum in the U.S. if they traversed a safe third country;

- End the disparate treatment of contiguous vs. non-contiguous unaccompanied alien children (UAC) under the Trafficking Victims Protection Reauthorization Act (TVPRA) and terminate the Flores settlement agreement that limits detention of family units to 20-days; and Raise the credible fear standard;

- Mandate and appropriate resources for completion of the border wall system;

- Increase CBP personnel & resources such as holding facilities and border technology, and clarify CBP's authority to issue Notices to Appear (NTAs);

- Increase ICE resources for Deportation Officers (DO) and detention beds so they are commensurate with the mandatory detention and removal requirements in the law, and clarify DO's authority to make custodial arrests;

- End the abuse of the parole authority;

- Restrict prosecutorial discretion to remove it as the catch-all excuse for limiting immigration enforcement;

- Mandate full implementation of the Migrant Protection Protocols (MPP), otherwise known as Remain in Mexico, and appropriate funds for permanent court facilities along the border at every POE;

- Codify *Matter of A-B-,* which clarified that gang violence and domestic violence are not grounds for asylum;

- Eliminate discretionary grants of employment authorization under 8 U.S.C. 1324A(h)(3);

- Clarify that the entry into the U.S. of any alien with known or suspected ties to, or association with, a terrorist entity is prohibited until that alien has been properly vetted and the Secretary has determined that no threat exists;

- Establish further restrictions on federal court jurisdiction to review claims brought by aliens and their associations/organizations; and

- Reverse *Arizona v. United States* and give states independent authority to participate in the enforcement of immigration laws.

These are the primary components that would constitute a robust border security bill. These are the fixes that, if enacted and enforced, would end the border crisis. Ending the border crisis will be a mandate from the American people. This is how you do it.

It's important to note, however, that this is only an initial step. Leadership should put additional, shovel-ready border security and immigration bills on the floor throughout the next Congress— from ending sanctuary policies to protecting American workers.

Congress will also need to conduct aggressive oversight and properly control federal funding mechanisms.

An Agenda for American Immigration Reform

From the Heritage Foundation immigration reform policy team of Kay James, James Carafano, John Malcolm and Jack Spencer comes the far reaching and comprehensive February 2019 "An Agenda for American Immigration Reform" policy agenda outline:

To address immigration and border security in a manner that keeps America free, safe, and prosperous, Congress must take a step-by-step approach to the full range of issues: Reject amnesty and open borders; secure our southern border; end "catch and release;" combat transnational criminal networks, fraud, humanitarian abuses, and human trafficking; restore the integrity of immigration enforcement; and sustain productive regional engagement.

Our flawed immigration system cannot be fixed without adoption and implementation of these initiatives. Legal immigration reform should include transitioning to a merit-based system, ending practices like birthright citizenship, and promoting patriotic assimilation. Moreover, legal immigration, border security, and enforcement reforms should stand alone and advance on their own merits, not bundled into a comprehensive package.

Foreword

Per Kay Coles James, past President of the Heritage Foundation:

The toughest policy issues call for honest, clear, and bold solutions. Throughout my career in government and public policy, few issues have presented challenges like America's flawed immigration system and broken borders. For decades, Congress has tried and failed to deliver satisfactory solutions. This situation cannot stand. Now is the time for action.

This is too important an issue not to get right and too important an issue to be driven by partisan agendas. Immigration, after all, is one of the fundamental building blocks that help to make America the unique nation that it is.

For over two centuries, the United States has welcomed millions of people from every corner of the globe. During the Constitutional Convention of 1787, James Madison expressed his wish "to invite foreigners of merit and republican principles among us. America was indebted to emigration for her settlement and prosperity." That open, welcoming attitude exists today, as evidenced by the fact that the United States lawfully admits over a million foreigners per year, more than any other country.

With that in mind, the research team at the Heritage Foundation set out to deliver a complete answer to the challenges posed by border security and immigration.

Fixing the problem requires some tough medicine. Amnesty is not the answer. We must stand strong against those who advocate open borders. Our borders must be secured—and yes, that means building more barriers (a wall if you will) along our southern border. Individuals who are here illegally do not have a right to stay. Our laws have to be enforced. It is only fair to millions of Americans (who have followed them) that we expect those who join our great nation to respect its laws and add to its wealth and welfare.

Introduction

Despite a protracted debate on illegal immigration and border security that has lasted more than a decade, Congress has failed to address these issues in a manner that will keep America free, safe, and prosperous. This must end. The role of Congress is critical in crafting a proper path forward. Congress must address the full range of issues but take a step-by-step approach.

Legal immigration reform is another important step. An effective legal immigration system is part of a powerful deterrent against illegal immigration, protects American sovereignty, respects the rule of law, preserves American identity, and contributes to the wealth and welfare of the nation. These reforms include transitioning to a merit-based system, ending practices like birthright citizenship, and promoting patriotic assimilation.

In addition, it is important that legal immigration, border security, and enforcement reforms not be bundled into a comprehensive package. They should stand alone and advance on their own merit.

The agenda for reform outlined in this paper was developed by:

Assessing the problem. Our current system stands on a clear constitutional foundation that established the sanctity of popular sovereignty, respect for the rule of law, and the protection of human liberty. Over many decades, that clarity has been lost through political compromise and contradictory impulses. In addition, shifting security, economic, and cultural challenges that often promote contrasting priorities must also be addressed.

Establishing principles. To remain true to the foundation established by the Constitution and adapt border security, enforcement, and immigration law to address contemporary challenges, our research identified four key principles to evaluate and prioritize our recommendations:

Respect the consent of the governed. There is no right to become a citizen or remain unlawfully present in the U.S.; there is no place in America for a policy of "open borders."

Preserve patriotic assimilation. This is a nation where immigrants become American, and it must remain so.

Do not compromise national security and public safety. We must know who is entering the country and have resilient and efficacious means to screen against malicious threats and remove people that break the law or are a danger to American citizens.

Respect the rule of law. Those who enter illegally are violating the rule of law; the Law of Nations Clause of the Constitution guarantees the power to control immigration.

Defining an agenda for action. This agenda provides a guide for mastering the challenges faced by legislators in crafting an effective agenda that addresses present-day conditions. These recommendations include border security, enforcing the law, and legal immigration reforms. They conform to the four guiding principles outlined above.

Taken together, this package of reforms addresses the scope of what needs to be accomplished to restore the integrity and effectiveness of border and immigration enforcement, preserve the sovereignty of Americans, and modernize the legal immigration system.

Assessing the Problem

Significant factors complicate the problem of reforming legal immigration, enforcement, and border security. The United States cannot have borders and immigration that better serve all Americans without addressing them.

Chain Migration and the Visa Lottery. For some time, the family reunification preference has been a means to extend green cards well beyond the nuclear family. In essence, once a family member is legally allowed within the country, a chain begins that extends out to the farthest reaches of a family. Similarly, while family-based immigrants contribute to the U.S. economy in some ways, depending on their education and skill level, the current system does not consider their skills or productivity, but merely their relation to someone already living in the United States.

A review of the economic literature from scholars of various ideological and academic leanings finds that higher-skilled and more-educated immigrants bring greater economic benefits from entrepreneurship and innovation than lower-skilled or less-educated immigrants bring.

Given the finite number of available slots for entering this country, family migration is coming not merely at the expense of the U.S. and its citizens, but also at the expense of other people who want to come to the U.S. legally.

The per-country limit has led to significant backlogs for immigrants from large immigrant-sending countries such as India, Mexico, the Philippines, and China. This policy ignores both the value of and the justification for individual immigrants coming to the U.S. exclusively because of their country of origin, and the result is clearly discriminatory.

Similarly, the Diversity Immigrant Visa Program, otherwise known as the "visa lottery" program, awards 50,000 visas per year drawn from a "random selection among all entries to individuals who are from countries with low rates of immigration to the United States."

A lottery is hardly a purposeful design for determining who can become an LPR—and eventually a citizen—in the United States.

Meritless Legal Claims. The current immigration court system has a backlog of over 800,000 cases. Immigrants with viable claims of asylum or other meritorious claims for legal status in the United States should have confidence that their cases will be handled in a fair, legal, and expeditious manner, but because our immigration court system is overwhelmed, outdated, and in dire need of reform, cases of merit are lumped in with meritless cases, each of which can takes years to resolve.

It is a common dilatory tactic for aliens to file applications for relief that lack legal and factual merit due to the length of time required for immigration judges to adjudicate them, especially those on a nondetained docket. This tactic is perhaps the single greatest reason for the backlog of cases pending adjudication in every immigration court throughout the Executive Office of Immigration Review (EOIR), especially for recent entrants seeking asylum and withholding of removal.

All trial participants know that if the alien expresses any sort of harm, the immigration judge is duty-bound to provide them a Form I-589 application for relief, grant a continuance for them to file the application, and then schedule an individual hearing on the merits and prepare an exhaustive oral or written decision if the application is denied.

Given the common practice by the Department of Homeland Security (DHS) not to appeal discretionary decisions favorable to the alien to the Board of Immigration Appeals (BIA), many immigration judges apparently grant relief from removal to avoid the considerable time required to prepare an oral or written decision.

In every state, federal, and administrative court system in the United States, judges routinely issue summary decisions in cases based solely on the documents filed in the record and without taking any testimony from the parties or their witnesses under oath in open court. If a typical state court judge were required to issue the same degree of precision, either orally or in writing, in every case and for any request by the parties, as is currently the practice in immigration courts, their docket would be at a virtual standstill.

Another issue of concern is the Ninth Circuit Court of Appeals misinterpretation of the *Flores v. Reno* settlement agreement or "Flores settlement," in which the Clinton Administration agreed to release unaccompanied alien minors within 20 days. This encourages illegal border crossing and fraudulent claims.

The Ninth Circuit recently held that the Flores settlement requires the DHS to release from its custody all children, even if they are with their parents, so when adults cross the border with a child, DHS is required to release the child within 20 days. Since the parents broke the law by crossing the border illegally, the government tries to detain and prosecute them after their asylum claims are completed, and since that will take more than 20 days, the DHS has to release the child, leaving the government with the choice of detaining the parents or releasing them all.

With the end of the zero-tolerance policy, the DHS has decided that it will simply release anyone accompanied by a child in order to comply with *Flores v. Reno*. As a result, the number of family units crossing the border is skyrocketing, overwhelming the DHS's ability even to figure out basic details of their travel and exhausting the immigration court system.

Legislative Missteps. The current structure of quotas based on the INA has put tremendous strain on the system, increasing illegal immigration and jeopardizing the ability of the United States to recruit and retain those who want to come to America to improve their own lives and those of other Americans. The resulting frustration with the immigration system from virtually every ideological perspective has contributed significantly to the demand for reform.

In the past few decades, the national debate has revolved around how best to enforce existing immigration laws, how best to stem the tide of illegal immigration into the United States, what we should do about the millions of illegal immigrants residing in the United States, and what should be done to change our legal immigration system.

One approach to solving these interrelated and vexing issues has been to pass a "comprehensive immigration reform" law. On its surface, that approach might seem reasonable, as we are a country of problem solvers, and anything Congress can do to fix a problem once and for all is necessarily appealing.

In practice, however, the fix-it-all-at-once approach has contributed to the problem and should not be repeated. The most recent example is the Reagan-era Immigration Reform and Control Act of 1986, otherwise known as the Simpson-Mazzoli Act.

Amnesty kicked in immediately, and over 3 million illegal aliens gained legal status in the United States. Employers found ways to skirt the new law: They complied technically with the verification requirements by accepting what looked like genuine work documents, regardless of what they reasonably should have known about the veracity of the documents.

In addition, money for increased border security was not appropriated immediately and by 1989, illegal immigration border crossings had increased as the lure of jobs and future amnesty drove millions to cross the U.S.-Mexico border. Strengthened border patrols in some areas merely dispersed illegal crossings to other areas. Today, millions of illegals are living inside the United States due to a lack of increased border security.

Cross-Border Criminality. While borders have been an uncommon avenue for terrorism, they have served as a common path for crime. Specifically, the activities of transnational criminal organizations (TCOs) pose significant challenges to the U.S.

The opioid crisis has refocused attention on the issue of drug smuggling. For example, in FY 2017, the U.S. seized 62,331 pounds of cocaine at POEs and 9,346 pounds elsewhere along the border as well as 1,196 pounds of fentanyl at POEs. DHS estimates that at ports of entry, it seized only 2.1 percent of the inbound cocaine, a percentage that has been dropping in recent years.

Human trafficking is another challenge posed by criminal organizations. Human trafficking involves the use of force, fraud, or coercion to induce some sort of labor or act. Thousands of individuals are trafficked into the U.S. every year for the purposes of forced labor and sex slavery. TCOs also engage in countless other illegal behaviors, including money laundering to move and hide their ill-gotten wealth and weapons smuggling, among many others.

Illegal Immigration Across Land Borders. However, illegal immigration is more problematic than the overall numbers indicate. The recent use of caravans (and now trains) to come to the U.S. threatens to overwhelm U.S. borders. The rise in children and family migrants also makes enforcement much harder by consuming additional resources. This includes the Flores settlement, which makes it very difficult to detain and remove unaccompanied children and family units, especially when combined with asylum claims, which also have increased drastically in recent years.

Furthermore, loopholes that prevent enforcement are drawing more illegal immigrants to the U.S. because the U.S. simply cannot remove them fast enough. An agreement with Mexico by the Trump administration to keep asylum seekers in Mexico while they apply for asylum is a significant step in the right direction, but the loopholes remain.

Illegal Immigration Through Visa Overstays. In recent years, about two-thirds of new illegal immigrants have been those who overstayed a visa, not those who crossed the border illegally. In FY 2017, 606,926 visitors and other non-immigrants overstayed their visas for more than 60 days, evincing a desire to remain in the U.S. illegally.

In FY 2016, there were 628,799 overstays for more than 60 days. Holders of student, work, or cultural exchange visas are the most likely to overstay, and Visa Waiver Program (VWP) visitors are the least likely: Overstay rates of countries like Djibouti, Eritrea, and the Solomon Islands were more than 20 percent, while rates for VWP nations like Japan, Monaco, and Singapore were less than 0.2 per cent.

Culture and Society. Over the past few decades, America has drifted away from assimilating immigrants. Elites in government, the culture, and the academy have led a push toward multiculturalism, which emphasizes group differences. This transformation has taken place with little input from rank-and-file Americans, who overwhelmingly support assimilation.

This oppressor–oppressed narrative is now taught to America's K–12 schoolchildren, reinforced in colleges and universities, and repeated constantly in the media and the culture. The rhetoric of victimhood has also had profound effects on policy toward immigrants.

It is not just that assimilation is no longer encouraged; it is now actively discouraged by governments at all levels, most perniciously in the schools, workplaces, and all other centers of public life. Rather than an invitation to be included in the American community, assimilation is now described as a humiliating demand that those who are presumed to be marginalized must conform to the identities of their supposed oppressors.

Previous immigrants assimilated to American life and succeeded, but indoctrinating people into the victimization narrative has not produced successful immigrants: Instead, it has only produced more and more people claiming victim status. Interpreting all disparities of outcome through a lens of racism preempts any serious discussion of differences in culture, behavior, and interests and how those differences might help or hinder someone from succeeding in this country.

Current Family-Based vs. Needed Merit Based Immigration System. The current family-based immigration system, which allows and encourages immigrants to go far outside their immediate family to sponsor dozens of other relatives to emigrate to the United States, takes away the ability of the American people to choose who gets to immigrate to this country and become members of our society. Instead, that choice is made by the immigrant and inures to the benefit of extended family members, leading to chain migration.

The opportunity for economic advancement is the key reason many come to the United States, but that leaves to chance who decides to take concrete steps to come to America and better their lives, and when and how they do that. A better system is one that expands and reforms employment-based immigration policies and moves away from a primarily family-based system. Attracting the best and brightest from around the globe, based on their skills and education and the demand signal of the market, while not injuring the economic and job opportunities of America citizens, is in our national interest.

Immigration programs like the diversity visa program and the per-country immigration caps may have made sense in the past, but they make little sense in a 21st century immigration system that is designed to select future Americans in a purposeful manner based on merit, their skills, and the demands of an ever-evolving and dynamic work force, regardless of their race, ethnicity, or national origin.

Inextricably intertwined with reforming the legal immigration system is the dire need to recommit ourselves to policies that live up to our national motto, *E Pluribus Unum*: out of many, one.

Welfare and Dependence on Government. Obviously, much more than education or skills should go into a decision about whether to admit this or that type of person. At the same time, however, ignoring those objective qualities and leaving to chance who one allows to become a citizen is not a prudent way to remain a country that can compete and thrive in the global economy.

Today, legal immigration by lower-skilled immigrants (those with a high school degree or less) imposes substantial fiscal costs on U.S. taxpayers. Congress must decide whether admitting large numbers of lower-skilled immigrants serves the national interest. Part of that decision must include the costs of doing so.

Legal immigrant households receive significantly more welfare, on average, than U.S.-born households. Overall, the fiscal deficits or surpluses for legal immigrant households are the same as or higher than those for U.S.-born households with the same education level, but the fiscal burden imposed by lower-skilled immigrants is not principally due to means-tested welfare. The welfare benefits received are large, but the combined benefits received from Social Security, Medicare, public education, and population-based services are significantly larger.

Over the past decade and a half, an average of 228,000 legal, lower-skilled adult immigrants have arrived in the U.S. each year. Around 45 percent of lower-skill legal immigrants did not have a high school degree, and 55 percent had only a high school degree. In addition to the annual inflow of 230,000 lower-skill legal immigrants, there was a matching annual inflow of 240,000 illegal lower-skill immigrants on average during the period.

Any effort to legalize the future inflow of illegal immigrants would, therefore, increase future fiscal costs.

Guiding Principles for a Reform Agenda

If it is to deal sensibly and effectively with immigration reform, Congress must rise above the politics of the moment and "take the time to deliberate and develop a clear, comprehensive, meaningful, and long-term policy concerning immigration, naturalization, and citizenship that is consistent with the core principles, best traditions, and highest ideals of the United States."

This is difficult in a political environment that is consumed with the topic of the moment.

The first step is to start with common-sense principles, as good policies flow from sound principles. To this end, based on the contemporary challenges that are frustrating effective reform, our research identified four principles that should guide Congress in reforming the nation's immigration system, enforcement, and border security.

Principle #1: Respect the consent of the governed. The United States is a sovereign nation. The very idea of sovereignty implies that each nation has the responsibility and obligation to determine its own conditions for immigration, naturalization, and citizenship.

Individuals who are not citizens do not have a right to American citizenship without the consent of the American people as expressed through the laws of the United States. Through those laws, the people of the United States invite individuals from other countries, under certain conditions, to join them as residents and fellow citizens. Congress has the constitutional responsibility "[t]o establish an uniform Rule of Naturalization" that sets the conditions of immigration and citizenship and ensures the fairness and integrity of the legal process by which immigrants enter the country legally and, in many cases, become American citizens.

Principle #2: Do not compromise national security and public safety. Every nation has the right, recognized by both international and domestic law, to secure its borders and ports of entry and thereby control the goods and persons coming into its territory. Americans have always been and remain a generous people, but that does not mitigate the duty imposed on the United States government to know who is entering, to set the terms and conditions of entry and exit, and to control that entry and exit through fair and just means.

This task is all the more important after the events of September 11, 2001. A disorganized and chaotic immigration system encourages the circumvention of immigration laws and is a clear invitation to those who wish to take advantage of our openness to harm this nation. Secure borders, especially in a time of terrorist threat, are crucial to American national security.

Principle #3: Preserve patriotic assimilation. The United States has always welcomed immigrants who come to this country honestly, with their work ethic and appreciation of freedom, seeking the promises and opportunities of the American Dream. This is because the founding principles of this nation imply that an individual of any ethnic heritage or racial background can become an American.

However, those same principles also call for—and a successful immigration policy is only possible by means of—a deliberate and self-confident policy to assimilate immigrants and educate them about this country's political principles, history, institutions, and civic culture.

This may be a nation of immigrants, but it is more accurate to say that this is a nation where immigrants are Americanized, sharing the benefits, responsibilities, and attachments of American citizenship. While the larger formative influence occurs through the social interactions and private institutions of civil society and through public and private education, the federal government has a significant, albeit limited, role to play in ensuring the success of this crucial process.

Patriotic assimilation is the bond that allows America to be a nation of immigrants. Without it, America either ceases to be a nation with a distinct character, becoming instead a hodgepodge of groups, or it becomes a nation that can no longer welcome immigrants. It cannot be both a unified nation and a place that welcomes immigrants without patriotic assimilation.

Principle #4: Respect the rule of law. Immigration is no exception to the principle that the rule of law requires the fair, firm, and equitable enforcement of the law. Failure to enforce immigration laws is unfair to those who obey the law and go through the regulatory and administrative requirements to enter the country legally.

Those who enter and remain in the country illegally are violating the law, and condoning or encouraging such violations causes a general disrespect for the law and encourages further illegal conduct.

Forgiving the intentional violation of the law in one context because it serves policy objectives in another undermines the rule of law. Amnesty is appropriate only when the law unintentionally causes great injustice or when particular cases serve the larger purposes of the law.

Those who break immigration laws should not be rewarded with legal status or other benefits and should be penalized on any road to citizenship.

The power to control immigration is built into the very definition of sovereignty.

Under the Law of Nations Clause of the Constitution, Congress is granted authority over immigration policy. The foundational writers of the laws of nations, whose works the Founders followed, agreed that immigration, because it necessarily deals with foreign governments and foreign nationals, falls under this clause. Nevertheless, the executive has clear authority to enforce our nation's immigration laws.

Essential Elements of an Effective Reform Agenda

Implement effective border security. Congress must appropriate funding for cost-effective border security measures paired with robust enforcement. The U.S. must build a system that welds all of the nation's border assets into a single coherent security enterprise that deploys the right asset to the right place at the right time. This will require key investments in border infrastructure, organization, technology, and resources. These initiatives include such controversial but essential tools as additional border "wall," expanded detention space, and (as required) the temporary and efficacious use of support from the Department of Defense.

Take a more deliberate approach to border staffing. With the Inspector General expressing serious concerns about Customs and Border Protection's ability to hire and use new agents effectively, Congress and the Administration should proceed deliberately and realistically in providing funds for this purpose.

Provide more funding for Coast Guard acquisitions. This will ensure that the Coast Guard can acquire the right mix of vessels, including Fast Response Cutters and Offshore Patrol Cutters, as well as appropriate unmanned aerial systems.

Improve U.S. government public affairs efforts to discourage illegal immigration. As a component of a broader regional strategy to prevent illegal immigration, a targeted public affairs campaign to inform would-be migrants about the dangers of the journey and U.S. immigration law would serve to deter caravans. In the past, a caravan was in Mexico City for nearly a week, and during that time, the U.S. government missed an opportunity to provide the migrants with information on entry requirements into the U.S. Instead, the migrants were provided with inaccurate information and coached by left-wing activists. Clearly, U.S. government efforts to dissuade migrants about illegal immigration to the U.S. are not working.

Align U.S. assistance funding levels to Mexico with U.S. national security interests. A safer and more prosperous Mexico will reduce the security threats to the U.S., alleviate the drivers of illegal immigration, and allow both countries to focus on productive matters in the bilateral relationship. Yet U.S. assistance to Mexico in the form of the Merida Initiative has decreased from the all-time high of $639.2 million in FY 2010 to $130.9 million in FY 2017.

Assess the efficacy of the Central American development package, the U.S. Strategy for Engagement in Central America. Following the 2014 unaccompanied-minor crisis at the U.S. southern border, the U.S., El Salvador, Guatemala, and Honduras launched this program to address the factors driving illegal migration in the region. Guatemala's northern neighbor Mexico collaborates with the U.S. in an effort to mitigate these shared challenges. The volume and frequency of illegal immigration toward the U.S. indicates a shortcoming. Congress should request impact reports from implementing agencies that gauge whether the programs are meeting their intended objectives.

Improve Central America's border security capacity. Uncontrolled borders in the northern triangle are a long-standing problem. The insecurity in these regions allows criminality to proliferate and mass movements of people across state lines. The U.S. and Mexican governments should work with their regional counterparts to improve their border security policies and programs. They should support El Salvador, Guatemala, and Honduras in expanding border patrols to ungoverned areas, modernizing border crossings, and encouraging the creation of joint border patrols. The U.S. Department of Homeland Security should host an annual high-level border-control working group to share best practices with the region.

Elevate the standard of cooperation with regional governments. Foreign aid investments by U.S. partners have led to few tangible improvements, and continued illegal immigration is causing U.S. policymakers to question the utility of foreign aid investments by the U.S. Rather than cutting assistance, Congress and the Administration should evaluate whether current foreign assistance conditions have produced measurable improvements in the region.

Dealing with Illegal Immigration and Unlawful Presence

Do not grant amnesty. Amnesty undermines the rule of law and encourages more unlawful migration.

Grants of amnesty, regardless of the form of the reward they give to aliens who knowingly enter or remain in the U.S., discourage respect for the law, treat lawbreaking aliens better than law-following aliens, and encourage future unlawful immigration into the United States.

If America suddenly awards legal status to aliens unlawfully in the United States, it will be treating them better than aliens abroad who follow America's immigration procedures and patiently await their opportunity to get a visa authorizing them to come to the United States.

Such action—as past amnesties have proved—will also spur more aliens to enter or remain unlawfully in the United States in the confident expectation that Congress will continue to enact future amnesties that provide aliens unlawfully in the U.S. a shortcut to legal status. The government should pursue a measured set of approaches to a wide variety of immigration issues, but in all events, it should exclude amnesty for aliens unlawfully in the United States.

Do not legalize Deferred Action for Childhood Arrivals (DACA). DACA was the unilateral executive program implemented by President Barack Obama without appropriate legal authority or the approval of Congress. This effort is fundamentally flawed, amounts to an amnesty, and will only encourage even more illegal immigration.

Give immigration law judges summary judgment and contempt authority. As of October 24, 2018, 786,303 immigration cases were pending in immigration courts, up from 186,090 in 2008. During that same 10-year period, the average wait time for the disposition of a case in immigration court went from 438 days in 2008 to 718 days in 2018. This is unacceptable and needs to change.

One of the main reasons for the huge backlog is the fact that immigration judges do not have the summary judgment authority that is common to federal and state court judges. Summary judgment authority allows judges to refuse to schedule cases that lack legal merit, but because immigration judges do not have that authority, meritless cases clog the dockets. Congress should amend existing statutes to give immigration judges this authority.

Amend the Immigration and Naturalization Act in response to *Sessions v. Dimaya*. In 2018, the U.S. Supreme Court held in *Sessions v. Dimaya* that a part of the Immigration and Nationality Act used to deport criminal aliens was unconstitutionally "vague."

The Court refused to approve the removal of a permanent resident alien after his second felony conviction for first-degree burglary because it was not one of a long list of specific offenses that are considered "aggravated" felonies that subject an alien to deportation and was not a "crime of violence."

Aliens who are legally in this country are guests who should be allowed to remain here only as long as they abide by our laws. When someone commits a felony of any kind, it is a very serious offense. When someone repeatedly commits misdemeanor crimes, that is also evidence that he or she has no respect for our laws and should not be allowed to remain as a guest in our country. This federal law is overly complicated and should be simplified to read as follows: "Any alien convicted of a felony offense or of two or more misdemeanor offenses, regardless of their nature, under the Federal or the State or the Territorial laws of the United States, shall be deported."

Do not change the authority for temporary relief from deportation to allow de facto amnesty or a path to citizenship. Any legislation that addresses the status of DACA recipients, persons in temporary protected status, or persons in other programs should not allow open-ended residence in the United States or grant a path to citizenship. Temporary relief from deportation or removal should be for a reasonable, defined period. Aliens should be required to reapply for admission to the United States after deportation or removal.

Adjust authorities for permission to reapply for admission based on significant reductions in illegal immigration. Aliens who have been unlawfully present in the United States for over one year (with the exception of aliens who entered the United States before April 1, 1997) and are deported or removed must wait at least 10 years before applying for permission to enter the U.S. Based on significant reductions in illegal immigration, it might be appropriate to adjust this requirement to offer an incentive to illegal immigrants to leave the U.S. voluntarily and seek to return through lawful immigration or a non-immigrant visa. Similarly, Congress might consider adjustments for requirements to qualify for cancellation of removal, but only after substantial and sustained reductions in illegal immigration. No program should include an automatic pathway to citizenship.

Allow for the sharing of Social Security no-match data with the Department of Homeland Security and expand E-Verify to the extent practical. The illegal workforce is too big to address through police action alone. The quickest gains in enforcement with the least effort and expense will come from giving employers the incentive to follow the law and avoid hiring illegal labor. Specifically, the government needs to target its enforcement efforts to encourage employers to verify the work statuses of employees whom they have reason to believe may be unauthorized to work—as they are already required to do by law—and to cease employing unauthorized workers.

Improving Immigration Enforcement

Increase funding for immigration court judges, prosecutors, and associated staff. The U.S. immigration adjudication and court system is falling farther and farther behind. More immigration judges, prosecutors, and staff to assist in immigration proceedings, as well as more U.S. Citizenship and Immigration Services (USCIS) asylum officers, are essential to enforcing U.S. immigration laws in a timely and effective manner.

Adjust the asylum claim process. Congress can improve the asylum system in many ways. Rather than applying for asylum at U.S. borders, asylum seekers travelling to the U.S. southern border should be required to have their asylum claims heard by a USCIS asylum officer at a U.S. consulate in Mexico. Interviewers should also ask the asylum seeker why he or she did not assert asylum in other countries, such as Mexico.

Immigration officials should consider failure to explain the refusal to pursue asylum in other countries in making their decisions. Congress could also consider new standards that make it even harder for illegal border crossers to claim asylum. The Administration should also pursue safe-third-country and other agreements with countries in Latin America to promote better control of the asylum process.

Close the loopholes. For example, Congress should reject the Ninth Circuit's recent interpretation of the Flores settlement. Flores has been interpreted to require DHS to release from its custody all children, even if they are with their parents. Thus, when adults cross the border with a child, DHS is required to release the child within 20 days.

Since the parents broke the law by crossing the border illegally, the government tries to detain and prosecute them after their asylum claims are completed, and since that will take more than 20 days, the DHS has to release the child, leaving the government with the choice of detaining the parents or releasing them all. Congress should legislate to allow accompanied children to remain with their parents while awaiting asylum adjudication or prosecution of misdemeanor violations of immigration law.

Strengthen immigration enforcement. U.S. laws must be enforced if additional illegal immigration is to be deterred. The U.S. should judiciously increase the number of Immigration and Customs Enforcement (ICE) agents; expand the 287(g) program that trains and deputizes state and local law enforcement officers to assist ICE in enforcing U.S. immigration laws; curb sanctuary cities; expedite removals of illegal immigrants caught at U.S. borders; streamline the removal process; increase resources to immigration courts; and ensure that aliens show up at court hearings by maximizing the use of detention facilities.

Strengthen the 287(g) program. Designed to enable state and local government to help enforce federal immigration laws, 287(g) was under assault during the Obama Administration, which sought to cut funding, access to, and use of the program. Congress should seek to widen 287(g) usage by increasing funding for the program and requiring DHS to enter into a 287(g) agreement with any state and local governments that request entry into the program—with significant consequences should DHS not meet this requirement in a timely fashion.

Ramp up comprehensive immigration-fraud evaluations. The U.S. is a generous nation that provides many people with immigration benefits, but there are many who abuse the system. Given the value of U.S. visas and citizenship, the U.S. should do more to investigate fraud, both on a case-by-case basis and through more complete assessments and investigations.

Do not address legal immigration reform in a comprehensive "deal." Instead, advance legal reforms on their own merit. In 2007 and in 2013, comprehensive efforts failed to get through the legislation process, and the policy faults of each of those efforts will be present in any bill that tries to address too many topics at once. In these cases and in all future efforts, the trade-offs that must be made to compromise with partisan demands will peel off potential supporters and mire the legislation in political and policy problems.

A compromise on immigration is not like a compromise on other issues: Satisfying partisan demands cannot be made without breaching principles. A comprehensive reform effort subjects the fate of policies with universal appeal to the fate of the most controversial topics. For instance, everyone agrees that asylum cases should be adjudicated much more quickly, but that reform has yet to be made because it is wrapped up in the failed comprehensive efforts of the past.

The key is to begin by working on the solutions on which many can agree rather than insisting on a comprehensive approach that divides Americans. Humanitarian reforms like asylum standards should be addressed in legislation that is separate from legislation that implements merit-based legal immigration. Washington must implement the mandates already on the books, follow through on existing initiatives, and employ the authorities that Congress has already granted before taking on new obligations.

Establish a merit-based immigration system. Congress should modify the family preference system and move to a new merit-based system of visas. This shift from family-based to merit-based immigration would prioritize economically and fiscally beneficial immigration and better serve the national interest.

Such a system should be designed in a way that recognizes that the market is the best and most objective way to identify those who will benefit the economy. This starts with requiring immigrants to have an offer of employment or financial means of self-support before entering the country. The government would not be picking winners and losers among industries, job categories, or immigrants.

The offer of employment is an objective market signal. If there were more requests for green cards than were available, Congress could consider a limited points system that again would place emphasis on the market. Another approach would be to implement an auction system whereby employers would pay for the permits of the immigrant labor they need.

One way to ensure that merit-based green card candidates are indeed working or otherwise providing significant benefit to the U.S. would be to make their legal permanent residence conditional for the first several years. In order to transition from a conditional lawful permanent resident (LPR) to full LPR status, immigrants should be required to maintain employment for most of the conditional period even though they would be allowed to switch jobs. The total period of time required to hold a green card before becoming a citizen—five years—would remain unchanged, but a requirement that the holder not be a public charge before becoming a U.S. citizen could be added.

Focus on the nuclear family and end chain migration. Congress should allow immediate relatives to remain uncapped while restricting the definition of immediate relatives to one's spouse and minor children. Congress should cut all or almost all of the current family preferences for extended family, thus ending chain migration. U.S. citizens could continue to sponsor their parents, but only for a renewable temporary visa that would not make them eligible for any welfare benefits and would require the citizens to provide proof of health insurance and financial support of their parents. It is worth noting that these extended family members may have other legal avenues for immigrating to the U.S.

End the Diversity Immigrant Visa ("Lottery") Program. Congress should eliminate the Diversity Immigrant Visa Program, which provides 50,000 immigrant visas annually to random individuals from countries with low rates of immigration to the United States. The United States should evaluate potential citizens individually. Rather than leave to chance the question of who gets an immigrant visa, Congress should decide on the qualifications of potential citizens and take into consideration their experience, professional credentials, and education.

The Diversity lottery treats people not as individuals, but as the means to create representation from various countries artificially. Congress should end this system because it does not serve the national interest and discriminates based on national origin.

End per-country immigration caps. Under the Immigration and Nationality Act, employment-based immigrants are subjected to a per-country ceiling or cap. The arbitrary per-country caps should be eliminated and replaced with a system that serves the national interest.

End universal birthright citizenship. The universal granting of birthright citizenship to all children born in the United States regardless of the parents' immigration status is the result of a misinterpretation of the Fourteenth Amendment and is inconsistent with the intent of the amendment's framers. The legislative history of the amendment makes clear that its purpose was to bestow citizenship only on those who owed their permanent, undivided allegiance to the United States and were subject to the fullest extent of its jurisdiction.

In particular, this meant the newly freed slaves, who were lawful and permanent U.S. residents and not subject to any foreign power.

Congress should clarify the federal definition of "citizenship" in a manner that is consistent with the original understanding of the Fourteenth Amendment by explicitly stating that only the U.S.-born children of individuals subject to the complete jurisdiction of the United States are citizens by virtue of birth on U.S. soil. This would include the children of lawful permanent resident aliens referred to in *United States v. Wong Kim Ark* but would exclude the U.S.-born children of illegal or temporarily present aliens.

Granting automatic citizenship has a serious and often devastating financial impact on American taxpayers by rewarding and encouraging illegal or exploitive immigration. Medicaid and its state corollaries dole out over a $1 billion annually just to cover the costs of physical births to illegal alien mothers, whose children are rewarded with citizenship—a status from which the entire family draws substantial benefits.

Promote Patriotic Assimilation. Congress must put an end to measures that coerce immigrants and their American children and grandchildren into pan-ethnic identity traps. We must stop categorizing them as victims with protected status and start mandating that they participate in all aspects of society. Immigrants came to be American, not to join synthetic nations within the nation.

Candidates for citizenship should demonstrate a strong understanding of America's language (English), history, and civic life. The patriotic rituals surrounding the naturalization ceremony should be augmented to reinforce the transformational character of the event. Once immigrants go through naturalization, they are expected to have no other national loyalty, whether to the lands of their birth or to a "nation within a nation."

The government should return to the ethos that once an immigrant is naturalized, he or she should be encouraged, in Washington's words, to "get assimilated to our customs."

Public schools should therefore reinforce these values and not, as they do now, divide school children into ethnic boxes to teach even math according to "culturally responsive teaching."

Government schools must do a better job of instilling civic values, and policymakers at the state level should provide more charter schools and private school choice options for families.

Their charters include their own mission statements and curricula and have a separate school board. We should be encouraging the growing number of civically minded charter schools, such as the Great Hearts and Barney Charter initiatives.

The Way Forward

Together, these recommended policies, if adopted and implemented, would address the contemporary challenge of the need to fix broken borders and a flawed immigration system in a manner that is at once fair, equitable, responsible, humane, and prudent. They represent an agenda that is focused on what is best for the welfare of all Americans.

With that in mind, a quote by President John F. Kennedy seems fitting as we close out this chapter.

"As each new wave of immigration has reached America, it has been faced with problems... Somehow, the difficult adjustments are made and people get down to the tasks of earning a living, raising a family, living with their neighbors, and in the process, building a nation."

Appendix

20 Ways States Can Prevent Illegal Immigration - Heritage Foundation:
https://thf_media.s3.amazonaws.com/2022/States_Immigration_Reform_Booklet.pdf

40 *MADNESS* Textbook Titles: https://www.fratirepublishing.com/madnessbooks

Biden's Border Crisis: Examining Policies That Encourage Illegal Migration:
https://www.risch.senate.gov/public/_cache/files/d/f/df4e21bf-322e-455c-a61b-bd7aeba13f70/BE79EBB318BE1CA8FD4B4AC24B661D6A.final-migration-report-biden-s-border-crisis.pdf

Center for Immigration Studies (CIS): https://cis.org/Immigration-Statistics-Data-Portal

Federation for American Immigration Reform (FAIR): https://www.fairus.org/

Fiscal Burden of Illegal Immigration on United States Taxpayers: 2023 Cost Study, The - FAIR:
https://www.fairus.org/issue/publications-resources/fiscal-burden-illegal-immigration-united-states-taxpayers-2023

H.R. 2 - Secure the Border Act of 2023: https://rules.house.gov/bill/118/hr-2

Heritage Foundation, The:
https://www.heritage.org/search?contains=illegal%20immigration&range_start=2020-10-01&range_end=2023-10-31&type=All&date_offset=&page=0

Judicial Watch: https://www.judicialwatch.org/jwtv/

Migration Policy Institute (MPI): https://www.migrationpolicy.org/

National Review:
https://www.nationalreview.com/immigration/?utm_source=footer&utm_medium=desktop&utm_campaign=topics&utm_term=seventh&utm_content=immigration

Numbers USA: https://www.numbersusa.com/

SAPIENT BEING PROGRAMS: https://www.sapientbeing.org/programs
- **Free Speech Alumni Ambassador (FSAA) Program**
- **Make Free Speech Again On Campus (MFSAOC) Program:**
- **Sapient Conservative Textbooks (SCT) Program**

Glossary

Adjustment of Status - The process through which certain noncitizens apply for permanent resident (that is, green card) status from within the United States, as opposed to applying from abroad. (Applying from abroad is referred to as "consular processing".)

Admissible - A noncitizen who may enter be "admitted" to the United States because he/she is not excludable for any statutory reason or has a waiver of excludability.

Admission - The decision of the Department of Homeland Security (DHS) to allow or not allow a noncitizen at a United States border or port-of-entry to enter the United States. Whether a person is admitted to legally come into the U.S. and on what date may determine whether that person will be eligible for immigration applications that he/she might file in the future.

Affidavit of Support - A form filed by a United States citizen or lawful permanent resident (known as the sponsor) on behalf of a noncitizen seeking lawful permanent residence (a green card) in the U.S. The affidavit is intended to verify that the sponsor has sufficient income to support the persons intending to immigrate to the U.S. It is a legally enforceable contract against the sponsor.

Affirmative Asylum - The process in which asylum-seekers in the U.S. voluntarily present themselves to the U.S. Government to ask for asylum. Noncitizens who have not been apprehended by DHS are eligible to file an affirmative asylum application.

Aggravated Felony - A term created by statute to refer to a list of specific crimes and categories of crimes that if attached to noncitizens, the government then determines them to be aggravated felons.

Alien - Or illegal alien, is a person who is not a citizen of the United States and who is in any immigration status, including lawful permanent residents (holders of "green cards"), temporary visa holders, and undocumented ("illegal") foreign nationals.

Alternatives to detention (ATD) - ICE programs using electronic monitoring or enhanced supervision which supplements use of formal detention.

Amnesty - A commonly-used term for programs established by the Immigration Reform and Control Act of 1986 (IRCA) that made it possible for many previously- undocumented non-citizen to legalize their immigration status.

Apprehension - In immigration terms, the capture of a noncitizen who may not be legally allowed to be in the U.S. Captures made at or near land borders or at "interior checkpoints" are generally made by Border Patrol agents, who work for the Customs and Border Patrol (CBP) division of the Department of Homeland Security. These usually entail noncitizens who are attempting to enter the U.S. or who have recently entered. In addition, agents within the Immigration and Customs Enforcement (ICE) division of the Department of Homeland Security apprehend persons in the "interior" of the U.S., that is, usually further from the border.

Arriving Alien - A noncitizen applicant for admission at a port-of-entry who either: (1) is coming or attempting to come into the United States, (2) is seeking to travel through the U. S. on to a foreign destination, or (3) has been intercepted by U.S. authorities in international or U.S. waters and brought into the U.S.

Asylum - A legal status sought by a noncitizen who claims to be afraid of harm in their home country.

Beneficiary - A noncitizen on whose behalf a United States citizen, lawful permanent resident, or United States employer has filed a petition. The purpose of the petition is for that person to receive legal immigration status as a result of this relationship.

Board of Immigration Appeals (BIA) - The highest U.S. administrative body for interpreting and applying immigration laws. It is within the Executive Office for Immigration Review of the Department of Justice. The BIA has nationwide jurisdiction to hear appeals from certain decisions rendered by Immigration Judges and by some officials of the Department of Homeland Security.

Cancellation of Removal - A means of avoiding removal (deportation) and obtaining permanent residence (green card). It cannot be obtained by direct application, but only during a removal hearing in Immigration Court.

Child - In legal terms, an unmarried person under 21 years of age who, if not a United States citizen, must meet certain legal requirements with regard to legitimacy (wedlock), parentage, or other factors, in order to be eligible for certain immigration benefits.

Citizen - A person who owes permanent allegiance to the United States, and who enjoys full civic rights (for example, the right to vote in elections and to run for elective office)

Citizenship and Immigration Services (USCIS) - A bureau of the Department of Homeland Security responsible for the administration of immigration benefits and services, such as processing applications for residency and citizenship

Conditional Resident - A noncitizen granted permanent resident status on a conditional basis due to a relationship with a qualified person, generally a United States citizen spouse. Conditional residents must file a second petition within a designated time frame in order to retain United States residency.

Credible Fear Interview - An abbreviated interview of a non-citizen who arrives in the United States with false or no documents (and is therefore subject to Expedited Removal) and who expresses a fear of persecution in one's own country or a desire to apply for asylum.

Customs and Border Protection (CBP) - A bureau of the Department of Homeland Security responsible for patrolling the borders and monitoring the movement of goods and people into and out of the U.S. and is also part of the Department of Homeland Security. The responsibility for protecting U.S. borders was transferred from the Department of Justice's now-defunct Immigration and Naturalization Service (INS) to the Immigration and Customs Enforcement (ICE) component of the newly-created Department of Homeland Security in 2003.

Department of Homeland Security (DHS) - Is the United States government agency charged with protecting the nation. The DHS also offers and administers immigration and citizenship services. These are the DHS-affiliated agencies that work with immigration issues: U.S. Citizenship and Immigration Services (USCIS). U.S. Customs and Border Protection (CBP). U.S. Immigration and Customs Enforcement (ICE).

Department of Justice (DOJ) - The Department of Justice also deals with some immigration matters. The Executive Office for Immigration Review (EOIR) makes determinations in immigration cases. The immigration courts and Board of Immigration Appeals (BOA) are independent of the DHS. The immigration courts are charged with interpreting, administering, and enforcing federal immigration laws, including appellate reviews and administrative hearings.

Deportation - The administrative process involving the removal of a person from the U.S. who is not a U.S. citizen. Under the Illegal Immigration Reform and Immigrant Responsibility Act of 1996, the formal term for deportation was changed to "removal".

Diversity Visa - An immigrant visa lottery program established by the Immigration Act of 1990. It makes up to 55,000 immigrant visas per year available to persons from countries with low admission rates to the United States, in an attempt to diversify the immigrant pool to the U.S.

Employer Sanctions - The employer sanctions provision of the Immigration Reform and Control Act of 1986 (I.R.C.A.) prohibit employers from hiring, recruiting, or referring for a fee non-citizens known to be unauthorized to work in the U.S. Violators are subject to a series of civil fines for violations or criminal penalties when there is a pattern or practice of such violations.

E Pluribus Unum - Out of many, one

Executive Office for Immigration Review (EOIR) - The full title of the office with oversight responsibilities for the immigration court and the Board of Immigration Appeals. It is within the Department of Justice and is abbreviated as EOIR.

Expedited Removal - A process in which federal immigration officials immediately remove noncitizens seeking to enter the U.S. who are not authorized to so enter.

Green Card - A card given to lawful permanent residents (LPR) of the U.S.

Homeland Security Act of 2002 - Congressional legislation that created the Department of Homeland Security (DHS). Passed by Congress in the aftermath of the events of 9/11, it was reported to be the largest government reorganization in 50 years. The law went into effect in 2003. It called for the placement of many government functions, previously spread over many agencies, into a single department. It placed most immigration responsibilities, formerly administered by the Immigration and Naturalization Service (INS), into the new department. The INS ceased to exist after the creation of DHS.

I-94 Form - The Arrival-Departure Record Card, is a form used by U.S. Customs and Border Protection intended to keep track of the arrival and departure to/from the United States of people who are not United States citizens or lawful permanent residents

Illegal Alien - Or alien, is a person who is not a citizen of the United States and who is in any immigration status, including lawful permanent residents (holders of "green cards"), temporary visa holders, and undocumented ("illegal") foreign nationals.

Illegal Immigration Reform and Immigrant Responsibility Act of 1996 (IIRIRA) - Congressional legislation that substantially revised the Immigration and Nationality Act.

Immediate Relative - An immigrant who is exempt from the numerical limitations imposed on immigration to the United States due to his/her close relationship to a U.S. citizen.

Immigration Act of 1990 - Increased the limits on legal immigration to the U.S., revised grounds for exclusion and deportation, authorized temporary protected status to noncitizens of designated countries, revised and established new non-immigrant admission categories, and revised naturalization authority and requirements.

Immigration and Customs Enforcement (ICE) - The responsibility for the enforcement of immigration laws within the U.S. borders was transferred from the Department of Justice's now-defunct Immigration and Naturalization Service (INS) to the Immigration and Customs Enforcement (ICE) of the newly-created Department of Homeland Security in 2003. These responsibilities include apprehension, detention, and removal of noncitizens.

Immigration and Nationality Act (INA) - The primary statute relating to the immigration, temporary admission, removal, and naturalization of noncitizens. Congress passed the I.N.A. in 1952 and has amended several times since, including in 1965, 1980, 1986, 1990, and 1996.

Immigration and Naturalization Service (INS) - The name of the former branch of the U.S. Department of Justice. It was responsible for a variety of immigration services and enforcement of immigration laws. The INS ceased to exist after its responsibilities were transferred to the newly-created Department of Homeland Security in 2003.

Immigration Court - An administrative court responsible for adjudicating immigration cases in the U.S. Cases involve noncitizens who generally have been charged by the Department of Homeland Security (DHS) with being in violation of immigration law.

Immigration Judge - An attorney appointed by the Attorney General to act as an administrative judge within the Executive Office for Immigration Review within the U.S. Department of Justice. Immigration Judges conduct formal court proceedings in determining whether a noncitizen should be allowed to enter or remain in the U.S., in considering bond amounts in certain situations, and in considering various forms of relief from removal.

Immigration Marriage Fraud Amendments (IMFA) of 1986 - Passed in order to prevent and/or discover immigration-related marriage fraud.

Immigration Reform and Control Act of 1986 (IRCA) - Legislation passed by Congress. A significant provision of this law established a mechanism to allow members of two groups of previously-undocumented persons to legalize their immigration status.

Inadmissible - The immigration status of a noncitizen who does not qualify to enter or remain in the U.S. because of a prohibited status or activity.

Inspection - The process by which U.S. immigration officials determine whether people can enter the U.S. It usually occurs at a port-of-entry at a land border or international airport. It is conducted by Immigration Inspectors who are employed by U.S. Customs and Border Patrol, which is part of the Department of Homeland Security.

Labor Certification - The process for U.S. employers to recruit and employ certain noncitizen workers.

Lawful Permanent Resident (LPR) - An immigrant who has been granted a status allowing him/her to live and work permanently in the U.S. Most LPRs are eligible to apply to naturalize after five years, though shorter waiting periods apply to certain categories of LPRs.

Migrant Protection Protocols (MPP) - In December 2018, the Trump administration announced the creation of a new program called the "Migrant Protection Protocols" (MPP 1.0)—often referred to as the "Remain in Mexico" program.

Moral Turpitude - A classification of crimes committed by noncitizens which might justify their deportation from the U.S. or denial of certain immigration benefits.

Naturalization - The process by which immigrants become U.S. citizens.

Non-Immigrant - A noncitizen who wants to enter the U.S. for a temporary period of time and for a specific purpose. Unlike "immigrants", visas for "non-immigrants" are limited to temporary stays in the U.S. and are restricted to the activity specified in their visa.

Non-Immigrant Visa - A visa issued to a person who has qualified for non-immigrant status.

Notice to Appear (NTA) - A document which alleges that a particular noncitizen has violated certain immigration laws and should be removed (deported) from the U.S. as a result. In most cases, the Department of Homeland Security (DHS) prepares this document, serves it on the noncitizen and files it with the Immigration Court which has jurisdiction over the noncitizen. The filing of this document commences removal proceedings against the individual.

Parole - Permission granted to an noncitizen to enter the United States who is or may be legally ineligible to enter. Parole is not a formal invitation to enter ("be admitted to" the U.S. with the legal benefits that this would entail.) Rather, parolees are given temporary status, requiring them to depart the U.S. when the conditions supporting their parole status cease or the designated time period expires.

Persecution - A type of harm that is central to applications for asylum. The term is not defined in the U.S. asylum statute. However, it has been defined by U.S. courts to mean "a threat to the life or freedom of, or the infliction of suffering or harm upon, those who differ in a way regarded as offensive." Generally, such severe forms of harm as imprisonment, torture, and rape as well as death threats are thought of as constituting persecution.

Port of Entry (POE) - Any location in the U.S. or its territories that is designated as a point of entry for noncitizens and U.S. citizens. At the present time, there are about 300 ports of entry.

Prosecutorial Discretion (PD) Program - Individuals allowed to stay, at least temporarily, in the country based upon the exercise of ICE's prosecutorial discretion.

Public Charge - Is a ground of inadmissibility that could bar an individual's admission to the United States on a visa or application for lawful permanent residence if the government determines the individual is likely to rely on certain public benefits in the future.

Refugee - A person who is outside his or her country of nationality and who is unable or unwilling to return to that country due to past persecution or a "well-founded" fear of (future) persecution in that country.

Removal - The expulsion of a person from the U.S. who is not a U.S. citizen. The more common term for this is "deportation." The process often involves a hearing before an Immigration Judge who also may determine whether any exceptions to deportation should be applied.

Removal Hearing - A court hearing to determine whether certain noncitizens are subject to removal (deportation) from the U.S. The hearings are administered by the Executive Office for Immigration Review (EOIR), also known as the Immigration Court, and presided over by an Immigration Judge. EOIR is part of the Department of Justice.

Special Agricultural Workers (SAW) - The term created by the Immigration Reform and Control Act of 1986 that refers to previously-undocumented agricultural workers who were eligible under the law to apply for legalization of their immigration status.

Special Immigrant Juvenile - A non-U.S. citizen juvenile who is physically present in the U.S. and may apply for lawful permanent resident status (green card.) The juvenile must have been declared, by an appropriate local juvenile or family court, to be "dependent" on the court or a state, due to abuse, neglect, or abandonment.

Temporary Protected Status (TPS) - A legal grant of permission for nationals of particular countries temporarily to remain in the U.S. Specific countries are designated for TPS by the Attorney General after consultation with government agencies. Countries are selected where unstable or dangerous conditions would pose a temporary threat to returning persons. TPS was created by the Immigration Act of 1990.

Undocumented Immigrant - A person who is not a citizen of the U.S. and who does not have lawful immigration status in the U.S. Most undocumented immigrants either entered the U.S. "without inspection" (i.e., they did not enter the U.S. at a designated port of entry with valid documents) or they were "inspected and admitted" with valid documents but violated the terms of that status. In legal terms, undocumented immigrants are "unlawfully present" in the U.S. Persons who are unlawfully present for more than a year and then depart the U.S. are ineligible to return to the U.S. for a period of ten years. Undocumented immigrants were formerly referred to, and still are, as "illegal aliens."

Visa - Evidence of official permission for a noncitizen to enter the U.S. and to remain there for a certain period of time and for a specific purpose.

References

20 Ways States Can Prevent Illegal Immigration. Heritage Foundation. Dec. 31, 2023. https://thf_media.s3.amazonaws.com/2022/States_Immigration_Reform_Booklet.pdf.

Alejandro Mayorkas Isn't Incompetent. He's A Man On A Nefarious Mission. FAIR. August 02, 2023. https://dailycaller.com/2023/08/02/mehlman-alejandro-mayorkas-isnt-incompetent-hes-a-man-on-a-nefarious-mission/.

Anderson, Jeffrey H. "Denying Reality on Immigration." *City Journal.* July 11, 2022. https://www.city-journal.org/biden-administration-denying-reality-on-immigration.

Ari Blaff 'They Will Hurt': Eric Adams Warns of Painful Budget Cuts to NYC Essential Services Due to Migrant Crisis *National Review* September 10, 2023 https://www.nationalreview.com/news/they-will-hurt-eric-adams-warns-of-painful-budget-cuts-to-nyc-essential-services-due-to-migrant-crisis/.

Arthur, Andrew R. "Two New Polls Show Biden Immigration Approval Further Slipping." Center for Immigration Studies (CIS). August 17, 2023. https://cis.org/Arthur/Two-New-Polls-Show-Biden-Immigration-Approval-Further-Slipping.

Bauer, Fred. "On Immigration, Republicans Are Starting to Think Creatively and Constructively." *National Review.* September 19, 2023. https://www.nationalreview.com/corner/on-immigration-republicans-are-starting-to-think-creatively-and-constructively/.

Bernstein, Brittany. "Biden Signs Executive Orders Ending Trump's Travel Ban, Stopping Border Wall Construction." *National Review.* January 20, 2021. https://www.nationalreview.com/news/biden-signs-executive-orders-ending-trumps-travel-ban-stopping-border-wall-construction/.

Bernstein, Brittany. "D.C. Mayor Declares Emergency over Migrant Buses: Crisis 'Certainly Not of Our Making'." *National Review.* September 8, 2022. https://www.nationalreview.com/news/d-c-mayor-declares-emergency-over-migrant-buses-crisis-certainly-not-of-our-making/.

Bernstein, Brittany. "Harris Defends Her Absence at the Border: 'I Don't Understand the Point'." *National Review.* June 8, 2021. https://www.nationalreview.com/news/harris-defends-her-absence-at-the-border-i-dont-understand-the-point/.

Bielskil, Vince. "America's Fentanyl Crisis Begins at the Southern Border." *National Review.* December 6, 2021. https://www.nationalreview.com/2021/12/americas-fentanyl-crisis-begins-at-the-southern-border/.

Blaff, Ari. "Massachusetts Becomes Latest in String of Blue States to Declare State of Emergency over Illegal Migrant Surge." *National Review.* August 8, 2023. https://www.nationalreview.com/news/massachusetts-becomes-latest-in-string-of-blue-states-to-declare-state-of-emergency-over-illegal-migrant-surge/.

Borders Bring Increased Crimes and Costs for Taxpayers. Heritage Foundation. Dec. 17, 2021. https://www.heritage.org/immigration/commentary/federal-report-shows-open-borders-bring-increased-crimes-and-costs-taxpayers.

Camarota, Steven A. "Our Missing Workers Are Not Missing Immigrants." *National Review.* April 13, 2023. https://www.nationalreview.com/magazine/2023/05/01/our-missing-workers-are-not-missing-immigrants/.

Camarota, Steven A. "What Happened When Immigration Fell?" *National Review.* May 16, 2023. https://www.nationalreview.com/2023/05/what-happened-when-immigration-fell/.

Camarota, Steven A. and Jessica Vaughan. "The Whole Justification for Sanctuary Cities Is Wrong." *National Review.* October 25, 2021. https://www.nationalreview.com/2021/10/the-whole-justification-for-sanctuary-cities-is-wrong/.

Davis, Hannah. "Fighting Human Trafficking and Battling Biden's Open Border." Heritage Foundation. Mar. 14, 2023. https://www.heritage.org/immigration/commentary/fighting-human-trafficking-and-battling-bidens-open-border.

Di Martin, Daniel. "Opening the Golden Door." *City Journal.* Nov 22 2022. https://www.city-journal.org/article/opening-the-golden-door.

Dougherty, Michael Brendan. "What Happens When the Darien Gap Is Overrun?" *National Review.* April 14, 2023. https://www.nationalreview.com/2023/04/what-happens-when-the-darien-gap-is-overrun/.

Downey, Caroline. "Biden Administration to Grant Legal Status to Nearly Half-a-Million Venezuelan Immigrants." *National Review.* September 21, 2023. https://www.nationalreview.com/news/biden-administration-to-grant-legal-status-to-nearly-half-a-million-venezuelan-immigrants/?utm_source=onesignal&utm_medium=push&utm_campaign=article.

Downey, Caroline. "Honduran Drug Dealers Say They've Flocked to San Francisco Because of Sanctuary Laws." *National Review.* July 10, 2023. https://www.nationalreview.com/news/honduran-drug-dealers-say-theyve-flocked-to-san-francisco-because-of-sanctuary-laws/.

Downey, Caroline. "San Diego Declares Humanitarian Crisis as Federal Government Drops Thousands of Migrants on Streets." *National Review.* September 28, 2023. https://www.nationalreview.com/news/san-diego-declares-humanitarian-crisis-as-federal-government-drops-thousands-of-migrants-on-streets/.

Downey, Caroline. "Trump: Border Crisis Could Have Been Averted If Biden Did 'Nothing'." *National Review.* June 30, 2021. https://www.nationalreview.com/news/trump-border-crisis-could-have-been-averted-if-biden-did-nothing/.

Dwinell, Erin and Hannah Davis. "The Costs of Biden's Border Crisis: The First Two Years." Heritage Foundation. March 13, 2023. https://www.heritage.org/immigration/report/the-costs-bidens-border-crisis-the-first-two-years.

Dwinell, Erin. "Biden Administration Is Playing Deceitful Shell Game to Claim Fewer Illegal Border Crossings." Heritage Foundation. Jan. 31, 2023. https://www.heritage.org/immigration/commentary/biden-administration-playing-deceitful-shell-game-claim-fewer-illegal-border.

Dwinell, Erin. "Law, ICE Are "Irrelevant" to Biden Administration." Heritage Foundation. July 12, 2022. https://www.heritage.org/immigration/commentary/law-ice-are-irrelevant-biden-administration.

Edlow, Joe. "For Biden Administration, Self-Reliance Is Not an American Value." Heritage Foundation. Feb. 28, 2022. https://www.heritage.org/homeland-security/commentary/biden-administration-self-reliance-not-american-value.

Fairless, Tom. "Immigration Backlashes Spread Around the World." *Wall Street Journal.* July 8, 2023. https://www.wsj.com/articles/immigration-backlashes-spread-around-the-world-142124bc?page=7.

Fund, John. "The Left's Latest Political Scheme: Let Noncitizens Vote." *National Review.* January 9, 2022. https://www.nationalreview.com/2022/01/the-lefts-latest-political-scheme-let-noncitizens-vote/.

Garcia, Uriel J. "Here's What You Need to Know About Title 42, the Pandemic-Era Policy That Quickly Sends Migrants to Mexico." *The Texas Tribune.* May 8, 2023. https://www.texastribune.org/2022/04/29/immigration-title-42-biden/.

Glebova, Diana. "Majority of Americans Think Cartels Have More Control Over Border than U.S. Government: Poll." *National Review.* September 22, 2022. https://www.nationalreview.com/news/majority-of-americans-think-cartels-control-border-more-than-u-s-government-poll/.

Gonzalez, Pedro L. "The Progressive Call for Compassion at the Border Is a Political Prop: Opinion." *Chronicles: A Magazine of American Culture.* March 22, 2021. https://www.newsweek.com/progressive-call-compassion-border-political-prop-opinion-1577896.

Governor Ron DeSantis Signs Strongest Anti-Illegal Immigration Legislation in the Country to Combat Biden's Border Crisis. Governor Ron DeSantis Staff. May 10, 2023. https://www.flgov.com/2023/05/10/governor-ron-desantis-signs-strongest-anti-illegal-immigration-legislation-in-the-country-to-combat-bidens-border-crisis/.

Green, Mark. "The Border-Crisis Numbers the Biden Administration Doesn't Want You to Know." *National Review.* October 27, 2023. https://www.nationalreview.com/2023/10/the-border-crisis-numbers-the-biden-administration-doesnt-want-you-to-know/.

Hankinson, Simon and Lora Ries. "Deceptive Numbers and Word Games Are Hiding Continued Mass Illegal Immigration Post–Title 42." Heritage Foundation. June 13, 2023. https://www.heritage.org/immigration/report/deceptive-numbers-and-word-games-are-hiding-continued-mass-illegal-immigration.

Hankinson, Simon. "6 Pillars" Border Security Plan Is Delusional." Heritage Foundation. May 24th, 2022. https://www.heritage.org/immigration/commentary/mayorkas-6-pillars-border-security-plan-delusional.

Hankinson, Simon. "Congress Should Fund Real Border Security, Not a Worldwide Welfare State." Heritage Foundation. Nov. 17, 2023. https://www.heritage.org/immigration/commentary/congress-should-fund-real-border-security-not-worldwide-welfare-state.

Hankinson, Simon. "Robbing Pavel to Pay Pedro: The Biden White House's New Refugee Plan." Heritage Foundation. Sep. 16, 2022. https://www.heritage.org/immigration/commentary/robbing-pavel-pay-pedro-the-biden-white-houses-new-refugee-plan.

Hankinson, Simon. "Senate Republicans' Report Condemns 'Biden's Border Crisis'." Heritage Foundation. Jun 27, 2022. https://www.heritage.org/immigration/commentary/senate-republicans-report-condemns-bidens-border-crisis.

Hansen, Claire. "How Much of Trump's Border Wall Was Built?" *U.S. News & World Report.* Feb. 7, 2022. https://www.usnews.com/news/politics/articles/2022-02-07/how-much-of-president-donald-trumps-border-wall-was-built.

Hanson, Victor Davis. *Mexifornia. Twenty Years Later.* Encounter Books: New York. 2021.

Heckman, Elizabeth. "Chicago Residents Explode With Anger Over Migrants, Sanctuary Policies: 'They Are Not Listening'." Fox News. November 8, 2023. https://www.foxnews.com/media/chicago-residents-explode-anger-migrants-sanctuary-policies-listening.

Heritage Hails Well-Timed Passage of Historic Proposal to End Border Crisis, Reduce Illegal Immigration. Heritage Foundation. May 11, 2023. https://www.heritage.org/press/heritage-hails-well-timed-passage-historic-proposal-end-border-crisis-reduce-illegal.

Hickey, Jennifer G. "Foreign-Born Workers in the United States." FAIR. December 2019. https://www.fairus.org/issue/illegal-legal-immigration-and-economy/foreign-born-workers-united-states.

Homan, Tom. "Effective Immigration Enforcement Can't Rely on Honor System." Heritage Foundation. March 8, 2022. https://www.heritage.org/immigration/commentary/effective-immigration-enforcement-cant-rely-honor-system.

Homan, Tom. "How Biden, Mayorkas Broke Our Immigration System From the Inside Out." Heritage Foundation. Jun. 29, 2023. https://www.heritage.org/immigration/commentary/how-biden-mayorkas-broke-our-immigration-system-the-inside-out.

How Many Illegal Aliens Are in the United States? 2023 Update. FAIR. June 22, 2023. https://www.fairus.org/issue/illegal-immigration/how-many-illegal-aliens-are-united-states-2023-update.

Huennekens, Preston. "Mayorkas' New Policies Effectively Abolish ICE." ImmigratoinReform.com. October 13, 2021. https://www.immigrationreform.com/2021/10/13/mayorkas-moves-abolish-ice-immigrationreform-com/.

Illegal Aliens Released From Local Custody Commit More Crimes – One Freed 10 Times. *Judicial Watch.* July 16, 2019. https://www.judicialwatch.org/illegal-aliens-released-from-local-custody-commit-more-crimes-honduran-freed-10-times/.

James, Kay, James Carafano, John Malcolm and Jack Spencer. "An Agenda for American Immigration Reform." Heritage Foundation. February 20, 2019. https://www.heritage.org/immigration/report/agenda-american-immigration-reform.

Korecki, Natasha. "How Texas Gov. Greg Abbott Divided Democrats on Immigration With Migrant Busing. NBC News. Dec. 17, 2023. https://www.nbcnews.com/politics/politics-news/texas-gov-greg-abbott-divided-democrats-immigration-migrant-busing-rcna128815.

Krikorian, Mark. "The Immigrant Population Is Growing Rapidly." *National Review.* June 2, 2022. https://www.nationalreview.com/corner/the-immigrant-population-is-growing-rapidly/.

Krishan, Ohan. "ESL Students Deserve a Better Education." *National Review.* July 27, 2022. https://www.nationalreview.com/2022/07/esl-students-deserve-a-better-education/.

Law, Robert and Kristen Ziccarelli. "The Biden Administration's Day One Immigration Proposal: Mass Amnesty and No Border Security." America First Policy Institute. February 20, 2023.

https://americafirstpolicy.com/issues/the-biden-administrations-day-one-immigration-proposal-mass-amnesty-and-no-border-security.

Mac Donald, Heather. California's Demographic Revolution: If the upward mobility of the impending Hispanic majority doesn't improve, the state's economic future is in peril." *City Journal.* Winter 2012. https://www.city-journal.org/html/california%E2%80%99s-demographic-revolution-13440.html.

Majority of Federal Arrestees are Foreigners, Thousands of "Unknown Citizenship. *Judicial Watch.* August 27, 2019. https://www.judicialwatch.org/majority-of-federal-arrestees-are-foreigners-thousands-of-unknown-citizenship/.

Malanga, Steven. "How Unskilled Immigrants Hurt Our Economy: A handful of industries get low-cost labor, and the taxpayers foot the bill." *City Journal.* Summer 2006. https://www.city-journal.org/html/how-unskilled-immigrants-hurt-our-economy-12946.html.

McArdle, Mairead. "Biden to End Trump Asylum Deals with Three Central American Countries." *National Review.* February 7, 2021. https://www.nationalreview.com/news/biden-to-end-trump-asylum-deals-with-three-central-american-countries/.

McCarthy, Charlie. "Biden Admin Wants Free Medical, Housing for 5.7M Migrants." *Newsmax.* October 16, 2023. https://www.newsmax.com/newsfront/joe-biden-admin-free/2023/10/16/id/1138475/.

More Than 100,000 DACA Applicants Have Been Arrested—Murder, Rape, DUI. *Judicial Watch.* Nov. 19, 2019. https://www.judicialwatch.org/more-than-100000-daca-applicants-have-been-arrested-murder-rape-dui/.

Morgan, Mark and Mike Howell. "How Feds Use Charities To Hide the True Cost of the U.S. Border Crisis." Heritage Foundation. Jan. 4, 2023. https://www.heritage.org/immigration/commentary/how-feds-use-charities-hide-the-true-cost-the-us-border-crisis.

Morgan, Mark and Tom Homan. "The Case for Impeaching Homeland Security Secretary Alejandro Mayorkas." Mar. 28, 2023. Heritage Foundation. https://www.heritage.org/immigration/commentary/the-case-impeaching-homeland-security-secretary-alejandro-mayorkas.

Morgan, Mark. "Cash to Illegal Immigrants Is the New Low in Biden's Open-Borders Push." *National Review.* November 8, 2021. https://www.nationalreview.com/2021/11/cash-to-illegal-immigrants-is-the-new-low-in-bidens-open-borders-push/.

Morgan, Mark. "The Got-Away Crisis at Our Southern Border." Heritage Foundation. Sep. 26, 2022. https://www.heritage.org/immigration/commentary/the-got-away-crisis-our-southern-border.

Nerozzi, Timothy H.J. "Texas Seized Enough Fentanyl to Kill 200 Million People This Year Alone, Officials Say." Fox News. December 9, 2021. https://www.foxnews.com/us/texas-seized-enough-fentanyl-kill-200-million-people-year.

O'Grady, Mary Anastasia. "How a Half-Million Migrants Moved North." *Wall Street Journal.* Nov. 19, 2023. https://www.wsj.com/articles/how-a-half-million-migrants-moved-north-latin-america-southern-border-policy-43dd3904?page=3.

Parks, Kristine. "CNN Host Admits Red State Strategy of Bussing Migrants to Sanctuary Cities 'Has Worked' to Pressure Biden." Fox News. December 29, 2023. https://www.foxnews.com/media/cnn-host-admits-red-state-strategy-bussing-migrants-sanctuary-cities-worked-pressure-biden.

Passel, Jeffrey S. and D'Vera Cohn. "How Removing Unauthorized Immigrants From Census Statistics Could Affect House Reapportionment." Pew Research Center. July 24, 2020. https://www.pewresearch.org/short-reads/2020/07/24/how-removing-unauthorized-immigrants-from-census-statistics-could-affect-house-reapportionment/#:~:text=If%20unauthorized%20immigrants%20in%20the,analysis%20based%20on%20government%20records.

Population Growth and the Environment. FAIR. Dec. 31, 2023. https://www.fairus.org/issues/population-and-environment.

Public Benefits for Noncitizen Residents in California Regardless of Status. Immigrant Legal Resource Center. Sept. 2022. https://www.ilrc.org/sites/default/files/resources/ca_public_benefits_for_noncitizens_sept_2022.pdf.

RAISE Act. Numbers USA. Oct. 3, 2017. https://www.numbersusa.com/resource-article/raise-act.

Raley, Spencer, Madison McQueen and Jason Pena. "Measuring the Trump Administration's Top Immigration Issues by the Numbers. FAIR. June 2021. https://www.fairus.org/issue/border-security/measuring-trump-admin-top-immigration-issues-by-numbers.

Rappaport, Nolan. "Biden 2.0: The US Could Double Its Undocumented Immigrant Population." *The Hill*. Nov. 6, 2023. https://thehill.com/opinion/immigration/4292447-biden-2-0-the-us-could-double-its-undocumented-immigrant-population/.

Rappaport, Nolan. "Biden's 'Catch and Release' System for Illegal Border Crossers is a Failure." *The Hill*. Sep. 18, 2023. https://thehill.com/opinion/immigration/4206842-bidens-catch-and-release-system-for-illegal-border-crossers-is-a-failure/.

Rappaport, Nolan. "How Alejandro Mayorkas is Shielding Almost a Million Deportable Immigrants From Removal." *The Hill*. Nov. 7, 2023. https://thehill.com/opinion/immigration/4083465-how-the-secretary-of-homeland-security-is-shielding-almost-a-million-deportable-immigrants-from-removal/.

Richwine, Jason. "Census Bureau: No End in Sight to Record-Breaking Immigration." *National Review*. November 9, 2023. https://www.nationalreview.com/corner/census-bureau-no-end-in-sight-to-record-breaking-immigration/.

Ries, Lora and Carla Sands. "Biden's Immigration Policies Have Turned a Win Into a Loss." Heritage Foundation. July 7, 2021. https://www.heritage.org/immigration/commentary/bidens-immigration-policies-have-turned-win-loss.

Ries, Lora and Mark Morgan. "Biden Encourages Massive Illegal Immigration and Tries To Hide It With Secret Flights." Heritage Foundation. Jan. 31, 2022. https://www.heritage.org/immigration/commentary/biden-encourages-massive-illegal-immigration-and-tries-hide-it-secret.

Ries, Lora and Mike Howell. "The Bipartisan Border Solutions Act: Rewarding President Biden for His Border Crisis." Heritage Foundation. April 30, 2021. https://www.heritage.org/immigration/report/the-bipartisan-border-solutions-act-rewarding-president-biden-his-border-crisis.

Ries, Lora. "Biden's Border Policies Are Taking Us Back To Pre-9/11 Homeland Security. *The Federalist*. Sep. 12, 2022. https://www.heritage.org/homeland-security/commentary/bidens-border-policies-are-taking-us-back-pre-911-homeland-security.

Ries, Lora. "Congress Should Reject Biden Administration's Asylum Rule and Ruin." Heritage Foundation. Aug. 30, 2022. https://www.heritage.org/immigration/commentary/congress-should-reject-biden-administrations-asylum-rule-and-ruin.

Ries, Lora. "The Biden Border Crisis Has Gone on Long Enough (How Congress Can Help)." Heritage Foundation. Nov. 28, 2022. https://www.heritage.org/immigration/commentary/the-biden-border-crisis-has-gone-long-enough-how-congress-can-help .

Rosenbloom, Raquel and Jeanne Batalova. "Mexican Immigrants in the United States. October 13, 2022 Migration Policy Institute (MPI). https://www.migrationpolicy.org/article/mexican-immigrants-united-states.

Rothman, Noah. "Migrant Busing Turned Out to Be a Political Coup for Republicans." *National Review.* May 11, 2023. https://www.nationalreview.com/2023/05/migrant-busing-turned-out-to-be-a-political-coup-for-republicans/.

Rumpf-Whitten, Sarah. "California to Offer 700,000 Illegal Immigrants Free Healthcare as Deficit Soars and Population Shrinks." Fox Business. December 30, 2023. https://www.foxbusiness.com/politics/california-offer-illegal-immigrants-free-healthcare-deficit-soars-population-shrinks.

Sanctuary Policies. FAIR. Dec. 31, 2023. https://www.fairus.org/issues/sanctuary-policies.

Seminara, Dave. "Migrant Millionaires?" *City Journal.* Nov 12 2021. https://www.city-journal.org/article/migrant-millionaires.

Seminara, Dave. "The Other Half of Our Immigration Crisis." *City Journal.* May 30, 2023. https://www.city-journal.org/article/the-other-half-of-our-immigration-crisis.

Solutions/Legal Immigration. Heritage Foundation. August, 2020. https://www.heritage.org/solutions/.

States Say ICE Stops Issuing Detainers for Illegal Immigrant Convicts, Revokes Them for Dozens. *Judicial Watch.* April 20, 2021. https://www.judicialwatch.org/states-say-ice-stops-issuing-detainers-for-illegal-immigrant-convicts-revokes-them-for-dozens/.

Stein, Dan. "Stein: The Biden Administration Has Finally Conceded We Have A Border Crisis. Now It's Time For Congress to Act." Daily Caller. October 12, 2023. https://dailycaller.com/2023/10/12/stein-biden-administration-conceded-border-crisis-congress-act/.

Stimson, Charles D., Hans A. von Spakovsky and Lora Ries. "Assessing the Trump Administration's Immigration Policies. June 29, 2020. https://www.heritage.org/sites/default/files/2020-06/SR233_0.pdf.

Swanson, Mark. "Foreign-Born US Population of 49.5M Highest in History." *Newsmax.* November 30, 2023. https://www.newsmax.com/newsfront/foreign-born-population/2023/11/30/id/1144290/.

Taer, Jennie. "Heritage Foundation Sues Biden Administration for Failing to Share Details on Limiting Deportations." Heritage Foundation. August 04, 2022. https://www.dailysignal.com/2022/08/04/heritage-foundation-sues-biden-administration-for-failing-to-share-details-on-limiting-deportations/.

The Fiscal Burden of Illegal Immigration on United States Taxpayers: 2023 Cost Study. FAIR. March 8, 2023. https://www.fairus.org/issue/publications-resources/fiscal-burden-illegal-immigration-united-states-taxpayers-2023.

Trump Administration Immigration Accomplishments. FAIR. Dec. 31, 2023. https://www.fairus.org/issue/biden-immigration-border-policy/trump-administration-immigration-accomplishments.

von Spakovsky, Hans A. "Biden's Border Crisis—Crime Problem in Texas a Bad Omen for Rest of U.S." Heritage Foundation. Aug. 2, 2021. https://www.heritage.org/immigration/commentary/bidens-border-crisis-crime-problem-texas-bad-omen-rest-us.

von Spakovsky, Hans A. "Impeaching Mayorkas Is a Must, He Violated His Oath and Committed 'High Crimes and Misdemeanors'." Heritage Foundation. Feb. 15, 2023. https://www.heritage.org/homeland-security/commentary/impeaching-mayorkas-must-he-violated-his-oath-and-committed-high.

von Spakovsky, Hans A. and Charles Stimson. "Enforcing Immigration Law: What States Can Do To Assist the Federal Government and Fight the Illegal Immigration Problem." Heritage Foundation. October 8, 2019. https://www.heritage.org/immigration/report/enforcing-immigration-law-what-states-can-do-assist-the-federal-government-and.

Ward, Nicole and Jeanne Batalova. "Frequently Requested Statistics on Immigrants and Immigration in the United States." Migration Policy Institute (MPI). March 14, 2023. https://www.migrationpolicy.org/article/frequently-requested-statistics-immigrants-and-immigration-united-states?gclid=Cj0KCQjw_r6hBhDdARIsAMIDhV-Hpf-0vx0DxVMXKGoyV3KC5_6KC7B0z6YuMcCx002O4SuA-VlREvIaAr7lEALw_wcB.

What Immigration Reform Should Look Like. Heritage Foundation. Dec. 31, 2023. https://www.heritage.org/immigration/heritage-explains/what-immigration-reform-should-look.

Why Amnesty Is A Bad Idea. FAIR. Dec. 31, 2023. https://www.fairus.org/issues/amnesty.

Wong, Bill. "Amnesty Is Unfair to Legal Immigrants Like Me." National Review. September 30, 2021. https://www.nationalreview.com/2021/09/amnesty-is-unfair-to-legal-immigrants-like-me/.

Zail, Cole P. "Immigration: Solidarity, Identity, And The American Dream. AMAC Magazine. Summer 2018. https://www.qgdigitalpublishing.com/publication/?m=40499&i=511026&view=articleBrowser&article_id=3132858&ver=html5.

Zimmermann, David. "Biden Administration Failed to Remove 99 Percent of Illegal Immigrants Released Into U.S., GOP Report Shows." National Review. Oct. 9, 2023. https://www.msn.com/en-us/news/politics/biden-administration-failed-to-remove-99-percent-of-illegal-immigrants-released-into-us-gop-report-shows/ar-AA1hWEvR.

Zimmermann, David. "New York City Asks Judge to Suspend Right-to-Shelter Mandate Amid Migrant Crisis." National Review. October 4, 2023. https://www.nationalreview.com/news/new-york-city-asks-judge-to-suspend-right-to-shelter-mandate-amid-migrant-crisis/.

Zimmermann, David. "Texas Passes Bill Allowing State Police to Arrest, Deport Illegal Immigrants." National Review. November 15, 2023. https://www.nationalreview.com/news/texas-passes-bill-allowing-state-police-to-arrest-deport-illegal-immigrants/.

Index

C

N

O

Author Bio

Author: Corey Lee Wilson.

Corey Lee Wilson was raised an atheist by his liberal *Playboy* Bunny mother, has three Anglo-Hispanic siblings, a bi-racial daughter, a brother who died of AIDS, baptized a Protestant by his conservative grandparents, attended temple with his Jewish foster parents, baptized again as a Catholic for his first Filipina wife, attends Buddhist ceremonies with his second Thai wife, became an agnostic on his own free will for most of his life, and is a lifetime independent voter.

Corey felt the sting of intellectual humility by repeating the 4th grade and attended eighteen different schools before putting himself through college (without parents) at Mt. San Antonio College and Cal Poly Pomona University (while on triple secret probation). Named Who's Who of American College Students in 1984, he received a BS in Economics (summa cum laude) and won his fraternity's most prestigious undergraduate honor, the Phi Kappa Tau Fraternity's Shideler Award, both in 1985. In 2020, he became a member of the Heterodox Academy, in 2021 a member of the National Association of Scholars and 1776 Unites, and in 2023 a member of Moms for Liberty.

As a satirist and fraternity man, Corey started Fratire Publishing in 2012 and transformed the fiction "fratire" genre to a respectable and viewpoint diverse non-fiction genre promoting practical knowledge and wisdom to help everyday people navigate safely through the many hazards of life. In 2019, he founded the SAPIENT Being to help promote freedom of speech, viewpoint diversity, intellectual humility and most importantly advance sapience in America's students and campuses.

The SAPIENT Being has three programs: Make Free Speech Again On Campus (MFSAOC) Program, Free Speech Alumni Ambassador (FSAA) Program, and the Sapient Conservative Textbooks (SCT) Program—all working together to promote its mission and vision of sapience.

If you're interested in the MFSAOC Program and starting a S.A.P.I.E.N.T. Being club, chapter, or alliance on or off campus, please go to https://www.SapientBeing.org/start-a-chapter, e-mail SapientBeing@att.net, or call (951) 638-5562 for more information.

If you're interested in becoming a conservative campus advisor or free speech champion for right-leaning campus organizations as part of the FSAA Program from the S.A.P.I.E.N.T. Being, please e-mail at SapientBeing@att.net, or call (951) 638-5562 for more information.

If you're interested as an educator, administrator, or student in the SCT Program and their 40 MADNESS series of textbooks from the S.A.P.I.E.N.T. Being, please check them out at the Fratire Publishing website at https://www.FratirePublishing.com/madnessbooks, for more information.

Hopefully, this textbook was enlightening and your journey through it—along with mine—made you aware of the issues and challenges ahead of us. If it has, your quest and mine towards becoming a sapient being has begun. If it hasn't, there's no better time to start than now. Come join us in creating a society advancing personal intelligence and enlightenment now together (S.A.P.I.E.N.T.) and become a sapient being.